Passing the Baton of Light

Saving a Family Tree

BEVERLY J. POWERS

WESTBOW
PRESS
A DIVISION OF THOMAS NELSON
& ZONDERVAN

WestBow Press books may be ordered through booksellers or by contacting:

WestBow Press
A Division of Thomas Nelson & Zondervan
1663 Liberty Drive
Bloomington, IN 47403
www.westbowpress.com
1 (866) 928-1240

ISBN: 978-1-4908-5488-5 (sc)
ISBN: 978-1-4908-5489-2 (hc)
ISBN: 978-1-4908-5487-8 (e)

Library of Congress Control Number: 2014917688

Print information available on the last page.

WestBow Press rev. date: 07/17/2015

- Unless otherwise indicated, Scripture quotations are from:
The Holy Bible, New King James Version © 1984 by Thomas Nelson, Inc

- COVER, photo taken by Beverly J. Powers. All Rights Reserved.
- THE VINE, photo taken by Beverly J. Powers. All Rights Reserved.
- FAITH, photo taken by Beverly J. Powers. All Rights Reserved.
- TELL THEM I'M ALIVE & WELL, photo by Beverly J. Powers.
  All Rights Reserved.
- THE LIGHT, photo taken by Beverly J. Powers. All Rights Reserved.
- THE WAY, photo taken by Beverly J. Powers. All Rights Reserved.
- PRAYER, photo taken by Beverly J. Powers. All Rights Reserved.
- BEHOLD, photo taken by Beverly J. Powers. All Rights Reserved.

PHOTO #14   The Largo
★ The Largo Nightclub, Courtesy of Mrs. Charles Landis.
  All Rights Reserved.

PHOTO #15   Jack Benny
★ The Jack Benny Program, "Don Breaks Leg", episode #14.18.
  All Rights Reserved.

PHOTO #16   Breakfast at Tiffany's
★ Breakfast at Tiffany's © Paramount Pictures, 1961.
  Courtesy of Paramount Pictures. All Rights Reserved.

PHOTO #17   Days of Wine and Roses
★ Days of Wine and Roses © Warner Bros. Entertainment, Inc. 1962.
  Courtesy of Warner Bros. All Rights Reserved.

PHOTO #18   Kissin' Cousins
★ Kissin' Cousins © Turner Entertainment Co. 1964.
  Courtesy of Warner Bros. All Rights Reserved.

PHOTO #20   Red Skelton
★ The Red Skelton Hour, "Sheriffs Are Bought, Not Made", 1968.

PHOTO #21   Regis Philbin
★ That Regis Phibin Show, aka "A.M. Los Angeles", 1965.

PHOTO #23   Comedy of Terrors
★ The Comedy of Terrors, © Orion Pictures Corp. 1963.
  Courtesy of MGM Media Licensing. All Rights Reserved.

PHOTO #24   George Gobel
  Summer Playhouse, "The Apartment House", 1964.
  Don Fedderson Productions.

PHOTO #26
  "Oscar Nominations Seen by Producer", May 31, 1972.
  Courtesy of The Valdosta Times, GA. All Rights Reserved.

PHOTO #31
  "Local Church Briefs", October 29, 1993.
  Courtesy of The Maui News, HI. All Rights Reserved.

This book is dedicated to my grandmother, Lena May Hatley,
the woman who prayed me out of darkness and into the light.

CONTENTS

FOREWORD xi

part one
THE VINE

1. THE ROOTS 3
2. THE GARDEN...28

part two
CHOICES

3. THE SINS...47
4. THE STARDOM..64
5. THE SEARCH 87
6. THE SORROW.. 102
7. THE SURRENDER 112

part three
FAITH

8. THE MOVE 123
9. THE TRAINING 138

part four
THE LIGHT

10. THE VOICE 157
11. THE DARKNESS 169

part five
THE WAY

12. THE FLEECE 179
13. FORGIVENESS 195

part six
PRAYER

14. THE FEARS 209
15. THE HOPE 220
16. THE LOVE 232

part seven
BEHOLD

17. THE CHILDREN 243
18. THE BLESSINGS 254

ACKNOWLEDGMENTS 267
NOTES 269

FOREWORD

The land You have given me is a pleasant land
Psalm 16:5

I wondered how I got here from over there. Then I connected the dots and discovered it had nothing to do with me, but rather everything to do with a plan put into action long before I was born.

How had it happened? The waters had been uncharted, murky, turbulent and often deadly. Yet, after decades of wandering lost at sea, I had arrived in paradise.

However, I soon discovered paradise was not the end of my saga, but really the beginning, and had nothing to do with my compass or navigational skills... but rather an ethereal course that had been set for me long ago.

The voyage had been difficult with only an occasional flicker of light, riddled mostly with darkness and confusion, false maps and belief systems, dichotomies, and unanswered questions; a twisted maze that eventually led me to my rightful place, where I came face to face with my destiny.

THE VINE

I am the vine, you are the branches

John 15:5

chapter one

THE ROOTS

Its roots reached to abundant waters
Ezekiel 31:9

I thought I would die. There I was on national television when Regis Philbin turns to me and asks, "What's a nice girl like you doing at night taking her clothes off for a living?" *Was he kidding?* How could he ask me such a thing in front of a bazillion people? *I was mortified.* And why was he acting like this? He had always been so nice to me before when I'd been on his shows. What happened?

The studio lights seemed unusually hot that day. I didn't know what to say. I was extremely proud of what I did for a living, and the name I had made for myself on stage as *Miss Beverly Hills*. I certainly didn't like his insinuation that what I was doing was wrong. It wasn't. At least I didn't think so. Until... maybe, at that moment.

The question haunted me long after I went home and the stage makeup came off. How *did* I, the oldest and precious granddaughter of Lena May Hatley, a devout and respected Southern Baptist, end up as the Queen of Burlesque? Even if my name was in lights on the Sunset Strip at one of the most prestigious nightclubs on the West Coast, where had the dichotomies crossed?

Mother was born in 1920, the year women were given the right to vote, and married my father straight out of high school in '38. Earl was tall, dark and handsome. Many blamed his good looks and wild nature on his Blackfoot Indian heritage. People whispered how outrageous Mother had been when she hopped on the back of his racy Indian motorcycle and eloped with him! "Whoever heard of such a thing?" they wanted to know. But, Mother was madly in love with my father and would have followed him to the moon riding on the back of a rocket, if he had asked her.

What neither of them anticipated was the birth of their first child, me, nine months later. So much for sowing their oats. Earl wasn't about to have a child dampen his fun, so Mommy stayed home and played house, while Daddy just went out and played.

From the beginning, Mother never let me forget how unwanted I was—how I had been an accident. Over the years, I heard Mother on numerous occasions tell of my painful delivery and how she had tried to abort me by drinking concoctions of iodine. Once, I even heard her actually admit she had tried using a coat hanger in hopes of aborting me.

"But, if you know Beverly Jean," she'd say, "she has always been stubborn. Even during labor she wouldn't come out. The doctors actually thought one of us was going to die. That's how long it was taking! Finally, after 24 agonizing hours, they gave Earl a choice: "It's either your wife or the baby--you choose." "Naturally, he chose me," she'd boast. "So the doctors went in with forceps and pulled her out. It was a miracle Beverly lived. But, as you can see," pointing at me, "she lived."

I hated her when she talked like that. Why did she have to tell everybody? She never spoke that way about the other two "accidents" she and my father had. Yet, I remember the day she came home from the hospital with my brother. My four-year-old sister Linda and I thought Jimmy was the cutest thing we had ever seen, but surprisingly not everyone felt that way. My eighth birthday was nearly here. Linda and I were on the front porch playing with our paper dolls. Mother was sitting inside on the big flowery couch nursing Jimmy when the phone rang. I heard Mother get up and go into the kitchen and pick up the receiver on the wall--my brother still sucking on her breast, never missing a beat. I hoped it was Daddy.

But, it wasn't. Instead it was a friend of his who, "... hated to be the one to tell my mother this... but..."

"What?" I heard Mother gasp. "I don't understand."

Then, I heard the word *bigamist*. Even though I didn't know what it meant, I knew it must have been really bad, because Mother began crying that day and never seemed to stop. My father had another wife and family hidden at the end of his truck route. Even after my brother started crawling, I could hear Mother sobbing in the middle of the night. In the morning, her eyes would be as red and swollen as her hands.

She now took in ironing to earn money to put food on our table. Her hands weren't like they used to be. They were calloused, blistered and often bled. The rickety ironing board she bent over for hours on end now stood in the middle of our tiny living room as a permanent fixture. Dozens and dozens of white, starched men's dress shirts hung everywhere, waiting to be picked up by the laundries that hired her. Mother vigorously tried to support us, but eventually we had to go on Welfare.

Money was scarce. Often we ate catsup sandwiches on white Barbara Ann bread. Sometimes we just ate peanut butter and jelly straight out of the jars. Afterward, when they were empty, we'd use them as drinking glasses. Eventually, we had a whole set.

Even before my father left, I hated mealtime. I remember the razor strap he would use to scare Linda and me into eating everything on our plates. "Don't you know there's starving kids out there who'd just love to have what you've got," he'd say, striking the door jamb with one loud crack of the razor strap, indicating that's what he was going to do to us if we didn't hurry up and eat. Deep gouges ran up and down the doorway. After Earl left, the threats stopped... but so did the food. The scars he left on the door jamb, along with the ones in my heart, remained.

Before Earl moved out, he would leave for work in the wee hours of the morning and head for his beloved eighteen-wheeler that took him out of town for days at a time. He always bent down and kissed me goodbye before leaving. After the front door shut, I would run and jump into bed with Mother. The sheets were always warm and his smell still fragrant on the pillow. But after that terrible phone call, my father's scent began to fade away.

I now slept with Mother all the time. Linda took over the couch that was once mine and Jimmy got the four-legged bathtub to sleep in. I wished the old days would come back, when I had the couch; Linda, the bathtub; and Jimmy still slept on the closet floor.

My beloved grandmother, Mamo, began visiting us several days a week. I would watch for her from our front porch on the days she was to come... anxiously waiting for her large frame to come into view. She was easy to spot. She was tall and always carried two shopping bags. One containing her work clothes, the other with food.

World War II was over. Soldiers were everywhere. On the streets. The buses. Downtown. As Mamo stepped off the trolley car, the soldiers would tip their hats as she strolled toward our little house on Windsor Road.

To help my mother care for us, Mamo took an extra job on weekends. Friday and Saturday nights, after working all day as a cleaning lady, she would get dressed up in one of her church-going dresses, rub a touch of lipstick on her cheeks, double-check the waves in her hair, then rush off to the grand La Monica Ballroom where she worked selling tickets, greeting people at the door with her shy smile.

Inside the large dance hall, a large, round, mirrored chandelier slowly rotated from the ceiling as couples swayed to the big bands. Duke Ellington was Mamo's favorite. She loved her new job and soon began urging Mother to go with her.

"Come on," Mamo would say. "The change will do ya good." G.I.s were home and raring to have some R & R. But, Mother's reply was always the same. "Who'd want a twenty-seven-year-old woman stranded with three kids?" Sadly, we were about to find out.

THE ROOTS

The fathers have eaten sour grapes
Jeremiah 31:29a

Everyone agreed. It must have been fate: Mother and Jerry meeting like that on her very first night out. Jerry was an ex-G.I. and Mother a recent divorcee. I heard Mother tell Mamo that Jerry had received a Dear John letter while off fighting the war. His wife had divorced him, disappeared, and taken their infant son with her. Everyone felt so sorry for him.

He only had a sixth grade education, but he had a promise of a steady job at his brother's sheet metal shop in downtown Los Angeles. Yes, this was certainly a match made in heaven. Mother would provide a built-in family, and Jerry would help support her and the kids. She made it perfectly clear, right from the start, she would never give him any children of his own, but he didn't seem to mind. He seemed to be content with hers. And so, the deal was made.

I didn't like him from the moment I met him, even though he came bearing gifts. He brought me a large helium balloon that popped the moment he handed it to me. Maybe the angels were trying to get our attention? If so, it didn't work, because within a very short time Mother and Jerry were married in a civil ceremony without any hoopla--and without a blessing.

Rarely were blessings or God ever mentioned in our home, except occasionally by Mamo. I never saw Mother pray. I don't think she ever thought to ask God if marrying Jerry was what He wanted for her and her three children. Was this really the best way? Or, was this the easy way: a way straight down a trodden path filled with hidden land mines and potholes? Being in love was not an issue. Lack and limitations were the motivating factors of the day. Sacrifices had to be made... and Mother ended up doing just that--by prostituting her life through the bondage of marriage. A marriage made out of convenience. A proposition made without love. A match obviously made by Satan himself. The sad part was... the children were put in harm's way, for unknowingly... Mother had married a pedophile.

When I was six, Mamo took me to a church where she used to worship when Mother was little. The Angeles Temple was founded by a woman named Aimee "Sister" Semple McPherson, who preached in flowing white dresses while telling colorful Bible stories.

Sitting in the balcony of the large, empty church, I could *feel* the quiet... the stillness. As we sat there beside each other, Mamo's eyes began to twinkle. When she finally spoke, her voice was soft and in a whisper, as if someone was listening. "Child, this is where I always sat," Mamo smiled. "I could see real good from here." She began to giggle. "I remembe' one Sunday morning before da church service, sirens and alarms began blarin' and goin' off real loud. Everyone thought there was a fire or somethin'. But then "Sister" came out from behind the curtains dressed up as a policeman and rushed over to a motorcycle that had been placed on the stage. She held up her arms and began waving to the people. "I have come here today to give everyone a warning!" she shouted. "I'm here to tell ya if ya don't stop speedin' down the road, and goin' the wrong way, you're gonna get a ticket--and end up in hell!'"

I could see Mamo's joy in her eyes. I could hear it in her voice. After a bit, she turned and put her arm around me. "Sister's passed on now child--but my, my, my, how she loved Jesus. She was a true blessin', she was."

As we left the Temple and began to stroll down Glendale Boulevard, a scruffy looking man ran up to us from behind, snatched me up me in his arms and began running across the street toward one of the entrances of Echo Park--a place, Mamo later said, known to be a home for winos.

I could hear Mamo's shrilling voice. "Let go of my baby!" she screamed. "Let go of my baby!" The rest is a blur, but I remember Mamo's voice. The fear. It was over as fast as it started, and I was back in Mamo's arms again. I never learned what the man hoped to accomplish by grabbing me, but I shall always remember the comfort of Mamo's embrace. In a short period of time, good and evil had graphically been illustrated to me that day. I may have been too young to understand the concept, but I wasn't too young to experience its reality.

The children's teeth are set on edge
Jeremiah 31:29b

Shortly after Mother and Jerry were married, Mother began working nights on the assembly line at Lockheed's Aircraft Factory. Within a short period of time, she had saved enough money for a down payment on a house, and with Jerry's G.I. Bill was able to purchase one. It was in Pacoima, a Hispanic and black community.

There was no warning--no announcement. One day we just up and moved! I panicked. How would my father ever find me? It had been almost two years since I last saw Earl. Why had he never come back? The question haunted me. The last time we were together, I was so excited to see him I bounced up and down on the bed and accidentally came down on his chest, jabbing him in the ribs with my elbow. He began to yell. He was really mad at me. Was that why he hadn't shown up at the park that day in the park?

Mamo and I waited all day for him to arrive. The birds were chirping their morning songs when we arrived at Los Feliz park and singing their evening serenades when we left. All day we sat on that hard bench and waited. But he never showed up. Eventually, the sun began to set and the colored lights surrounding the park's large water fountain came on. Red. Pink. Blue. Yellow. Green. The water looked like dancing rainbows with the sun shining from behind. But my heart wasn't dancing.

Slowly Mamo stood up, as if it took great effort, and began collecting her things, putting them into her shopping bag. Her voice broke the silence. "Come child. It's time to go."

"But what about Daddy?" My eyes began to sting.

"I don't think he's comin' Sweetpea. Somethin' must've happened. Come on now," her hand reached for mine as tears exploded from within me and I began running toward the restroom. One hand covered my mouth as I tried to hold back the tears. The other pressed hard between my legs, hoping I wouldn't pee in my pants. I was grateful no one was inside the small bathroom as I let go of my bladder--along with the pent-up tears I had been trying to keep hidden from Mamo. Sorrow that was hidden behind a mask that read, "It's okay. Daddy probably just got busy and forgot." But, I couldn't help but wonder--had Mother even told him I would be in the park to meet him that day? I never asked. And, I never found out.

Life proceeded as usual with one day following another. Mamo dropped by as often as she could and I continued looking for my father everywhere I went. Anyone who even resembled Earl had my attention. I watched Tennessee Ernie Ford on our small black and white TV and pretended he was singing to me. I fantasized about how he would someday come and find me. I missed him so much. I knew if he knew where I was, he'd come and save me from my life of unhappiness. Mother rarely spoke to me anymore, except to tell me the list of chores she wanted me to do. She always seemed angry.

Mamo, on the other hand, was the opposite. She was the rose in my garden of weeds. I'd tell her stories of how I felt and she'd soothe me with her comforting words. "Beverly Jean, no matta what," she'd say, rocking me back and forth in the leather armchair she favored, "God has a plan fer you (Jer. 29:11). An' child, don't ya forget it, 'cause yer special to Him an' yer certainly special to yer Mamo." Maybe so. But I sure didn't feel special. I felt more like a piece of rotten fruit that nobody wanted around.

Mamo was always trying to bridge the gap between Mother and me. "Yer mother loves ya child. She jest has a strange way of showin' it, thet's all," she'd explain. "Ya shouldn't blame her. She's always had a hard time expressin' love. It's not her fault, ya know. When she was a little tyke, I had to leave her by herself while I went off to work. I'd give her a jar of pennies to play with an tell her to stay there until her brothers, yer uncles, came home from school. She'd sit there in the middle of thet big ol' bed countin' those pennies an' entertainin' herself. Yer mother is a good person child; she's jest had a hard life, thet's all."

I had heard the story before. I also heard how my grandfather, whom I never met, once tried to kill my mother when she was little. I overheard Mamo say how she came home one day after work and found my mother, four years old, hiding high up in a tree, with my drunken grandfather beneath it brandishing a knife. That was the end of Melvin, my grandfather. He and his belongings were out of the house before the sun went down. Her only explanation was, "Yer grandpa was mean when he was drunk." I wondered how Mamo had ended up with such a nasty man.

She was born in 1897 near the time the first automobile and telephone were invented. Mamo was the oldest of seven and at twelve years of age, stood 5'8" tall--a full head and shoulders over her parents. People teased her, saying she was the "largest of the litter." They lived on a tiny backwoods farm in Sulphur Springs, Texas. When Mamo turned eight, she was forced to quit school to help out around the house and farm. She picked cotton, brought water in from the well and had the cows milked and the eggs gathered long before the sun was up.

In her early teens she married Melvin, the boy from the neighboring farm, and within five years they had three children. They lived with his parents until Mamo learned of the bootlegging Melvin was into. A quarrel had broken out over the ownership of the illegal operation and Mamo's brother-in-law was murdered. They fled to California, where Mamo watched as her husband became a worthless drunk, leaving her to raise three children by herself. My mother was only two years old at the time.

It was the Roaring '20s and society dictated protocol. Topics of politics and religion were off-limits. Consumption was out and assumptions were in. You never crossed party lines. Church was for women and children, both of which were to be seen and not heard--and good parents bred only good children. Work ethics were crucial, and if you were fortunate enough, your children could read, write and do arithmetic.

Mamo had been forced to quit school at an early age; consequently, she insisted her children attend and finish school. No matter how hard she might have to work, she would provide an education for them. She instilled good values in my mother and two uncles: they were to work hard, keep their word, and above all, graduate from high school! Those were the rules! Mamo was embarrassed she could barely read or write, though no one seemed to notice but her. To me, Mamo was the smartest person I knew. I just loved her to death.

We lived with her, Mother, Earl, and me, until I was five. When we finally moved into our own place, I begged Mother to let me visit Mamo as often as possible. Oh how I loved those visits. I'd stand in the kitchen watching her make chicken and dumplings, along with her famous mincemeat pies. She rarely used measuring spoons. Instead, everything was a pinch of this and a speck of that. The best part was how she always had leftover dough, and together we would make cinnamon and sugar cookies, which were always better than the cookies we got from the Helm's Bakery truck that drove by each week. Only Mamo could make something so wonderful out of something so simple.

Behold, the maidservant of the Lord
Luke 1:38

Mamo worked as a maid six days a week, leaving home long before the sun was up to catch a bus and trolley car that would take her from her modest home in the foothills of the San Fernando Valley to the prestigious homes she cared for in Brentwood. Each week, she tirelessly took care of other people's homes so she could care for her own. Her job was to serve, and she did it with dignity and efficiency.

She worked for a different family each day of the week. My favorite was the McCallisters. They had a grown son who worked in the movies, a daughter my age, and another cute son two years older than me. When I was allowed to go to work with Mamo, I'd hold the tokens and transfers as we rode in and out of the foothills until we arrived at the beautiful homes in the Los Feliz area. It took two buses and one streetcar to get us to the McCallisters, but once we were there, it was like stepping into another world. They had chandeliers in huge rooms with velvet furniture and large rugs. Mamo washed and ironed, making sure their clothes were as sparkling clean as their homes. Her employers thought of her as their white Aunt Jemima; large, sweet and very much appreciated. Everyone adored her. And, I was her little helper.

At seven years old I would sit under the large mahogany tables and polish the ornate wooden legs until I could see my reflection. I loved helping Mamo. She always bragged on me, and gave me a nickel so I could buy one of those large dill pickles sitting in a jar at the grocery market we stopped at on our way home. Mamo made me feel special. At Mother's house, I was often degraded and sarcastically called *Queenie*. But, at Mamo's house, I was always made to feel like I really was a *Queen*.

Mamo would tell me over and over how much she loved me. She'd smooth my feathers when they were ruffled and fluff my bruised spirit when needed. She comforted my saddened heart with words she'd whisper in her Southern drawl. "Thet's all right, Sweetpea," she'd coo. "Yer not an accident, fer goodness sake. Yer someone special. Remembe'? God has a plan fer you. He knew what He was doin' when He gave you to us." She'd squeeze me. "Ya know, Mamo couldn't get along without you, an' yer helpin' hands." I loved being around her. She made me feel wanted in a world that didn't.

The first weekend Mamo visited our new house in Pacoima, she woke me early Sunday morning, whispering for me to get dressed. Without a word, she scooted me out of the house before anyone could wake. Once outside, she reached into a brown paper bag she was carrying and brought out four cinnamon-sugar cookies wrapped in waxed paper. She handed me two, took the others, tossed the bag in the trash can, and began walking down the road. Where were we going? She didn't say anything. We just walked together eating our crusty breakfast in silence. Soon we were kicking a loose rock here and there. After strolling for several blocks, we came to a church. The sign on the lawn read, "The Evangelistic Tabernacle. All are welcome."

Mamo turned to me and said, "Let's go in."

Once inside the small room, I realized we were the only white people in there. But Mamo didn't seem to mind, so neither did I. She just sat there, all 250 pounds of her, gazing up at the large cross that hung behind a small podium. Soon, organ music began booming out and goose bumps raised up on my arms. I scooted closer to Mamo, sitting there motionless as she listened to the choir. Then a preacher got up and started saying we were the branches in God's garden, and His Son, Jesus, was the Vine. He kept calling God, "The Gardener."

I looked up at Mamo and could tell she was really enjoying herself. He must have been talking her language. She never flinched a muscle as her hand rested on my shoulder. But, soon her thumb began rubbing back and forth, slowly making little small movements, over and over again, until my skin began to burn. I didn't want to move. I knew when she did that she was just lovin' on me; that the discomfort was really an expression of her love. But it hurt. I snuggled closer to Mamo so her rubbing would continue further down my arm. It worked.

The preacher drawled on about how we are to stay grafted onto the Vine if we ever hope to produce lasting, delicious fruit. I was too young at the time to understand just how lasting the fruit would be that Mamo fed me that Sunday morning so long ago.

I wanted the moment to go on forever. But, it didn't. Soon, everyone stood up and began singing "The Old Rugged Cross," then left. Mamo and I walked home without saying much, just holding hands, watching our shadows dance in front of us. Then Mamo began chuckling.

"Oh, child. If my Mama could have saw us in church today. Our white skin stickin' out like white cat hairs on Papa's black jacket." She laughed. It was good seeing Mamo having fun. Suddenly she stopped, turned, and with a serious look asked me, "Beverly Jean, ya think ya could find yer way back to that church again by yerself iffen ya wanted to?"

"I think so," I said, not knowing for sure why she asked.

"Ya wouldn't be scared?"

"No," I nodded, wondering what I should be scared of.

"Well... Sweetpea, I was thinkin' thet it may be real nice if ya started goin' to church on Sundays. What ya think? Could ya do thet fer yer Mamo?"

"Sure," I said, not realizing the wonderful gift Mamo was giving me. I'd do anything for her. I'd even go to an all-black church by myself if that's what she wanted. As we continued walking down the wide dirt road, a breeze washed over us, like a caress. Soft like Mamo's touch. Comforting, like her sweet hugs.

Because it was difficult to get to our new house in Pacoima, Mamo only visited us once in awhile. But when she did, she always asked about church. She encouraged me to join the junior choir. Oh, how I loved the music! I wanted to sing like Doris Day. I looked forward to going to church. And, when they told us girls shouldn't wear lipstick, I swore I never would. When they said, "Thou shall not dance," I was glad Mother had pulled me out of dance lessons after Earl left, saving me from a life of damnation.

Mamo coaxed Mother into letting me attend their Summer Bible Camp. I would be camping out for an entire week away from home, surrounded by pine trees, in the middle of the Angeles National Forest! I was so excited. Each girl was required to make her bed with pine needles found on the ground and place their blankets on top. For seven nights, we would be sleeping under the stars and massive trees.

Mounds of makeshift beds dotted the hillside. I chose to make my bed of needles as far away as possible from the noisy activity inside the commissary. In the evening, faint music and laughter could be heard softly echoing through the trees. It was like being in heaven. I could feel God's presence. I could smell Him. He was everywhere. In the trees. The clouds. The stars. Oh, how I loved those times, being alone with God. Just me, Him... and all those other kids I could hear in the distance. By the third summer, I gave my life to Jesus and was baptized.

With each passing year, Mother's hatefulness toward me seemed to grow. By my twelfth birthday, it was in full bloom. "Oh here she comes now," she'd say, trying to be funny. "The one who thinks she's gonna save the world." I hated her when she taunted me like that. But, I hated the feelings I had for myself even more. I prayed at night that God would forgive me.

I also resented what was happening to my body. I wasn't even in junior high and already I had started my period. Only "Miss Show Off" from our sixth grade had started menstruating. She even bragged about it! I sure didn't want to be like her. The night I became "A Young Lady," it was Jerry who was home and had to improvise, making me my first sanitary napkin from an old rag he'd found around the house. He handed it to me through the bathroom door, along with two large safety pins that were really my brother's old diaper pins that Mother kept in the goody drawer. "Pin it to your panties," he instructed. I was horrified.

But even more than that, I hated what was happening to my breasts. They were growing so fast I couldn't keep them hidden anymore on my small, short frame. Boys cupped their hands over their mouths and yelled "Moo!" whenever I walked by. I began wearing Jerry's extra large work shirts in hopes of hiding them. But nothing worked. I tried slouching my shoulders hoping nobody would notice them, until someone said it only made them look long! I felt like a freak. Why was God punishing me with such big boobs?

I wanted to be built more like my mother than Mamo. Mamo was big all over. Extra large breasts looked good on her, but looked stupid on me. I wasn't even twelve and already I was having to wear bras that needed to be made for me. And of course, Mother never let me forget how much the one she bought me had cost. "Don't think Jerry and I are gonna support you in bras young lady. You're gonna have to get a job and start making some money if you want another one."

"32 Double-D Bras" weren't sold in department stores and had to be special ordered. Miss Paulette's Brassieres were made with the finest starched muslin available. The extra wide straps were capable of holding up any amount of weight, impossible to bend or adjust. Each cup was made like a cone, all darts carefully sewn to stop an inch from the center where the material poofed out... apparently where the nipple was supposed to go. Well, mine didn't. So, each morning I would stuff the flattened gathered material at the end of my massive bra with toilet paper. And, the rest of the day I spent trying to avoid getting too close to anyone, for fear they may press against me and hear the toilet paper crackling inside my shirt.

Yes, I *really* hated my boobs. To me they were a curse. *Why had God given them to me?* The kids teased me, Mother's dislike for me grew with each increase in cup size, and men began looking at my chest as if I didn't have a face.

But, that wasn't the way it was with the man who moved in next door with his family. Louie was tall, dark and handsome, just like Earl. He was always smiling and obviously loved his family. I'd see him in the afternoons playing in the yard with his two little boys. And, in the mornings giving them and their mother a kiss before leaving for work. I noticed the younger boy right off. His name was Philip. He was four, the same age as Jimmy, my little brother, who I thought was adorable… so much so, that one day I even took him to school with me for "Show and Tell" because I thought he was so precious. It shouldn't have been much of a surprise to anyone that I found little Philip also adorable.

Sometimes, from my window I could see Philip, the new kid on the block, sitting on his porch, watching the neighborhood kids play Kick-the-Can or Hide-n-Seek. He never joined in. He never said anything. He just sat there. Occasionally he would holler into the crook of his arm with his hand cupped over his ear, which I thought was rather strange. Then I learned he was deaf and couldn't speak.

When Philip was an infant, he had caught a serious illness and an experimental drug saved his life. However, the drug that saved his life also took away his hearing, and for some unknown reason also made him unusually strong. Philip had no idea of his own strength and was kept away from the other kids "for their own good. Otherwise, someone is always getting hurt," we were told.

One dreadful day, someone did get hurt. Him. The front gate where they last lived had been left open and Philip got out. A neighborhood search began. Eventually he was found on the floor of a neighbor's garage. He was unconscious and pinned under a washing machine. He had accidentally pulled the heavy appliance down upon himself while trying to free his arm from the wringer he'd been playing with. The electricity was on and the wringer still spinning. With each rotating spin, his skin was being ripped away. After numerous operations, the hideous scars under his arm and across his chest resembled stretched rubber that had been pulled this way and that across his torso. I felt sorry for him at first. But then I got to know him and my sympathy was replaced with admiration and love.

Philip was sweet, kind and receptive. He always had a smile for me like his father. From the moment we first met through the chain-link fence that separated our properties, we became friends. He would hang onto the fence and holler his melodious sounds when I came home from school, trying to get my attention. Eventually, I began going over to his house and sitting on the porch with him. I was curious about his hearing and why he was always cupping his ear and making those melodic sounds. Over and over again, I would yell "Ouch" in his ear, pinching him lightly each time I spoke, hoping he'd hear me. Then one day Philip pinched me and hollered "OUCH!" in my ear. I couldn't believe it. I was ecstatic and jumped for joy. I couldn't wait to tell everyone. I was completely baffled when no one shared my excitement.

"He's not stupid, Beverly Jean," Mother said. "He can't talk because he can't hear. Don't you understand? He's just aping you." Wasn't that the whole point? He was mimicking the correct sound for the correct reason. I was only eleven, yet even at my age I understood the significance of what Philip had done. "I can't believe you, Beverly Jean. Stop going around giving everyone false hope. *The boy is deaf!*" She shrugged and rolled her eyes. "Boy, I'll be glad when summer vacation is over and you get back to school and forget about all this nonsense." Well, it may have been nonsense to her, but it wasn't to me. I knew what had happened--Philip had heard me!

Not longer after, Philip's mother began working nights with my mother at Lockheeds' and I became the official babysitter for both families, taking care of Philip and his brother along with my own brother and sister until our fathers got home.

"Now you can start earning some money and start buying your own stupid bras." Mother was pleased. "Your good-for-nothing father isn't helping. He doesn't care about you kids. The sooner you find that out for yourself, the better off you're gonna be." Mother rarely raised a hand to me, yet she knew how to hurt me.

When the school counselor heard of Mother's plight and how much I was needed at home, they granted my release early from school each day--so both mothers could go to work and I could take care of their kids. The school referred to us as a "hardship case." Every afternoon I would gather my books and leave school before my last class and walk to the bus depot where filthy men, in filthy clothes, slept on filthy benches. Most had a brown paper bag with a bottle inside clenched under his arm.

Each day, I arrived home just in time for Philip and me to wave goodbye to our mothers. Then together we would sit on the porch and I would yell vowels into his ears as we waited for our siblings to come home from grade school. My responsibility was to watch over the children, feed them a snack and keep them busy until our fathers came home and took over.

When Mamo heard what I was doing, Mamo called me Philip's little angel. But, she was wrong. Philip was my angel, because just about the time I needed one, Philip showed up. He'd jump up and down and squeal with joy when he saw me. He always made my heart smile. "Ther's no doubt about it," Mamo said the first time she saw us together. "The twos of you have formed yer own 'mutual admiration society.'" And... she was right.

And a little child shall lead them
Isaiah 11:6b

On my twelfth birthday, during a roller skating accident, I fell and broke my tailbone. The doctor at the emergency room told Mother the remedy was "complete bed rest for a week and to wear a rubber girdle which you'll have to buy for her--along with a large round cushion she'll need to sit on once she's up," he added. I thought I heard Mother growl. "In the meantime," the doctor assured her, "it's Absorbine Junior and lots of bed rest, and in no time your daughter will be as good as new."

I was upset with myself for falling and breaking my tailbone. My summer vacation was ruined! I should have never fallen. The stupid boy that came racing toward me was just trying to flirt and get my attention. He wasn't really going to bump into me. But I got scared. I was just learning how to skate backwards and panicked when I saw him rushing towards me. I lost my balance and fell... hard. I don't remember which hurt worse as I tried to get up--the injury to my back, or the embarrassment of Mother yelling from the sidelines. "Get up. What's the matter with you? You're acting like a cry baby." She was right of course. Now that I was twelve, I needed to start acting my age.

THE ROOTS

And, the wolf shall dwell with the lamb
Isaiah 11:6a

The following Saturday afternoon as Mother readied herself for work, I went into her room to use the heating pad on her bed as I had done the day before. It seemed to have helped. I was seeking relief for my sore body. Gingerly I crawled onto the bed, turned on the heating pad, and attempted to make myself comfortable. I was surprised when Jerry came in the room. I had forgotten it was his day off. I thought perhaps he was coming in to offer me comfort. But I was wrong. Within moments, I soon realized the comfort he wanted to offer me was more than sympathy. Confused and frightened I propelled myself off the bed and scrambled out of the room. As I hobbled past the closed door where Mother bathed, I wanted to go in--to feel safe--to tell her what had just happened. But I couldn't. What would I say? That Jerry had scared the daylights out of me? *Oh yeah, that would really go over well.* Plus--she hated to be bothered when she was trying to get ready for work.

Later that evening after Mother left, I was in the living room lying on the couch watching Cliffie Stone's "Hometown Jamboree" on our small black and white TV. Linda and Jimmy were sprawled on the floor. We were laughing at Minnie Pearl and her silly hat when Jerry walked into the room. Glancing at the TV, he came over and took the pillow from under my head and slid onto the couch, replacing his lap for the cushion I had been using. Settling down, he began watching television with us.

I was shocked; taken aback. For the second time that day, which I didn't understand, I was suddenly filled with fear. I wanted to jump up and run, as I had done earlier—but I was frozen. Laughter, from the television and the kids on the floor, swirled around me. My head began to spin. Then suddenly, without warning, Jerry jumped up and quickly raced toward the bathroom. He was acting so weird. He was really frightening me.

The following morning, I couldn't wait to get to church. I needed to talk to Ruth, my Sunday school teacher, and find out what was going on. I squeezed into my rubber girdle and hurried out of the house before anyone was up. With each step, the rubber panties squeaked between my thighs, making me walk like a zombie. But I couldn't stop. I didn't know what Jerry was up to, but it didn't feel right. I wanted him to stay away from me. But, how? We lived together in the same house. I couldn't tell Mother. I had been on her "poop list" ever since my skating accident and was unable to help out around the house. My fear made me walk faster. I began to sweat. By the time I got to church, my thighs were chafed and raw. I ached all over. But, I had to talk to Ruth. I just had to! She was smart... she'd know what to do.

After church I whispered to Ruth that I needed to talk with her. I told her that what I was about to tell her had to be a secret. "If Mother finds out, she'll really get mad. I know she will." I made Ruth promise not to say anything. She agreed and I believed her. So I told her. "Please, help me and tell me what to do to make him stop whatever he's doing." Ruth didn't say anything. For a moment she just stood there. Then she reached out and took me in her arms, and began rocking me. Eventually she spoke. "Darlin', everythings' gonna be all right," she whispered. But it wasn't. And, it took decades before I stopped secretly blaming her for the trouble the church brought me the following day.

Mother wasn't dressed for work when I got home from school. She was always ready for work when I arrived home. Her shift started at three and she never missed work. "We can't afford it," she'd say. As I entered the kitchen, I could tell she was angry. I clenched my schoolbooks when I saw her expression.

"Guess who came over today and paid me a visit?" Mother asked, trying to be nonchalant.

"I don't know," I trembled. But I suddenly had a pretty good idea.

"Ruth, your Sunday school teacher." I felt my bowels turn to water. I waited.

"And guess what she told me?"

I shrugged, unable to move.

"She said you accused Jerry of trying to molest you. Is that true?"

I stood there frozen, my heart pounding. Could she hear it?

She took a step toward me. "Young lady, did you say that or not? Has Jerry been trying to molest you!?!"

Why had Ruth told? She said she wouldn't. She promised. I told her Mother would be angry if she found out. Why hadn't she believed me?

Mother grabbed my arm. Her strong grip from years of ironing squeezed deep into my flesh. "Beverly Jean, answer me." I could see the veins in her neck. She was really upset. I tried to look away.

"DID YOU SAY THAT OR NOT?" she hollered, stretching out her words. She paused for a moment. Then in a slow growl she spat, "If he's touched you, so help me God, I'll kill him." I heard my schoolbooks fall to the floor. I knew Mother was telling the truth. She never lied. She always followed through with what she said. She was always saying how she didn't love Jerry. She'd even say it sometimes in front of him.

"I only married him because he wanted a family and I needed his help," she'd say. "I told him I wouldn't give him any kids of his own, but he said he didn't mind." When she talked like that, I felt embarrassment for her and Jerry. Her for talking like that, and Jerry for having to listen to it.

She was really angry and I believed, without a shadow of a doubt, Mother would kill Jerry if she knew the truth. I didn't want him dead. I just wanted him to stop whatever he was up to.

"I'm asking you for the last time. Did you say that or *NOT*?" Her fingers dug deep into my skin.

I denied everything. I didn't know what molesting was, but I denied it anyway. Mother's face froze. Her grip weakened.

"Well... if you didn't say that, why would Ruth come over here and tell me a lie? Answer me that, huh?" Again, there was a long pause. I could tell she was still upset. "I don't understand. Hasn't

Jerry been good to us, helping me support you kids--buying you bras and school clothes because your shiftless father won't?" She began to shake me. "Beverly Jean, I'm asking you a question. Why would Ruth lie to me?"

"I don't know," I cried, bowing my head, tears streaming down my face. I hated Ruth for tattling. I don't remember what happened next. It was never discussed again. But now, instead of being called *Holier Than Thou*, I was referred to as *The Trouble Maker... The Black Sheep of the Family*. Thankfully, what he was doing stopped, and Jerry never touched me again like that. However, from then on, his touch brought welts and bruises to my body and scars to my heart. Darkness had only changed its form. Truly, my life was never to be the same. My home had become a war zone, and I... the enemy.

The year was 1951. World War II was not a history tale but rather a vivid memory. People wanted to be left alone to rebuild their lives. It was the era of McCarthyism and the witch hunt for communists. Each week, newsreels told of "The Hollywood Ten" and the lives that were ruined because they knew too much. The attitude of the day was what you didn't know can't hurt you. People didn't want to stick their noses into other people's business. They were afraid. "The less we know, the better off we are." There were no such things as Social Services or Children's Advocacy Groups. Children were on their own.

Mamo's hands were tied. She encouraged me in every way she could. On weekends, her home became my sanctuary, Mamo's solution to keep Jerry away from me. It was a blessing in more ways than one.

The book *Angel Unaware* had just been published, and one day Mamo brought it home for me to read. It was the true story of Robin, a child with Down's Syndrome, born to Dale Evans and Roy Rogers, that died at age two. It told of Robin's short life and the impact she had made while she was here on Earth. Robin had brought joy to everyone just by being born! Just by showing up!

I instantly loved the book and read it several times. It spoke of a God I didn't know. The book spoke of a personal and caring God. A God I could talk to. A God who would listen. I began imagining His "Holy Ghost" as "Casper the Friendly Ghost." I would talk to Him at length in the privacy of my thoughts and prayers as I lay at night, under the large window over my bed, looking up at His numerous stars. On cloudy nights, when I couldn't see the stars, I knew they were still there. Just like I couldn't see Casper... I could feel Him. I knew He was there.

You send forth Your Spirit
Psalm 104:30

Dale Evans' book explained why Robin had been born, but it didn't answer my question: why had *I* been born? I began spending time alone in our den wondering about my purpose. I would go outside to feel the wind blow on my face and pretend it was Casper, my new-found friend, stroking my hair, soothing me. Little did I know, He was (Ps. 18:10).

"Beverly Jean, are ya listenin' to me?" Mamo was saying. "God don't make mistakes."

"Well, how come He gave me this life? Didn't He know I wasn't wanted like Robin?" Nothing made any sense.

"Jest remember child, God won't give ya more than yuz can carry."

Oh, that was just great. Did that mean God was the culprit responsible for the mess I was in? For the first time in my life, I had the thought, "I wish I were dead." Sadly, it wouldn't be the last time the thought entered my mind.

Ruth visited our house only one more time after her initial visit. She came by, again while I was at school, this time to drop off a book instead of the bombshell. The Bible was on my bed when I got home. My name, Beverly Montgomery, had been engraved on the cover. Inside she simply wrote, "Proverbs 3:5, 6."

Lean not on your own understanding but trust in the Lord,
and He will direct your path
Proverbs 3:5,6

It took nearly thirty-five years before I understood what that scripture meant and nearly that long before I ever attended another church service. It took me that long to realize that, indeed, Ruth had helped me. She had brought out into the light an area of great darkness that had infiltrated my home (1 Cor. 4:5b). I felt the church had betrayed me. They couldn't be trusted. I was finished with all of them along with their God. Or, so I thought. But apparently God wasn't finished with me. In fact, He had just begun.

###

Mother with Beverly, 3 months old

Beverly's Father, Earl Montgomery

First Stage Appearance, age 7

chapter two

<u>THE GARDEN</u>

They were in the garden of God
Ezekiel 31:9

The summer I was to enter the eighth grade, we moved from the dirt streets of Pacoima to the white, middle-class neighborhood of Panorama City, where every house looked alike. Jerry continued working at his brother's sheet metal shop in Los Angeles and always expected his dinner on the table exactly at 5:05 p.m. when he got home from work. If it wasn't, I paid for it by having extra chores placed on me... leaving me no time for myself or my school work.

Mother had quit her job and began working at Von's Grocery Market in Van Nuys. She took to it quickly and people loved her. She was very pretty and vivacious, and soon became *Checker of the Month*. She finally seemed to have found a place she fit in and it made her happier. I was happier, too.

I liked my new school and enrolled in Mrs. Waldorf's glee club. I loved singing. I applied for a weekend job using my new Social Security number, at a hot dog stand near our house where I could sing to my heart's content while I prepared for the day's business. I began to feel like I was a part of a normal family.

When I was thirteen, I learned from a classmate that there was going to be a beauty contest at the Devonshire Downs Faire Grounds for the title of *Miss Junior San Fernando Valley*. First prize was a year's worth of paid tuition to a local modeling school.

"Please, please, please!" I begged Mother. "Some of the other girls at school are going to be in it. All I need is a one-piece bathing suit." She finally agreed and signed the permission slip.

The day the faire arrived, I was excited and filled with nervous energy. My entire family was there. Mamo, Mother, Linda, Jimmy and Jerry, who took all the pictures. When my name was announced as the winner, they jumped up and down and screamed for joy. I had never seen Mother so excited. As photographers were taking my picture, Mother was making sure they had my named spelled right.

When my photograph hit the newspapers, Mother landed me my first modeling job. A coworker of hers was married to an amateur photographer with a makeshift studio in his garage. He was willing to give us a set of 8" x 10" glossy head shots I needed for the modeling school, in exchange for some cheesecake shots--slightly revealing photos he could hopefully sell to various magazines. So, another deal was made without consulting God, and at age thirteen I did my first *Pinup* job.

It seemed innocent enough. Mother promised that I'd always be covered and she would chaperone. So, from the shadows of a darkened garage, Mother looked on as I began a career at mastering the art of revealing little while wrapped in nothing more than a towel, a sheet, or a man's large, unbuttoned, white tailored shirt. That was the summer I turned fourteen.

Mother and I joined a local gym that promoted beauty contests, and within a short time the two of us were being used for their newspaper ads in lieu of a membership fee. Each Sunday our picture appeared in local newspapers, posing together in identical shorts and halter tops, with an ad that read:

Which one is the mother? Which is the daughter?
You too can look young & beautiful
by joining Butcherman Bruce's Gym

Any considerations I may have had in the past about my body were soon forgotten. It was obvious which side my bread was buttered: The outside. Wasn't it God who gave me my body in the first place? It was a gift, like my naturally curly hair. It was certainly nothing I could take credit for. I didn't like it when people noticed my looks and disregarded what I thought. They obviously cared more about my body than about me. But, I remembered the words Ruth once taught in Sunday School: "It's a sin if you don't use the gifts God gives you." So I decided to do just that.

Trophies soon began lining my bedroom wall: *Miss Marines, Miss Mt. Baldy, Miss Bay Beach*, Miss This, Miss That. Seventeen titles in all. I was wanted for store openings and ribbon cuttings, and I appeared on local television and radio shows. I was receiving a lot of attention, though some might say for all the wrong reasons. But not my family. For the first time, Mother seemed proud of me. She loved seeing my picture in the newspapers. My love for the stage, she said, was inherited from my great-great-grandfather on Earl's side. "In the 1800s, he was one of the first aerial acts in the circus, you know. Beverly Jean comes by her talent naturally," Mother would boast.

That year I began attending Van Nuys High School. The school bus service didn't include the area we lived in, and I was forced to walk several miles to catch the city bus that would take me to school. My back still hadn't completely healed from my skating accident, and each day I'd grumble to myself, shifting the weight of the heavy school books from one hip to another. *Why doesn't anyone ever stop to give me a ride?* I didn't understand. They did it all the time for Mamo. Neighbors would see her walking down the street carrying her shopping bags, pull over and offer her a lift.

"Where ya' going, Hattie?" they'd ask. "Hop in an I'll give ya a ride."

I couldn't understand why they didn't do that for me? Nearly every car that went by only had one person in it. The driver! The rest of the car was empty! As I continued walking, my back writhing in pain, I couldn't believe how unfair it was, and how uncaring people were.

By the time the bus dropped me off for school that first day, I was exhausted. With or without the books, my back was killing me, and I still had another forty minutes before the bell rang. The gates weren't open and there was no place to sit. I noticed a group of girls sitting on the lawn outside the school's chain-link fence. I was still the new kid on the block and quietly sat down on the perimeter and leaned against a big sycamore tree, which offered my back some relief.

I recognized a few of the girls from last year in junior high but didn't know the older ones. Sitting quietly, I listened in as they swapped stories of their summer escapades with their boyfriends. The tales became more and more graphic as each girl described her lover's abilities. They were going into great detail describing ALL the parts of their boyfriends. I sat in the background with my mouth open, wishing the school bell would ring, too embarrassed to get up and leave before anyone else.

The following morning as I walked toward school, I dreaded the thought of sitting with those girls again. But then I spotted St. Elisabeth's Church across the street. I hadn't noticed it before. She sat there quietly with her staircase spreading out wide, like beckoning arms, inviting me to enter her open doors.

I walked into the foyer and I dipped my finger into the water bowl, as I had seen people do in the movies, and made the sign of the cross upon myself. Timidly I entered the cathedral. It was magnificent. Nothing like the church in Pacoima. But there was something similar about both. It wrapped around me like a hug.

The morning service had just finished. The church was empty. I could hear faint voices coming from another part of the building with an occasional clang of silverware and dishes. Standing there in the empty sanctuary, I suddenly felt something I hadn't felt since years earlier: the feeling of being alone with God Himself. Morning sunlight filtered through the tall stained glass windows lining the massive room, sending shafts of light streaming across the sanctuary in a rainbow of colors, with flecks of lint floating in the air.

I was drawn toward the front where an enormous stained glass window of Jesus loomed behind the altar. I knelt, not moving, my eyes transfixed upon the Lord's figure depicted before me. The school bell rang from across the street. I didn't want to leave. The air inside the church seemed different than it did across the street, where kids gathered in school rooms to recite *The Pledge of Allegiance*.

Three years earlier, I had sworn I would never enter another church. I blamed them for the mess in my life. But, here inside *this* church, I felt safe. The contrast *inside* the walls versus *outside* was tangible. And so, St. Elisabeth's became my oasis, my safe haven, for the next two-and-a-half years. Before every school day, I could be found inside the empty church, hanging out with myself... and God. I looked forward to our time together, and even on days I ditched school--which were many--I still went to church first. *Then*, I played hooky.

Occasionally someone else would be in church with me, and in silence we would drink up the quiet peace together. Sometimes I sat in the front. Sometimes in the back. Sometimes under the choir loft. Sometimes *in* the choir loft. Sometimes I knelt. Sometimes I sat. But always, I was there every morning before school. Praying. Listening. Looking. Watching. Searching. Did God really have a purpose for me, like Mamo said? Or, was I an accident like Mother said? I don't remember getting any answers. I just remember feeling good when I left there, like I used to in Ruth's church. I couldn't explain why.

God's glory filled the church
2 Chronicles 7:1

As time went by, kids at school began asking, "Are you Catholic?"

"No," I'd answer.

"Then why are you always over there?"

"Because...." I'd shrug. I didn't know why I was there. I just knew I wanted to be there. They thought I was strange. So did my family, except for Mamo. She seemed to understand what the others didn't. If truth be known, neither did I.

My popularity wasn't helped any by my photograph being in the local newspapers each week. Girls thought I was *stuck up*. Others thought I was one of those Jesus freaks who didn't do anything except read the Bible. Little did they know that the only Bible I had was the one Ruth gave me years before, which still sat in its original box somewhere in my closet. I couldn't explain today why I did things any more than I would be able to explain, tomorrow, the miracle God was about to send me.

My scrapbook began filling up with newspaper clippings and magazine articles showing me smiling from ear to ear. I was getting a lot of attention for my looks. I loved the applause from an audience, but didn't like the attention one-to-one. The few times I had been alone with a boy was disastrous. They wouldn't keep their hands off me. When I refused their advances, they would spread lies about me at school how they had *felt me up*. I had very little time for any of them.

Then I met Billy. He had a gymnast body, dark eyes, jet black hair, olive skin and a phenomenal sense of humor. What wasn't to like? He was shy and the first boy that didn't trip all over himself when he first met me. He had dropped out of school the year before while in the tenth grade, and was the youngest of the notorious Powers brothers. His mother was the same age as Mamo but half her size. They lived near the school, and I would often see her leaving St. Elisabeth's after the morning mass. She was a devout Catholic and had nine children to prove it. Billy was her seventh son, her "baby boy," and I loved her from the moment we met.

In a world that often made me cry, Billy made me laugh. I laughed at his silly jokes and enjoyed his simple ways. He didn't seem to care what others thought. Once he even picked me up at school on horseback! You should have seen everyone's faces.

He didn't seem to care what they thought or that I modeled, and we rarely spoke of either. We soon became best friends. We saw each other alone seventeen times before he tried to kiss me. I know, because I began keeping track. I started thinking something was wrong. But then one day, he kissed me.

Mother didn't like Billy at first. "He comes from the wrong side of the tracks," she said. I couldn't believe my ears. *Was she kidding?* Who did she think we were? Any *Father Knows Best* image we may have had was only a facade.

Billy's father was abusive. He was also a drunk. I learned he often beat Billy's mother, until one night the older brothers stood up to him and kicked him out. He died six months later, shortly before Billy and I met. His sentiment was "good riddance." He told me once, "I never even cried." I could understand why!

Shortly after his father's death, Billy and his family moved from their converted pigsty on Sherman Way (where the garden hose was also the family shower), to a small one-bedroom apartment perched over a grocery store. Breakfast consisted of coffee and bread, with a bit of sugar and occasionally some cinnamon sprinkled on top.

The Powers brothers had a bad reputation, and I was nervous about meeting them. But, I quickly learned this group of "Black Irishmen" were full of fun and mischief. I liked all of them. They were very polite and never used foul language. And, oh how they loved to tease and make me blush! Some of them had been in jail. Even prison. One had actually died in San Quentin. Rumor had it that a few of them had robbed a post office and sold marijuana, though I never saw any evidence of it. But, Billy wasn't like that. He wanted to get away from the path his older brothers had paved and make something of himself. "I have to," he said. So, at seventeen he convinced his mother to sign enlistment papers for him, and he joined the Navy.

I thought my heart would break the day we said goodbye. He gave me his gym ring on a chain and placed it around my neck. I swore I'd never take it off. We made an oath to write each other every day. Then he was gone, and I was alone. I sat in our den for days, playing the same seventy-eight records we owned, over and over again, songs that reminded me of him. *Little Things Mean A Lot* by Kitty Kallen was our favorite.

THE GARDEN

It didn't take long for word to get around that Billy Powers and I were going steady. Having his ring around my neck was like having a personal body guard tied to me. Everyone knew the reputation of the Powers brothers and no one bothered me. I would often drop by The Chili Burger after school looking for the guys. It was only a few blocks from school, and I knew it was their favorite hangout. I hoped for a ride home after physical therapy, which I now took, so I wouldn't have to take the bus and walk that long distance carrying my school books. Usually there were at least two or three brothers around, and one of them was always willing to make time for me and give me a lift. To these guys, I was their baby brother's little girlfriend. They never took advantage of me and always treated me like I was a lady.

The following year, Billy and I officially became engaged. We picked out our rings. Since he was stationed in San Francisco, each month we would go down to Hart's Jewelers and pay the monthly installment together, counting the months until the rings would be ours. The elderly owner would go behind the counter and take out the rings from inside the safe and let us look at them. We were so excited.

Eventually my back improved somewhat. In addition to my occasional modeling jobs, Mother got me a job bagging groceries at the market where she worked, and I started baby-sitting at night to earn extra money. Billy and I were trying to save up enough money to buy our first car. Eventually we succeeded.

I couldn't believe my eyes when Uncle Leo drove up the driveway that Monday afternoon in the most beautiful car I had ever seen. My uncles, Leo and Ray, owned a body & fender shop and had found a car they knew Billy and I would love, a 1949 Ford Coupe. They painted it candy-apple red, put in white tuck-n-roll upholstery and added four shiny new whitewall tires to match. They had outdone themselves! This was more than I could have ever imagined. I couldn't wait to show Billy. He would be home on leave in less than a week from San Francisco.

Summer was over and school was starting the following week. I couldn't wait for those snooty girls at school with their fancy cars to see mine. I was now a sophomore. My career was just starting. Natalie Wood, *Miss Popularity*, had moved on from Van Nuys High, where the two of us had gone to school, to Hollywood High. Which left me... *Miss San Fernando Valley Junior Beauty Contest Winner Herself,* in person, with her cool car, bright and beautiful for everyone to see. I really thought I had it all as I cruised down Van Nuys Boulevard sporting my new car, and driving through Bob Big Boy's drive-in.

It was extra hot that Wednesday, even for September. Mother left me instructions to take my sister shopping for some new school clothes. "They're having a sale at Sears & Roebucks," Mother hollered as she ran out the door to work. As we drove up Ranchito Street, Linda chatted incessantly about the neat things she wanted. I could see the steeple of Saint Genevieve in the distance. My eyes glanced upward toward its cross as something from my left caught my eye. I instantly reacted but it was too late. The speeding '53 Dodge crashed into my '49 Ford, propelling me out of the car and onto the hot pavement, careening me across the asphalt with my beautiful new car tail-spinning counter clockwise right behind me.

Gravel ripped at my skin before I skidded to a halt. I watched in horror as the tires under the car's red fender raced toward my face. Then, it just stopped... as if it hit an invisible wall. One moment it was racing toward me, and the next, it had stopped, slamming into something so powerful that it sent Linda, who was still inside the car, flying across the front seat crashing into the passenger door, leaving an indentation in the side panel and breaking her breastbone. I watched in terror as my car quivered and quaked over me before landing upright. I could smell the rubber. I don't remember much else. I blacked out. When I came to, the paramedics were working to get my long, thick, brown hair out from under one of the whitewall tires. They finally used scissors.

The ambulance raced us to Valley Receiving Hospital where Mother was waiting. She was upset. The good samaritan who had called her on the phone said they thought the one laying in the street was dead. Mother wasn't sure which one of us they were talking about. The paramedics agreed, saying "the one laying in the street should have been dead, given any logic."

You will stretch out Your hand... and save me
Psalm 138:7

The hospital kept me overnight for observation, and released me the following day with severe skin lacerations and abrasions that ran up and down the left side of my body. It was nearly a year before all traces were gone. But, the new short hairdo? That took much longer to grow out after the savage haircut the ambulance driver had given me while trying to release me from the grip of my new car. My tailbone was also rebroken, which created a chronic spine problem that never completely healed. And once again, I was forced to wear a panty-girdle that squeaked when I walked.

But, I was alive! That was all I could think about, along with wondering what had really happened. When I tried to explain what I saw that afternoon as I lay in the middle of the street, the story didn't sound real.

"But honest to God, Mamo, the car actually teetered back and forth over me. I could smell the burnt rubber. Honest!" I could tell she didn't understand. Or, maybe she did. But, *I* didn't! How could I explain the unexplainable? How could a car racing toward me one minute suddenly just stop on a dime? Had it really hit some invisible wall? How crazy was that? I stopped talking about it after awhile. But, I knew what I had seen.

I began to wonder if the God I visited each morning before school had anything to do with what had happened. The same God Mamo said she prayed to each night, covering me with a blanket of prayers and asking for a hedge of protection (Ps. 139:5) to surround me as I, her darling Sweetpea, ventured out into the world, vulnerable, unaware of any dangers that may be lurking around the next corner. Yes, God's hand was upon me that day. Years later, I would come to realize that it was Mamo's prayers that placed God's hand upon me. He was the One who protected me, as He would throughout my life. All because of the one praying grandmother I was given.

"Your daughter is lucky to be alive, Ma'am," the policeman said to Mother as he left my hospital room the day of the accident. I heard what he said, but I knew he was wrong. Luck had nothing to do with it. I knew I had been saved by the invisible hand of God.

Any feeling of euphoria I had that I survived and was still alive was dimmed by the ugliness of living inside my house. Especially after Jerry had been arrested. He had sexually molested a five-year-old girl at our local movie theater during the Saturday afternoon children's matinee. He had been caught red handed. I was mortified. But not nearly as much as when Mother began sticking up for him.

"That little girl is just lying through her teeth," Mother defended. "Obviously her parents coached her. Otherwise, how could someone her age be able to describe such a thing?" *Maybe because it's true!* I wanted to scream. I couldn't believe my ears. Had everyone except me forgotten what Ruth had told them about what Jerry had done to me four years earlier? This time, he had been caught in the act by an usher who had seen it firsthand when he flashed his light on the exposure. I couldn't understand how anyone could make excuses for Jerry. But they did. EVEN my own mother!

Mother pleaded to the court for leniency. "This is his first offense, your Honor," she told the judge. "And, his financial support is very much needed at home to help support my three children." The judge obviously agreed with her and sentenced Jerry to six months of weekends only at the Los Angeles County Jail. During the week, he was free to come and go as he pleased. So, every Friday night he would report to jail. Then, on Sunday nights he would come home just in time for dinner and tell us horror stories of what he had seen that weekend while he was *inside the tank*. We heard the words "Homosexuals" and "Transvestites" and learned what they meant. We learned of other things we had no business knowing. My mind screamed, *Please. Please. Please. Stop!* But, no one seemed to notice.

Our good neighbors couldn't wait to send us nasty letters after Jerry's arrest and conviction hit the newspapers. We also began receiving late night phone calls from anonymous callers with hateful voices. "No doubt from one of our so-called Christian neighbors," Mother concluded. "They're all hypocrites!" The entire community seemed to be talking about the man who lived down the street. Neighbors pulled their children inside and closed their doors when any of us went outside. Each day I walked by their houses, going back and forth to school, and felt like every eye was on me. I truly wanted to die and just disappear. Maybe I could be born again into someone else's family and have parents like Dale Evans and Roy Rogers.

"Child, ya stop thet foolish talk," Mamo said when I finally shared my thoughts. "I know dis is difficult on ya, but child, God isn't gonna give ya any more then yuz can handle. Don't ya forget thet."

How could I? She was always telling me that. Okay, so maybe God wouldn't give me any more than I could bear, but with each passing day, it was becoming more unbearable. And, it wasn't the wounds from the neighbors, or Jerry's vicious tongue, that I couldn't bear. It was Mother's continued denial to look at the truth.

Once Jerry began serving time, any free weekends I had to be with Mamo came to an abrupt halt. Mother needed me at home, and again I had the responsibility of watching the kids. The last weekend I slept over at Mamo's, she raised her eyes from the breadboard she was working over and said, "Child, I don't knows all da details of whet's goin' on. But, Beverly Jean, I do knows God has a plan fer yuz. Jest like He has fer everyone." Softly she began stroking my cheek with her floured finger as if trying to soothe away my inner torment. "Yuz jest mark Mamo's words, Sweetpea. Someday God is gonna use you. He's jest preparing ya like dis dough I is workin' on."

There! She said it again! What did that mean? That God was orchestrating this misery today in preparation for some mystical purpose for me tomorrow? That just didn't make any sense, not for a loving God. I struggled with the question as Mamo's hands went back to work, sprinkling more flour on the mound of dough before her.

Our house became a silent battlefield between Jerry, myself and my growing resentment toward Mother's complacency. All she ever preached was for me to stay out of Jerry's way and get "your bloody high school diploma so you can get out of here." Boy, I wanted that too. Each night I would gaze up at the stars from my bed and pray, "Please, dear God, help me." Then, one day the answer came. And, ironically it came from Jerry himself, when he asked Billy and me, "Hey, when are you kids getting married?"

Married. Of course! That was the answer. We had been sweethearts for nearly four years, but we had never actually discussed a wedding date. It was always, *someday.* Obviously, *now* was that *someday*, and so the wedding plans began. Billy became my "Knight in Shining Armor," my ticket out of there. I could hardly wait. The thought of getting married to my adorable sailor became my main focus. But first, I had to graduate.

I had enough credits to skip a grade from the two years I attended summer school and was given permission to graduate early. My graduating class voted to attend the Moulin Rouge, a dinner and nightclub theater in Hollywood, for *Senior Night.* Billy got a weekend pass and rented a tux. We were mesmerized as we were greeted at the nightclub, first by the valet, then by the hat-check-girl, surrounded by fur coats of every color and length hanging neatly in a row. The cigarette girl, with her low-cut "merry-widow" black mesh hose and spiked heels, really caught our eyes. We tried to look nonchalant as we sat in the audience waiting for the show to begin. I felt like I was in heaven as my eyes took in the grandeur, and my ears listened to the musical sounds of the band warming up in the orchestra pit. When the lights dimmed and the curtain went up, the dancers appeared and I was mesmerized. I wanted to be up there, on stage, doing what they were doing. "You should," Billy whispered. "You're as pretty as they are."

Maybe so. But as dancers they were way out of my league. I had taken tap lessons for several years when Earl was still around. At age five, Mamo had taken me to see a movie with Ann Miller tap dancing in front of mirrors, giving an illusion of a hundred pairs of shoes all tapping together in perfect harmony. I knew then that's what I wanted to do. To *Dance*. I loved it and couldn't stop imitating the tap steps. I pleaded with Mother to take lessons. It was Earl who enrolled me the following week at the Joan Lot Dance Academy. Within three months, I was in my first show, twirling a parasol sprayed with glitter and singing *April Showers*. I danced my way into the audience's heart as only a five-year-old can. But they had entered into mine, too. Smiling from ear to ear, I took my first bow, loving the applause. They said I was a natural. Sadly, when Earl left, so did the lessons.

Now, nearly a decade later and graduating from high school, with Billy's encouragement I returned to the Moulin Rouge and auditioned for a job. I lied about my age and got a job as a chorus girl. I was ecstatic. It didn't take long before it became obvious that my limited training and prior back injuries had taken their toll on my talent and flexibility. Those legendary Donn Arden kicks and Cancan Tillers were nearly impossible. I stretched my hamstrings and worked extra hard on the routines in hopes of keeping my job, but the grueling task master of a choreographer saw I was struggling during rehearsals and would scream at me, embarrassing me to the point of tears. Each day, I waited for that dreadful pink slip to arrive. It never did. But, my union card did. And, I soon became a bona fide American Guild of Variety Artists member, earning $63.00 a week and loving every minute of my new profession.

Jimmy Durante was the main attraction, with a cast of nearly fifty. The opening production could have been from some Cecil B. DeMille movie with its cascading staircase and tall showgirls, elegantly costumed and coifed with sequins and yellow plumes sprouting everywhere. The dancers were known as ponies, and my height of five feet, five inches, made me the shortest of them all. Standing next to those six-foot, six-inch show girls, I felt more like a Shetland than a pony. When we received the news back stage that a movie studio was out front filming our routine for Lana Turner's film, *Imitation of Life*, the excitement became electrified! But it was our grand finale, *The Frankie & Johnny Production*, with its outrageous rendition of the San Francisco fire, that drew so much attention. It was rowdy, explosive, and had all the drama and excitement of the infamous 1906 fire. Things in my life were changing, and I was starting to truly enjoy myself.

In November, Billy and I were married at The Little Brown Church of the Valley--he in a tuxedo and me in a white wedding dress with veil, proudly symbolizing my virginity. There were about a hundred-and-fifty people in attendance, a mix of our old school friends and new ones I'd made dancing on the Sunset Strip.

The hooligans from the Powers clan were outside drinking beer and decorating the car that would soon whisk Billy and me away for our honeymoon. Inside the chapel, my side of the family looked normal, but in reality, Aunt Helen was drunk having one of her crying jags. Earl, the bigamist, who Mother said could not attend, secretly snuck in and sat in the shadows in the back of the church so no one would see him. And then there was Jerry, the convicted pedophile, who led me down the aisle. In this company, Billy and I stepped into our future and began our new life together. Each promising the other to love, honor and obey, until death do we part.

We rented an adorable furnished apartment in North Hollywood near Lockheed Airport, so it would be easy for Billy to travel to and from San Francisco, where he was still stationed at the naval base. As I put our wedding gifts away, the strawberries on the dishtowels Mamo had embroidered reminded me of the Bible lesson we heard together so many years before. "You are the branches and God is the vinedresser (Jn. 15:5). Now, go and produce good fruit."

"Mamo, there's no doubt in my mind that Billy and I will produce good fruit," I said to myself as I placed the dishtowels on the closet shelf. Billy and I had felt the sting from the briers and thorns our family trees had produced. The bad and the ugly, the hateful, the outlaws. We both wanted to do better than that. We weren't going to produce rotten fruit and hurt each other like our parents had done. Our love was going to be nourishing and lasting. We were going to live happily ever after.

But then the honeymoon was over and Billy was shipped overseas for *Operation Hardtack* and the "Bikini Island Bombings." This time my beloved would be gone for nearly a year. I didn't know what to do. The show at the Moulin Rouge was closing and I refused to go back to Mother's. Then I heard about, and tried out for, an *All Girl Traveling Review*. I lied about my age as I had with the Moulin Rouge, and one month later was headed for Las Vegas. And once again, God had not been consulted.

###

THE GARDEN

Billy and Beverly's Wedding

Renaissance Faire Beverly & Billy

St. Elisabeth Church

CHOICES

I have set before you life and death,
blessing and cursing;
therefore choose life,
that you and your descendants may live

Deuteronomy 30:19

chapter three

THE SINS

Forgive us our debts
Matthew 6:12

Ina Rae Hutton's *All Girl Review* was booked for three months at the Royal Nevada Casino, which later became the Stardust Hotel. From the moment I arrived in Las Vegas, I knew I was going to love it. I could feel the excitement. I loved the lights, the adrenaline, and the applause of the audience. I still wasn't the greatest dancer, but I was improving. What I had was a great stage presence. The audience was so busy watching me, they never seemed to notice that my kicks weren't as high as the dancers beside me. I thought I had found my calling. I was using the looks and personality God had given me, and doors were beginning to open. I gave little thought to where those doors would lead.

My future looked rosy when I first started. Obstacles and land mines were nonexistent. The thrill of the unknown filled my being. The future looked bright. My path was well-lit with all the dazzle of the neon lights. The world sang out, *This way to fame, fortune, and fun!* Without any thought of ramifications, I innocently and ignorantly jumped with both feet into my future.

Las Vegas was everything the girls at the Moulin Rouge had said it would be. Excitement was everywhere. The atmosphere was exhilarating. From the moment I got off the plane inside the airport's small terminal, I could hear slot machines going off. People were laughing... having a good time. Two girls that had boarded the plane in Burbank whizzed passed me, giggling and laughing. They were dressed in the most luxurious outfits. They looked like they just stepped off a magazine cover instead of a small bouncing airplane. They waved to me as they slid into the back seat of a limousine that was waiting for them. It had a large Mustang emblem engraved on its door. I wasn't familiar with the symbol, but it looked so glamorous as the limo pulled away from the curb. I was glad a taxi was nearby. The flight had been bumpy and the breakfast Mother insisted I eat was hard to keep down.

The Vegas Strip ran between The Dunes at the west end and the Sahara at the other. In between sat the Royal Nevada, my destination. It was the grandest sight I had ever seen. When I was younger, I fantasized about my name being in lights. And, here I was, standing under a million of them. I couldn't wait to tell Billy the next time I wrote.

The *All Girl Review* opened after a two-week rehearsal. The cast of dancers and showgirls came from everywhere. Sitting in the dimly lit showroom on that first afternoon of rehearsals, I wished Mamo were there. I didn't have nearly as much stage experience as some of the girls, but I made up for it with a big smile and lots of enthusiasm. And, my assigned roommate turned out to be a true Godsend, helping me with routines in our room late into the night. When I was finally able to call Mamo, she could hardly contain her laughter over the telephone when I told her my roommate's name was Chuckles. She was from Ohio, and engaged to a boy back home who was studying for the ministry!

"Child, doesn't God have the greatest sense of humor?"

It wasn't long before I became known backstage as *Mascot*. Naive and shy, the older girls knew I was younger than the required "twenty-one" written on my Nevada work permit. They laughed at me one night when I overheard some of the girls say they were going to do some "tricks" after work, and I asked, "Can I come too?"

Chuckles explained to me that some of our coworkers were prostitutes after hours, and the word *trick* was really a term used for the performance they gave while laying on their backs and pretending to have fun. Their treat came later in the form of payment. *How could they earn money like that?* I asked myself. Some of them were really nice. I was shocked to learn that was the primary purpose for many of the dancers working in the show. This is when I learned the glamorous girls I saw get into the limo at the airport worked at the Mustang Ranch. It wasn't for cattle ranching at all, but rather a brothel for ranching the cowboys.

My original plan was to work in Las Vegas for three months with the show, then return to Los Angeles with the money I saved and wait for Billy. I received letters from Mamo telling me I was welcome to come and stay with her while I waited for Billy's return. Her chicken scratches on the stationary told of the prayers she "held up" for me each night. She always closed with "I love you, Beverly Jean. Be a good girl. XXX OOO Mamo." But, I wasn't being a good girl, or at least I was afraid that's what she would think. As time went by, I wrote less and less, to her or Billy.

When our *All Girl Review* closed at the Royal Nevada, I jumped at the chance to audition for the well-known and adored choreographer Barry Ashton at the El Rancho Hotel. What I didn't know was the hotel was more than a hotel, and the dancers were expected to do more than just dance. Without realizing it, I had entered a world where Mamo's prayers would be the only thing that would save me. Within a week, I was saying goodbye to Chuckles and hello to my new roommate, who would share the adjoining bathroom located between our individual private sleeping quarters.

My new job was grueling, and with little glitter. Every two weeks our dance routines changed, as did the marquee announcing the new coming attraction. We rehearsed by day and performed by night with stars like singer Eartha Kitt, comedian Joe E. Lewis, and stripper Candy Barr. Her entourage included mobster and boyfriend Mickey Cohen and Manager Joe DeCarlo. They were always close by. Mickey was short. But Joe was tall, dark and handsome, just like Earl. He was also kind and witty like my Billy.

It was mandatory that the girls at the El Rancho remain in the casino after the show, unless otherwise instructed, mixing with the customers until 4 a.m.. Each night, after the last show, I would slip into the cocktail lounge and sit in a booth by myself and listen to performers from other hotels who often dropped by for a jam session. Fats Domino, Louie Prima, Keely Smith, even Frank Sinatra sat at my table one night for a brief moment and chatted. Later in the gossip columns, he found himself somehow linked up with me, though I'm sure he didn't have a clue who I was. Me, a nobody, having the time of her life, sipping on one Slo-Gin-Fizz after another, in her new, low-cut, very tight dress that she could barely sit in... acting cool, calm and collected, watching stars such as Anthony Quinn, Debbie Reynolds, and Eddie Fisher all enjoying the impromptu performances. I truly felt I had died and gone to heaven.

On slow nights I gambled. The craps tables were like a magnet, and soon I became the *darling* of the graveyard shift. The dealers knew I tipped well and went out of their way to be friendly. I quickly learned that by sitting at the tables with the visiting gamblers from one of the East Coast Junkets, I could make money without having to lay on my back. Many of the "Johns" just wanted a pretty face to gamble with, and I was always available. I became quite good at stashing gambling chips in my skin-tight dresses with low-cut necklines. Within a short time, I had enough money to buy my first Cadillac, a 1955 black sedan, which I soon traded in for a '58 pink Cadillac convertible.

When I gambled by myself, I always bet with the house. Often I'd see patrons walk away from the table angry after losing everything. But I, on the other hand, nearly always walked away with a smile on my face and a purse full of hundred dollar black chips. I couldn't wait to tell Billy about all the money I was saving. I just loved my new life.

I met the new lifeguard the hotel recently hired. I had never seen anything like him before. Muscles everywhere. Even at Butcherman Bruce's Gym, where Mother and I use to go, none of those guys could compare. As he dove into the pool that afternoon, I thought

I was seeing Tarzan in person. Big. Bronze. Beautiful. I learned he recently had won the title, *Mr. Venus.* He was single. He had been married but was divorced, twice apparently. He had two small sons, whom he rarely saw. On top of everything, he was polite, nice, and worldly. What started out as a friendship soon escalated into something else. Soon I was sneaking out from my mandatory hours in the Casino after the shows and placing gambling on temporary hold. I had found something much more compelling.

I became obsessed with the enchanted rendezvous awaiting me in my tiny hideaway. I used every pat excuse to justify my affair: I wasn't hurting anyone or doing anything wrong, we were both consenting adults, it wasn't like I was a virgin any longer. Like they say, what people don't know won't hurt them. I decided I had been struck by Cupid's arrow and didn't question it.

One afternoon I was summoned to Beldon Cattleman's bungalow. The owner of the hotel wanted to see me! My knees shook. I wasn't sure what I had done, or hadn't done, but I was as nervous as a child as I approached his door. I had only seen him occasionally when he entertained friends at his private table in the hotel's dining room. We had never met. I tried to stay out of his way. There were horrible rumors how he could be cruel; that girls had actually vanished, never heard of again if they didn't go along with his requests. I was terrified.

"So you're the one they call the Mascot," he said, sizing me up as I entered the large living room. The girls had been right. Maybe he did know everything that went on in his hotel.

"How do you like your new car?" he asked after a moment of painful silence.

"I love it," I stammered, wondering why he cared, and how he knew.

"I heard you're good at the tables? Is that true?"

"Yes, I guess so." I was becoming more uneasy.

After a long pause, he looked up at me and stared into my eyes, as if challenging me to look away, and simply asked, "Is it true you are married?"

| 51 |

The question took me by surprise. I nodded.

"And, your husband is overseas, right?"

Again, I nodded.

"Then why, *Miss Mascot*, are you cheating on him... with *my lifeguard*? Tell me that."

At first I was speechless. Then frightened. Instinctively I stepped back. *How had he found out?* I knew we weren't supposed to fraternize with the help, but we had been so careful to not let anyone know. *What difference did it make to him anyway?* We were still doing our jobs and weren't hurting anyone.

Before I could answer I heard a phone ring in the distance. Suddenly, someone appeared in the doorway and whisked my accuser off to who-knows-where and I was escorted back to my bungalow. Again, I found myself waiting for that dreaded pink slip. And though it never came, my romantic affair with the handsome lifeguard was relocated to afternoons at Lake Mead.

Everyone received pink slips when it was learned the Folies Bergere, a packaged nude stage show from Paris, was taking over. Even Barry Ashton, our choreographer, was being terminated.

"What're your plans now that the show is closing?" he asked me one night after we learned the news. We were sitting in the lounge, sipping frothy cocktails in tall slender glasses with cherries floating on top.

"I don't know," I confessed. "I don't want to go back to Los Angeles just yet. I heard from my mother that my stepfather has suffered a serious heart attack and won't be able to work for awhile. I was hoping to find another job to help with the expenses."

His pudgy body leaned toward me and whispered, "Darling, you know after Candy Barr starred here last month she went to work down the street at the Silver Slipper. Her contract is up in two weeks and she will be heading to Beverly Hills to work at a place called The Largo. The Silver Slipper is gonna need a new headliner," he paused, then leaned back in his chair.

Headliner? Did I hear him right? Is he talking about me taking her place? *Yikes!*

"They're paying five times what you're making now," he whispered, pulling his chair in closer. "I know you are modest and all, Darling, but I was thinking, if I promise to choreograph the numbers for you... so there'd be no bumps or grinds... just a little tease here and there, and perhaps a pirouette or two." He smiled, raising his eyebrows. "Then at the very end, as you slip off your bra, the curtain comes down, and nobody sees a thing. That's the tease." He paused. "So what do ya think? Could you do it?"

Of course I could do it. Anyone could do it. But, was I *willing* to do it? That was the real question. He had thought of everything, and had made it sound tempting. I was flattered. I could certainly use the money, but I was way too shy to get on stage and reveal myself to a bunch of strangers. My earlier pin-up days had been an illusion.

"I know you are modest," Barry added. "That's why I went ahead and asked Lloyd Lambert, Eartha Kitt's designer, if he'd design you the most elegant breakaway gown you've ever seen."

My eyes widened; *I'd never seen ANY breakaway gowns, except for Candy's!*

"And Lloyd said, *'YES!'* Can you believe it? He said he'd design you a gorgeous gown with panties and bra just like the bikini swimsuit you wear now at the pool, except instead of polka dots he'll use bugle beads and fringe. We'll cover your breast with rhinestone pasties, which nobody will see anyway because the curtain will be coming down." Then he quickly added, "Don't worry, Darling, you'll do just fine. It'll be like wearing one of the costumes you wear now. Except it'll be far more glamorous."

I was speechless. I finished off my drink, gobbled up the cherry (pulling the stem from between my lips) and ordered another drink.

"I think your solo should be done as a *real teaser*, you know... like Sally Rand, with fans, but much grander."

Solo?

"We can do it like Lily St. Cyr, using the art of illusion."

Who were these women?

"We'll call you, 'Miss Beverly Hills, The Sophisticated Lady of Burlesque.' And we'll use Duke Ellington's hit-song, *Sophisticated Lady*, for your theme. I'll be sure to get you top billing, just like Candy Barr." I could feel his eyes on me.

"What do you say, huh? Ya want to give it a try? Come on; it'll be fun. What can it hurt?"

My head was swirling. I loved his energy—his creative self. He had thought everything out. I had already decided. I was beginning to see my next money making opportunity.

"Come on, Darling. Trust me."

Trust him? I already did. He was safe, like a girlfriend. I genuinely liked being with him. Barry knew I wasn't the greatest dancer, yet he always found ways to showcase me whenever he could. He always covered for me when I left the casino early to meet my lifeguard. He never tried getting me into bed. What was there not to trust? So, giving it little or no thought, I stepped into my future thinking only of what I could gain and not of the consequences. Fame and fortune were calling. And once again, I suspect the angels were gasping, "How long will it take, dear Lord, before this woman learns for every action there's a cosmic reaction?"

The devil, the father of lies
John 8:44

For three years, everyday before high school, I had faithfully visited God's house at St. Elisabeth's. I prayed to Him. I hung out with Him. Yet, within a year of graduation and the marriage of my high school sweetheart, I was having an illicit affair with someone I barely knew, and working nights as a burlesque queen. But, my name was in lights! My picture graced the cover of numerous magazines. I justified my behavior, and looked down upon anyone who disapproved. I was proud of what I was doing.

THE SINS

The Silver Slipper was a honky-tonk casino with nightly Vaudeville Skits featuring Hank Henry and Sparky Kaye, of the *Ocean's Eleven* movie fame, and who supposedly had connections with the Sinatra Clan. In the days leading up to the opening, I was becoming more and more nervous. Especially when Mamo called and told me she and Uncle Leo were driving up for my opening. Was she kidding? I couldn't have my Mamo in the audience when I took off my clothes! What was she thinking?

The night of my performance arrived. My family was somewhere in the crowd, and I was about to go on. I was terrified. I thought of something my mother would say, "A lady can be a lady anywhere." That must include the stage too, I thought. At that moment, I said a little prayer. It became a nightly ritual before I went on stage. "Please, God, help me to not trip, or make a fool of myself."

Afterward at the cast party, I learned that Earl, my father, who seemed to keep sneaking in and out of my life, had come to Vegas to take a bow for siring such a outstanding filly, his daughter. I nearly died of embarrassment when I later learned he had been in a drunken brawl with one of my coworkers after the cast party, and had passed out in the parking lot.

The next day at breakfast when Mamo learned of Earl's horrendous behavior, she appeared disgusted. She didn't want to hear anything about it. Instead, she spoke about my newfound profession. She immediately started with the truth.

"Beverly Jean. I must tell ya. I don't like it one bit what ya doin." She hesitated, fiddling with her napkin for a moment. She softened, "But I must admit, yuz do it like a lady." And, with that, for Mamo the subject was closed. Uncle Leo looked up from his bacon and eggs and glanced around uncomfortably. Changing the subject, he said, "Hey, Little One. Sure do love your pink Cadillac. I bet Billy's gonna love it too when he gets back from sea duty." I could tell he was thinking of something more he'd like to say about my new profession, or maybe Earl, but he didn't say anything and went back to dipping his toast in his eggs.

The three-week contract at The Slipper extended to four months. Everyone loved me. I was modest, young, and quickly became the hit of the Vegas Strip. Headliners from other hotels came to experience the late night Lounge Show. I wore beautiful gowns like Barry promised and had a floor length cape covered in sequins that weighed a ton. And then, though I was a hit, and loving every bit of my newfound freedom, it was time to leave. Billy was coming home! It was time for me to get out of my Vegas dresses and get into the apron. Billy was finally being discharged from the Navy! I couldn't wait. There was much to do. We would both need to find new jobs. I needed to find a place for us to live and gather our things being stored at Mamo's. So, I said "Goodbye" to the life and fame I had only known for a short time, and headed home.

But our reunion, which should have been wonderful, turned out to be a terrifying nightmare. Shortly before Billy and I were to meet, after nearly a year's absence, I discovered I was pregnant! I felt that what should have been the beginning of our new life together, would begin with a massive lie. A lie that nearly killed me trying to keep it a secret. Not to mention my shame.

As it turned out, some people eventually learned the truth. The abortion I elected to have cost a lot more money than I had saved, and I was forced to borrow from my mother. I felt guilty that I was living up to the label she had given me years before. Even though my name had been in lights on the famous Las Vegas Strip, I was still the *black sheep* of the family.

Arrangements were made for the abortion. Billy would be home in a week, and in the meantime I could stay with Mother and Jerry. *Gee, this wasn't fitting my expectations at all!* I had envisioned Billy's homecoming quite different; as a happy occasion we would remember forever. But here I was, my knees shaking and sick to my stomach as a taxi dropped me off on a deserted corner of the outskirts of Beverly Hills for an illegal surgery. It was eleven o'clock at night, and I was alone, waiting for some unknown person to come and whisk me off to who-knows-where, promising to return me in three hours. *Prayerfully in one piece*, I thought to myself. Had I lost my mind? Why had I chosen to do this? Oh, yes, because I didn't want to tell Billy the truth... that I had been unfaithful to him and was pregnant with another man's child!

A black sedan pulled up and the back door swung open. A voice whispered firmly, "Get in."

I jumped into the back seat. As the car sped off, a dark blanket was tossed to me. "Lie down and put this over your head," the obscured driver ordered. After several minutes, with many stops and turns, the car came to a halt and the back door quickly opened. I was whisked down a walkway lined with hedges. With the blanket still over my head, all I could see was the sidewalk, then two stairs that led to a dimly lit room. The blanket was taken off from behind as the door closed. Adjusting my eyes to the lighting, I could see an examination table with stirrups in the middle of the room, with a single light fixture hanging from the ceiling. Beside it was a table with surgical tools and an examining light.

A woman entered the room from another direction. She wore a blue surgical mask.

"Beverly?"

"Yes."

"You have something for me?"

"Yes." I assumed she was referring to the envelope filled with money wadded up in my pocket. I handed it to her.

She quickly took it, glanced inside, and tossed me a white sheet with instructions, "Remove everything from the waist down and lie down on the table with your legs in the stirrups. The doctor will be with you shortly."

She returned with a man dressed in doctor's attire, wearing a mask. The woman came over to the table I was lying on and checked my pulse and heart rate, which I'm sure was racing a mile a minute.

"Don't be nervous," the doctor said. "I'm here to help you. When you leave here it will be all over. In the meantime, you must not make any noise. Even if you feel discomfort, you are to keep quiet.

Do you understand? If you make any noise, I will be forced to quit the procedure."

I nodded.

His eyes squinted as if he was smiling. "Very well. Let us begin."

The procedure didn't take long. But, the pain was so excruciating, I'm sure I would have fainted if the surgery had taken any longer. It took every ounce of strength I had to put my clothes back on so the sedan with the black blanket could whisk me back to reality. It had been torture. But it was over. Behind me. And now I hoped Billy and I could begin our life... anew.

I feigned the excuse of having a serious menstrual period the first night Billy and I were together. The lie kept us apart long enough for me to recover. So once again, Billy and I entered our future together. This time, however, I entered it with more hidden baggage than ever before.

To say Billy was surprised when he learned of my burlesque career would be an understatement. The year before he left for duty overseas, he was married to *Miss Prim and Proper*. Upon his return, he finds *Miss Tease*, revealing to strangers what should have been for his eyes only. He was puzzled by the change but quickly learned to accept it. Especially after I received a phone call from Chuck Landis, owner of the Largo, wanting to meet with me at his plush nightclub on the Sunset Strip. Candy Barr, who was currently starring at his Beverly Hills nightclub, had been arrested in Texas the year earlier for possession of marijuana and given a stiff, fifteen-year jail sentence. She was out on bail and working while she waited for an appeal, which had just been denied. She was to give herself up to the authorities immediately for extradition. Landis was calling to ask if I could come in the following afternoon to talk business. He was looking for a replacement.

It wasn't long before Billy and I were giggling all the way to the bank each week as we deposited large paychecks into our checking account from my new career. Billy found a job at night working on the assembly line at General Motors, and we would often meet up after work at a local coffee shop and talk away the rest of the night. Billy was my best friend. I loved him so much. I had been so afraid I had blown it earlier, but now dancing in Beverly Hills, with the love of my life picking me up on weekends in our pink Cadillac, I knew my decision had been the right one. But my memory was short-lived, for within a year, I was once again heading in a direction that would nearly kill me, and my marriage.

After Candy Barr left her boyfriend, mobster Mickey Cohen, continued coming around the club with his sidekick, Joe DeCarlo. Sometimes they invited me to join them at an after hours joint, along with a dozen or so other people. More and more my picture was showing up in the tabloids.

I loved the attention I was getting as headliner of The Largo. I had bought into the lie "there's no such thing as bad publicity, as long as they spell your name right." I hired a press agent, a man who slaved for his wages. The publicity stunt began, "Mobster Mickey Cohen & Stripper Miss Beverly Hills are to be married." Billy, of course, was in on the hoax. The ten-carat, emerald-cut diamond ring I wore on my finger flashed on the front pages of newspapers around the world. The tabloids ate it up.

But, it wasn't long after the borrowed diamond was returned to its rightful owner that I pulled up to Rondelli's Cafe in Studio City one night after work to meet up with everyone, when DeCarlo came running out of the club waving his arms for to me to not stop. I rolled down the window, the engine still idling. Jack Whalen, The Enforcer, had just been murdered. His bullet-ridden body lay inside. The police had not yet arrived.

"Get out of here, Beverly," Joe ordered. "I'll call you later."

I was frightened. I raced home, immediately woke Billy and asked him to drive me to the Little Brown Church of the Valley where we had been married. It was open all night, and while Billy waited in the car, I slipped inside and begged God for protection.

A few months later, I was subpoenaed by the Grand Jury inquiring about Mickey, his goings on, and the murder. I didn't know anything except I was still frightened. Especially when I was shown photos of me wearing Mickey's engagement ring; pictures taken outside my apartment, on the walkway, in my garage, carrying groceries, holding my house keys. Where had the photographer been hiding when these shots were taken? I told the Grand Jury everything I knew, which was nothing. "I was just along for the publicity ride. Honest." Thankfully, they believed me.

Shortly afterward, Landis, who had become my manager, sent me out of town for awhile to San Francisco to work at the *Fax Nightclub*, where I would follow comedian Don Rickles, who, despite his gruff persona, was very kind to me. The club paid me $6,000 for six-weeks! It felt like a fortune. Having been through so much in Hollywood, it felt good to get away. Billy was now attending hairdressing school and would have to stay in Los Angeles. But we promised to talk each night on the telephone.

I loved San Francisco, especially the red carpet treatment I received. Nearly every day, requests for appearances and interviews came in from local newspapers and television shows, for which I was paid even more money. A helicopter was occasionally used, picking me up for an appearance in another county, only to fly me back for my nightly show. It was the first time I had ridden in a helicopter. It was exciting. I felt like royalty. I was in demand and I loved it. I also loved the personal attention I was receiving from my new press agent... however, I soon regretted it.

Mother always said I had a thick skull and she was right. I don't always learn a lesson the first time around. Often, it takes several thumps on my head before a lesson sinks in. Apparently, my past shenanigans with the lifeguard hadn't taught me the error of my ways. Upon my return home from San Francisco, I found myself pregnant again. And, of course, the timing made it such that it couldn't be my husband's child.

Once again I arranged to have an abortion. This time I would find the abortionist at an abandoned duplex located next to the railroad tracks in downtown Los Angeles. I would be met on the second floor. The voice on the phone ordered, "Be sure to bring the money."

"Yes sir," I sputtered.

On the appointed day, horror gripped me as I cautiously stepped up the rickety staircase. I could see curtains from the top floor window open, then close. I knew I was being watched. By whom? No one knew where I was. Suddenly I was even more scared than before. Billy thought I had gone shopping.

I said a frantic prayer, "Oh Lord, please be with me. I promise I'll be good from now on. Please, please, please."

I slipped the ten $100 bills, as instructed, under the door on the left and then entered the door on the right. I glanced over the dingy quarters. In the middle of the room was that lonely table like the one I had seen before, with stirrups facing the window. The familiar tray with instruments, along with one single lamp, stood beside it. There was a note on the table:

"Remove all clothing from the waist down. Get on table. Drape sheet over yourself and the doctor will be with you shortly."

Voices drifted from the other room. Suddenly a man in street clothes appeared in the doorway wearing a familiar green mask. He introduced himself as The Physician and asked me to lie back and put my feet in the stirrups.

"Scoot down," he ordered. Suddenly, with very little warning, he injected something deep into my vagina. I could feel my cervix scream. I yelled.

"DON'T MOVE! It's almost over. Just a little bit more and I'm done." He was done all right. I pushed myself backwards away from him, as fluid squirted from the syringe he was holding. He quickly stood up.

"I suspect there's enough in her," he said to the nurse who had entered the room. "In a few hours her body should begin to abort." He turned to me as if annoyed. "Just go into the bathroom when it does, and flush the blood clot down the toilet. You'll be fine." With that, he gave me a good luck pat on the arm and left.

And then I was alone. It seemed to take forever to get dressed and make it down the stairs to my car. Hours more to get home. Blood was everywhere. The front seat cushions were saturated. Pools of blood had formed below on the floor and ran all the way under the seat to the back floor board. My blue jeans were crimson red. I couldn't move. I laid on the horn as I drove up the driveway and waited for my Billy to find me.

I awoke in St. Joseph's Hospital. Tubes ran out of my arms. I was hooked up to a machine.

"Welcome back, young lady," the nurse said as I opened my eyes. "How do you feel?" *How did I feel? Like I had died!* Then, it dawned on me what I had done and I really did want to die.

"You nearly did," Dr. Alex later told me. "Girl, what were you thinking?" *What was I thinking?* That seemed to be the problem; I wasn't. I never seemed to think. I rarely prayed. I was a mess. I promised myself things were going to change. I would see to that.

That evening from my hospital bed, I begged Billy for his forgiveness. I was so filled with shame. What had I done? And, why? Because I could? I thought I could get away with it without anyone finding out. What kind of excuse was that? What kind of a person had I become?

"I promise on everything that is sacred to me, Billy, I will never do this to you again. Ever. I promise. I will be faithful to you for as long as I live, so help me God. Please forgive me, Billy. Please. Please. I wasn't trying to hurt you." But I had. Tears ran down both our faces as we confessed our undying love for each other. "Till death do us part," we promised once again. We had been through so much, the worst, thanks to me and the awful choices I had made. But, now it was time for the best. And, the best it was to be, for a very long time to come.

Godly sorrow produces repentance
2 Corinthians 7:10

\#\#\#

Las Vegas, Nevada

The Largo, Hollywood, CA

chapter four

THE STARDOM

Things that are seen are temporary
2 Corinthians 4:18a

Billy and I never spoke of my indiscretion again. Soon I was back headlining at the Largo on the Sunset Strip, and Billy on the assembly line at General Motors. His demonstration of love, through his forgiveness, humbled me. For the first time in my life, I was happy. Truly happy. I had a home of my own. I had married my high school sweetheart and best friend. We played. We giggled. We danced 'til our hearts nearly burst after hours at the Whiskey-A-Go-Go. During the summer months, we played make-believe at the Renaissance Pleasure Faire.

It was the '60s. We were living in the now. Method acting was in. Boundaries were out. It was a decade of decadence... of sex, drugs and rock-n-roll. The Vietnam War raged on, and the *Peace* and *Human Rights* movements fervently pushed forward. Ardent crowds across the country shouted, "Peace, brother, peace." The motto of the day was, "Make Love, Not War."

Yet, right in front of our eyes, both President Kennedy and Martin Luther King were murdered. Political unrest, and social and economic grievances had spawned wars in our streets. In Los Angeles, the Watts Riots were fueled by the outrage and unrest of the African-Americans living in the Watts neighborhood. With emotions running high, it sparked a six-day siege by Americans... against Americans... on American soil! Sadly it caused thirty-four deaths, over a thousand injuries, nearly thirty-five-hundred arrests, and more than $40 million in property damage.

Backstage at the Largo, the dancers and I watched on live TV as Senator Robert F. Kennedy was assassinated. It was only miles from where we sat in horror. We couldn't believe what we were seeing. We could hear sirens whizzing by the club as police and ambulance vehicles sped toward the Ambassador Hotel in an attempt to save the Senator's life. But it was too late. Our nation had gone mad! How had *America the Beautiful* become a *Country of Conflict*? *Ah, yes*, it was that age-old pull of *Ying and Yang*—the forces of good and evil. It was during this period of time I began questioning my own mortality and purpose—but only briefly—then the reality of my current fantasy life whisked me off to yet another wondrous place.

The early '60s arrived with a dazzle. It became the start of my whirlwind extravaganza. It began with a formal invitation to attend the 31st Academy Award ceremonies as the guest of Arthur Freed, the producer of that year's Oscar-winning movie *Gigi*. Mr. Freed had seen me in Las Vegas and sent a letter asking to have my agents contact him for a future screen test when I returned to Los Angeles. My life resembled *Cinderella's*, except the pumpkin coach I rode in towed a matching ski-boat to play in. And the *Prince Charming* I sat next to was my lover, my escort, and husband, my biggest fan... cheering me on to the end.

I'm not certain how it happened, but Billy became friends with various studio casting directors and soon was on a first name basis with many of them. Everyone loved Billy. The press adored him. They referred to him as *Mr. Hills*, and even wrote about him when he left General Motors to become a hairdresser. One article read, "he has just returned from Rome where he studied under the latest hair guru..." Not exactly true, but it made for great publicity.

We were surrounded by press agents, theatrical agents, and managers. All with one purpose: to advance my career. They weren't focused on God, or joining the Peace Corps. But rather, initiating me into the various unions[1] *required to further my career.* They were doing a great job. Far better than I could have ever imagined. The name *Miss Beverly Hills* shined in large letters across the massive marquee on the Sunset Strip. Negotiations for appearances on various Hollywood shows were all proof of the great representation that surrounded me. I never imagined it might be Mamo's prayers that were pulling me further and further away from my chosen career as an exotic dancer, covering me each night with prayers and asking God to set me on the straight and narrow (Matt. 7:13).

Radio Talk Shows filled my daytime calendar. Bob Crane, on KNX radio with his notorious drum set tucked in the corner of his tiny sound stage, put me at ease and made for a pleasant interview. I felt I was in a dream when I taped the *Armed Forces Radio Show* and rubbed elbows with Robert Taylor, my mother's favorite movie idol. Billy was sorry he hadn't gone with me on the interview. But he did accompany me the following year, as I tried my hand singing at the USO show with Johnny Grant at Camp Pendleton. The marines hooted and hollered over my rendition of *Give Me A Little Kiss, Will Ya Huh?* I suspect they couldn't actually hear my voice quivering over the roaring cheer of five thousand men in uniform, excited to see a woman dressed in a miniskirt and tight sweater. The experience bolstered my ego, and the press fueled it. Billy and I, two kids from the wrong side of the tracks, were having the time of our lives.

Television offers began to come in. My first was portraying a stripper, who was brutally murdered in a Boris Karloff's *Thriller* episode, "Jack the Ripper." Ironically, it was directed by actor Ray Milland, trying his hand for the first time at directing, as I, a stripper, was trying mine at acting... *pretending* to be a stripper.

During this time the San Francisco Examiner referred to me as a *junior* Rita Hayworth, and the Los Angeles Examiner said I was "one of the nicest and most respectable ladies in the body beautiful business." My looks and name were in demand, and the studios were willing to pay. My agents were earning their keep. Paramount Studios hired me to portray myself in *Breakfast at Tiffany's* with Audrey Hepburn. I only worked on the closed set for a few days, yet I was paid more than Billy and I earned together in a good month.

The first thing I did was buy myself an orthopedic king size bed—for my constantly aching back, and Billy's pleasure.

The two of us were lost in a large wonderland of make believe. We played together privately, locked behind doors where a red night-light burned aglow. But, we also played in public in my professional world of pretend. I loved the limelight. And Billy, he loved the image of being my protector, always on the perimeter.

However, one time my agents got us booked on a television show... together. Billy didn't like that one bit, but I thought it was wonderful. It was an opportunity to get paid and have some fun and free publicity.

We were hired to be on Bud Collyer's television game show *To Tell The Truth*, a popular quiz show. Businessman Chuck Landis, my manager and Largo owner, along with friend Gary Owens, a distinguished radio disc jockey and later *Laugh-In* star, would be joining Billy as contestants. Their task was to convince the panel that they were my true husband. All three knew me well, and answered the questions from the celebrity panelist without much difficulty. The contestant with the least votes was the winner.

Billy was adorable the way he kept fidgeting with his clothes. He was nervous! I could hear it in his voice as he attempted to answer the panel's questions, desperately afraid he might get something wrong. At the conclusion of the show, Collyer asked the candidates, "Will the real husband of Miss Beverly Hills please stand up."

Landis pretended to stand. But then wavered and sat back down. Owens did the same, pretending to be my spouse. No one had voted for Billy! The audience shouted with joyful surprise when they learned Billy was my husband. The ruse had worked. Billy's quiet demeanor had fooled everyone, and he was proud that he had made it through as the winning contestant and had overcome his nervousness. We both had lots of fun and walked away with a new set of the Encyclopedia Britannica and a nice size paycheck in our pocket.

It was around this time that I was crowned California's *Bowling Tournament Queen*. With the title and publicity pictures came public appearances at various bowling alleys, where I was expected to be more than a pretty face. I was expected to bowl! *YIKES!* My back! I was good in front of a camera, but behind a bowling ball? The team named me *Captain of the Largoettes* and had me pose for photos while they practiced their game. We bowled opposite well-known stars and local disc jockeys whose radio stations were also looking for publicity. With the history of my back, I was surprised I was able to bowl with only an occasional gutter ball. Together, Billy and I were meeting and becoming friends with many Hollywood celebrities.

It was during this time that I had my embarrassing appearance on TV with Regis Philbin. A few days later, Mamo and I were having our daily talk over the telephone when she shocked me by saying, "Remember when thet man on TV asked ya, 'How'd a nice girl like yuz end up doin' what ya do at night?'"

"Yeah?"

There was a pause. "Well, I was thinkin', child. Maybe he was right. I mean... I don't really think God meant ya to show yerself off in front of strangers. Thet's 'spose to be only fer yer husband. Maybe God's openin' up other doors fer ya."

Maybe so. I knew she was right about my job at the Largo, but was surprised to hear her say so. I had suspected how she felt, but she had never said anything. It had nagged at me too, wondering if what I was doing was right. But, I loved the glamour and the attention. It wasn't like I was hurting anyone. In fact, it was quite the opposite. I was making lots of money and spreading it around. I was generous and employed numerous people. People knew "I wasn't the typical bump-and-grind girl."[2] As a columnist once wrote, "even women should be able to see the beauty in what Miss Hills does." I suspect Mamo wasn't one of them.

With my prior back history, I knew I'd never be a ballerina. But I enjoyed the dance. The tease. And, the sensuality. I became an expert at revealing little while tantalizing many, projecting an image that had little to do with the real me. By night I was seen as *Miss Beverly Hills, The Sophisticated Lady of Burlesque,* but by day I was *Mrs.*

William Powers, madly and passionately in love with her husband. We were soulmates enjoying our newfound fame and fortune along with the attention it was bringing. But that was about to change. This lucrative profession I delighted in was about to come to a screeching halt. And even though its ramifications would unknowingly linger for a lifetime, I'm sure the heavenly angels were saying along with Mamo, "Enough, is enough. There will be no more dancing for Miss Beverly Hills!"

The headlines in the papers read, "Stripper Hurt in Car Crash." Trying to be funny, another wrote, "2 Dolls get Sudden Roles in 'Smash Hit.'" They were referring to me and actress France Nuyen, who was not hurt in the accident. Her car had slammed into our car that Billy was driving. My leg injury, that was originally reported to be severe, was nothing compared to the news the doctors later reported.

"Luckily," the doctor began. *There was that word again, "luck."* The word echoed from the past. "It was lucky Beverly didn't break anything, but she did receive a nasty knock on her head. She has suffered a brain concussion which will take her out of the limelight for quite some time."

I didn't feel lucky! I was hospitalized for more than two months and only released after agreeing to use a wheelchair. My equilibrium and vision had been severely affected, and doctors feared I could fall and reinjure my old back injuries. When Mother came and visited, she remarked, "A brain concussion? Well, at least we know you have one." I strained to bite my tongue, and Billy pretended he didn't hear her.

I was temporarily in a wheelchair and unable to work, and Billy lost his job because he stayed home and took care me. For awhile, we both collected unemployment. We had never thought to save money and had spent it like crazy. We had nothing saved, so we began to barter. First, we sold the pink Cadillac I had bought in Vegas with my gambling winnings. Uncle Leo came through again and found us an old coupe so we could get around. We sold my jewels. Then, the furs. We stopped short of selling Roulette, the toy poodle that Billy had bought me, and dyed pink to match our Cadillac. Ultimately it wasn't enough. We were broke and had no place to live.

That's when God sent us an angel disguised as a realtor. He was looking to hire new management for a twenty-seven-unit apartment building located in North Hollywood. If we managed the complex, we would get our own apartment free! Billy and I jumped at the chance, figuring if we could run our one apartment, how hard could twenty-seven of them be? We soon found out. It was around then that we learned God had blessed us in another way. We were going to be parents. Billy and I were going to have a baby.

A son makes a glad father
Proverbs 10:1

We were overjoyed. God had forgiven me and not held my past sins against me. He had given me another chance. "Thank you, dear God. Thank you," I wept that evening as I slipped between the satin sheets and snuggled up to Billy. This child had been created out of love. Not lust. Billy and I cherished the thought of having a child. A child due to be born on Christmas Day, but who arrived two days early. We named him Derek, after my friend and actor, John Derek.

Shortly after the delivery of Derek, I was ready to reenter public life. While I was pregnant, I had been unable to attend the Hollywood movie premiere of *Breakfast at Tiffany's*. Pregnancy and sexy were just not mentioned in the same sentence. Public appearances were totally out of the question, especially when you looked like you were going to pop any second. But, shortly after the delivery of Derek, my agents were back with offers. A character of "Party Girl" opposite Jack Lemmon in *Days of Wine and Roses* was the first. We worked together for several days. Before each take I would see Mr. Lemmon whisper to himself, "It's magic time." I figured that was his way of asking for a blessing, like I had done when I first started dancing, "It's show time. Bless me, dear God. Don't let me mess up."

That was definitely my prayer. "Please, God. Don't let me mess up and embarrass myself by forgetting my lines." I hated memorization and wasn't very good at it. But I knew I had to get better at it. My dancing days were over because of my injuries, and I needed my new acting career to gain steam, even if I felt nervous that I had little talent. But my agents believed in me. As did Billy. And Mamo! She was beside herself with pride and joy.

"Maybe yer auto accident wasn't an accident after all child," she chided one day. "Cuz, look whet's happened. Out of ashes, God has given ya a precious son and da beginnin' of a new career." I suspected she was right.

Success was going to take more than a curvy figure and a big smile. I began taking acting classes several times a week with various notable teachers. Then I began singing lessons, and later I studied dance at the American Academy of Ballet, hoping it would strengthen my body. I wanted very much to excel at my new profession as a serious actress.

Billy and I were ecstatic when the Hollywood Reporter ran a 4"x5" head shot of me smiling from ear to ear with headlines that read:

MISS BEVERLY HILLS
Guest Starring
TONIGHT
THE JACK BENNY SHOW
9:30 P.M.
Channel 2
★

In Release:
"Comedy of Terrors"
with Vincent Price and Peter Lorre

The training had paid off. "Not since Gypsy Rose Lee had a stripper rated such a good break," Louella Parsons wrote in the L.A.

Herald. She was right. Even though I was working hard in my new profession, I still needed the breaks. I felt like a kid in a candy store, surrounded by all the goodies of Hollywood, but not sure which ones I would be allowed to have. I was nonchalant on the outside, and screaming with joy on the inside.

My excitement was over the top when my agents booked me on *The Lucy Show.*[3] I was to portray the starlet at a movie premier that a crowd had gathered to see. I was being escorted down the "Red Carpet" beside legends Edward G. Robinson, Kirk Douglas, and Jimmy Durante, real-life stars who were portraying themselves. My heart raced a mile-a-minute, and my cheeks were frozen in a grin plastered across my face, as we arrived together and waved to the crowd.

In the scene, my handprints were to be placed in cement for posterity. Lucy, who plays an enthusiastic fan, is so excited she actually falls into the wet cement... face first! She comes out spitting and sputtering, dripping with muck. Always the master comic!

Later, as I was leaving my dressing room after the shoot, Miss Ball came up to me and tapped me on the shoulder. I jumped, shocked to see her standing behind me.

"I'm sorry if I startled you," she said sweetly. Her voice was tender and encouraging. "You remind me of Judy Holiday." As she walked away, I thought to myself, *Judy Holiday?!* What a compliment. Holiday was a popular actress and well-known comedian! When Lucy's words sank in, those brief moments created a powerful, pivotal shift in my very soul. It was time to pay serious attention to my goals and choices.

I was becoming known around town as a reliable actress, always on time, knowing her lines. The image felt much better than the "sizzling dancer" that headlined on the Sunset Strip. In the San Francisco Chronicle, one headline read, "The bluenose stripper takes to the drama." But on the inside, I was still a starstruck kid. Especially when I met Elvis Presley. It was nearly impossible for me to act nonchalant.

MGM had hired me to be one of his back-up dancers in *Viva Las Vegas*. That should be simple enough, I thought to myself. I wasn't prepared though when we first met. When I was introduced to Elvis, all I could do was stammer, "How do... you do... sir," I said, extending out my arm in hopes of a handshake.

Sir? Yikes... was I crazy? I sounded like a young school girl.

He gave me that charming crooked smile and said, "I do jus' fine, Ma'am. Thank ya."

We instantly became friends. He had that southern charm I recognized in Mamo. Later, I was cast as Trudy in his movie, *Kissin' Cousins*. Elvis sent me a telegram congratulating me on the good news. I spent nearly two months on location with Elvis in Big Bear, and on the back lot of MGM. When the studio threw a cast party, Mamo and Billy came as my guests. Elvis was immediately smitten with Mamo. I think her large frame and Southern drawl reminded him of his mother. During the evening, Elvis jokingly kidded Billy about someday going on the road with him.

Not long after my third movie with Elvis playing *Miss Speedway* in the movie of the same name, he actually called and invited Billy and me to be guests at his opening in Las Vegas!

"I wanna give this to you and Billy for your birthday, Beverly," he crooned over the phone. How had he remembered my birthday? When August came around, there we were, Billy and I, sitting ringside at the International Hotel in Vegas as Elvis held the audience spellbound. Being there reminded me how much I loved being around the applause of a live audience. Recognition from television and film had its moments, but it was the love of the audience and joy of performing on stage that I truly missed. Watching Elvis rekindled that love.

After returning to Hollywood, I begged my agents to find me some legitimate stage roles. Soon I was portraying Hedy LaRue, the dumb blonde in the seven-time Tony Award-winning musical, *How To Succeed in Business Without Really Trying*. The six-week contract played out of town. I kissed Billy goodbye, took the hand of our son Derek, now four years old, and headed north to experience the thrill of Theater In-The-Round, where the audience surrounds the stage and there's no place to hide. It was grand!

"Wow! She's Somethin' Else," the headline read.[4] The article went on to applaud me for making a "difficult choice which in effect meant a complete new start in show business." They acknowledged, "While at the top, so to speak, she decided to change as well her image to the theater and since that time... well, she just loves comedy... and, if her performance as Hedy is any criteria for credibility, she is successful in her new ambition."

Jack Bailey was the star of the play. He had been one of my heroes when I was younger and had made an indelible impression on me. He and his television show, *Queen For A Day,* transformed women's lives by taking a wish, usually borne of pain and suffering, and turning it into a reality of healing and grace. I always remembered an episode I saw with an elderly woman who was the *Queen for a Day.* What was her one deep desire? The removal of the tattooed serial number, etched across her wrist by the Nazis while held captive in a German concentration camp during World War II. The compassion and gratitude I witnessed was overwhelming. Jack Bailey, with his classic *applause meter,* had made a phenomenal difference in the woman's life. Each show ended with its signature trademark, "Make every woman a queen for the day!" Now, years later, here I was in a play, feeling like a queen... rubbing elbows with Bailey each night!

One night during a performance, I was on stage when suddenly, without warning, my back went out and I couldn't move. One minute I was on top of my game, the next I was frozen in pain. I had to be helped off the stage, and was taken to the local hospital. I had ruptured a disc in my lower back. The following day, Billy drove up and took Derek back home with him while I remained in the hospital, praying I could somehow get well enough to complete my contract.

"Bit Player Takes Over For Hurt Star," the Fresno Bee reported. "Early in the show," the newspaper reported, "Miss Beverly Hills injured her previously broken back, yet despite the pain which the cast says is obviously intense, she continued the show to the end. But, because Miss Hills is in 'a lot of pain' a stand-in was used for three nights." The remainder of my days were spent alone in traction before reporting each night for work. What a relief when the show was over. My body ached and I was ready to go home. I longed to sleep in my own bed under Billy's tender, loving care. Once at home, physical therapy soon had me strong enough to return to work. I was overjoyed to accept a new role, portraying Crystal Allen in Clare Booth Luce's play, *The Women,* at Melodyland--another Theater-in-the-Round.

It was a dream come true being cast as the "other" woman, the role Joan Crawford made famous in the film. This was my first dramatic role. All I had to do was remember my lines and walk straight. No twisting or turning. Yet, I was scared to death.

"Please, dear Lord, please be with me," I prayed on my way to the theater.

Each day, Billy would fluff my confidence and say, "Sam, I know you can do this," using the pet name he'd given me. "You just wait and see. The audience is gonna love you." And, when the reviews came out confirming his prediction, he actually gloated. The L.A. Times wrote, "Surely worthy of higher billing is Miss Beverly Hills... who plays the brassy, uncouth, wily sex kitten to the hilt and produces some of the show's high spots..."

In Al Capp's *Li'l Abner,* I played Stupefyin' Jones. The Times praised me again: "It's the stupefying Miss Beverly Hills who puts some desperately needed zing in the show with her double whammies. The remaining members of the cast are either forgettable or best forgotten." Critics were being very kind to me, and my agents used it to my advantage. They managed to get both Billy and me hired to do a film together shooting in the Philippines. Me as an actress; he as my hairdresser. He had been working at Gene Shacov's Salon in Hollywood, but was willing to say "Goodbye" to his day job for the opportunity to do a movie.

Billy's mother agreed to care for Derek, and off we went on what seemed to be the longest flight in history. Holding onto Billy's arm, smiling and waving at the press as I boarded the plane, I looked like a true Hollywood actress. Skin-tight dress, spiked high-heel shoes, nylon stockings, and a massive hat. I was adorable. However, twenty hours later after landing at nearly every island to refuel, we finally arrived in Manila. By then I resembled something the cat dragged in. I have never been so happy to arrive at any destination in all my life.

Brides of Blood Island took six weeks to film, all shot in the jungle. Everything about the location was foreign to me. The jungle was as I had pictured it, but we had none of the comforts of home. Six days a week we worked on location where there was no running water or bathrooms. Billy ended up constructing me a toilet in the middle of some bushes he had cleared, placing large rocks in a circle as my new toilet. The thought of snakes scared me, but it was the water buffalo that came browsing through the brush to investigate what was going on that had terrified me. The Orient itself had always frightened me, ever since watching numerous Charlie Chan cloak and dagger movies as a child. Even in Manila, when we weren't on location, I still felt uneasy. Having Billy by my side made me feel safe. Safe enough to venture out of my comfort-zone and into an unknown culture... leaving behind my precious son.

I was happy to be at home until the movie reviews came out. Before leaving the Philippines, the film's soundtrack had somehow been damaged, and the entire movie had to be lip-synched in Manila in a makeshift soundstage. It was a poor attempt to recreate the acting done while on location. It was horrible. The script was horrible. The soundtrack worse. Any chance I may have thought I had in the acting profession vanished while viewing the atrocious film.

Kevin Thomas of the Los Angeles Times, however, was more than nice to me. "Everything and everybody in this film is blah...

except for Miss Beverly Hills, also seen this week in *More Dead Than Alive* as a redheaded Beverly Powers—here she's a blonde. Either way or name, she looks sensational and works diligently at her acting career. Possibly because she has encountered the hypocrisy strippers traditionally face when they try to go legit. She never fails to make the most of every assignment, no matter how small. This movie is a hopeless mess, yet she emerges vital and sexy."

Even columnist Louella Parsons noticed me and wrote something that really made me think, "If Miss Beverly Hills is really serious about a legitimate career she might think about taking on a new name." Maybe the universe was trying to tell me something. Isn't that what Regis had insinuated on his TV program years earlier? This time I would listen, and change my name to my married name, Beverly Powers. But it wasn't easy. Some casting directors still saw me as an ex-stripper, no matter what I did. Others, thank God, judged me on my hard work, fortitude, and talent.

My tireless agents were loyal and believed in me one hundred percent. We were all very excited when they said they had gotten me a television pilot for a new TV series playing opposite George Gobel for Don Fedderson, the creator of the television smash hit, *My Three Sons*.

When "The Apartment House" aired on *Summer Playhouse*, I was too nervous to watch. It was Billy and Derek who came running to me with excitement after the show aired. Derek, of course, was too young at the time and couldn't figure out how "Mommy got inside the television." He kept coming into my bedroom during the show, checking to see if I was still there.

Even though the critics loved it, the television show didn't sell. So the studio tried me in another TV pilot, *The Newlyweds*. It starred Ben Cooper and used a new technology called video-taping using three cameras simultaneously. That show also didn't sell. I was disappointed and wanted to work, but I didn't mind, because I now had extra time to spend with my family. I was glad for the time at home and was thoroughly enjoying my "role" as housewife and mother.

But when CBS came knocking at the door offering me a semi-regular spot on *The Red Skelton Show*, I immediately accepted. A regular job working approximately four days a month, playing a straight man opposite Skelton, one of the funniest men in the business! It was more than I could have imagined. I could continue to stay at home with my husband and sons the rest of the month! It was surreal. Mamo seemed to be even more overjoyed than me. When I was little, Mamo and I would watch Red Skelton together on her small black and white television. She always remarked on his closing words, *God Bless*. "I jus' love it when he says thet," she'd smile.

Normally, I worked every other Monday and Tuesday playing a sex kitten opposite Skelton in his famous "black-out skits." On Monday mornings, the cast would gather around a large round table and run their lines. Writers were there, as well as that week's guest star. Skelton's humor was deliberate and always delivered with precision. One week during morning rehearsals, method actor Jack Palance, who was that week's guest star, wanted to know what his motive was for crossing the stage at a particular moment in the scene. Skelton simply leaned forward and jokingly giggled, "Your paycheck." Even Palance had to laugh.

During three seasons at CBS, I encountered many famous celebrities. Jane Wyman. Burl Yves. Van Johnson. If they had a *name*, they eventually appeared on Skelton's show. I was in awe of them all. Once again, I struggled with my lines, fearing I may undermine one of Skelton's jokes. The respect I had for him grew with each episode. While other comedians were wallowing in filthy language and obscene innuendo, Skelton raised the bar. Not only was he the best mime in the business, though he claimed Marcel Marceau was, he also had the cleanest mouth. So when a large mouth, vulgar comedian from Vegas showed up on the set, my respect for Skelton shot up another full notch.

Monday nights were for dress rehearsals. We would rehearse skits mainly for the cameramen and stagehands. It was also a chance to review wardrobe and props. Usually Skelton was not present at these before dinner rehearsals. Such was the case that particular evening. From the old days of being backstage with strippers, I had become accustomed to foul mouth ladies—and often was one myself. But this week's guest star made even the hardcore-mouths shudder.

That evening, I watched from the wings as the dress rehearsal of the hillbilly skit was being rehearsed. A stand-in read Skelton's part. The guest, a big mouth comedian, was dressed in a wholesome hillbilly costume with many petticoats. She was ready for her cue, to fall backwards onto the mound of hay that lay behind her. And, on cue she did. But when her skirt and petticoats went up in the air, she revealed to the shocked spectators that she was wearing no underwear! From backstage I could see the men's different reactions. Some roared with laughter thinking it was hilarious. Others seemed embarrassed, shaking their heads in disbelief, while others simply walked away in total disgust.

After the meal break, I was again standing in the wings watching the Monday night taping of the show, when Skelton quietly came up from behind, startling me. He rarely came out of his dressing room until his curtain call. After a moment, he leaned over and whispered, "I understand you were in the wings during rehearsal when our guest decided to display her wares."

Her wares? I shook my head, "Yes."

"On behalf of the studio and myself, I'm sorry for any embarrassment you may have experienced." And with that, he turned around and walked back to the other side of the stage. I couldn't believe it. *The Master of Mime* was apologizing to me, an ex-stripper. It was never discussed again. But, from then on I would have voted for him as President if he ran; he had enormous integrity.

Not everyone, however, was as gracious and forgiving of my past. Some areas of show biz were strictly taboo for a girl with a name in burlesque. Even though the name was only on the West Coast, the East Coast Television CEOs controlling the money for commercials were not willing to take a chance. I was ecstatic when my agents told me I had landed a coveted national toothpaste commercial. But before a contract could even be drawn up, the commercial agency learned of my background and immediately I was replaced. They couldn't have a girl representing toothpaste that had stripped. It broke my heart. I was learning the hard way that choices we make carry consequences, whether we realize it at the time or not. As Mamo said, "Child, ya can't toss a pebble into a pond without makin' a ripple."

My bruised ego didn't last long. Paramount Executives came calling, offering the role of Carmelita, a foul-mouthed, aging carnival stripper, infatuated with a sixteen-year-old country boy in *Like a Crow on a June Bug*. The legendary Mercedes McCambridge would portray the boy's protective mother.

The studios seemed determined to typecast me. However, I felt I could use this role to redeem myself, by portraying Carmelita as no one else could. The role felt comfortable, and her filthy mouth all too familiar. Would I ever shake the persona I had worked so hard to create? Probably not. But maybe this was my chance to prove I was more than a stripper. At one time, I had been one of the most respected and highly paid exotic dancers in the business. I was hoping this role as a brassy carny dancer would launch me onto a new and different path. The choices I had made yesterday had followed me into my today, casting a negative shadow into my future. However, with this new role "my past" could launch "my future." I was being given another chance. A chance to show my talent as a legitimate actress. A chance to end my dancing career on a high note. So, when the movie reviews came out, I was thrilled. My determination had paid off.

"Oscar Nomination Seen By Producers" read the Valdosta Daily Times headline. "I think she'll get nominated for an Academy Award," the producer said, referring to Miss Powers' performance. "She dominates the screen from the time she first appears until she goes off."

My portrayal as the brassy carney Carmelita in *Like a Crow on a June Bug* was getting attention. My agents and I couldn't have been more excited. However, the glowing prediction never came into fruition. Shortly after the movie's release, a legal battle ensued over the ownership and distribution, and the film was not made public until years later. Under a new name, *Sixteen*, the film now collects dust on the shelves at video stores.

Despite the disappointment, the '60s were good to Billy and me. We were excited to see what the '70s would bring, especially after learning we were going to have another baby! Derek now seven, was the apple of our eye, and now was going to have a little brother! Billy and I were about to receive another gift from God. I wondered if life could get any better?

###

THE STARDOM

JACK BENNY and BEVERLY
Guest Starring on The Jack Benny Show

BREAKFAST at TIFFANY'S
Audrey Hepburn and George Peppard, watching Beverly
whose reflection can be seen in mirror

JACK LEMMON & Beverly
Days of Wine & Roses

ELVIS PRESLEY & Beverly
Kissin' Cousins

```
WU TLX LSA₪

MGM INC CULV

WUB152 SSK090 L CYA080 PD

CULVER CITY CALIF 26 954A PDT

MISS BEVERLY HILLS

   MGM STUDIOS TELEX LOSA

WELCOME AND GOOD LUCK ON THE START OF YOUR NEW PICTURE SPEEDWAY.

SINCERELY

   ELVIS AND THE COLONEL


154P PDT ..₪

MGM INC CULV
```

Elvis' Telegram

Red Skelton & Beverly
Valentine's Day Episode

Regis Philbin & Beverly
That Regis Philbin Show

DEAR BEV:

JUST SAW THE SEGMENT WE DID TOGETHER LAST NIGHT AND IT'S ANOTHER GREAT ONE. WE'RE A TEAM.

NO KIDDING, YOU LOOK AND SOUND TERRIFIC AND I THINK YOU SHOULD ALERT AS MANY PEOPLE AS POSSIBLE WHO CAN HELP YOU WITH YOUR ACTING AMBITION BECAUSE IF THIS DOESN'T DO IT, I'LL GIVE UP. I'M SO CONFIDENT ABOUT THIS ONE EVEN THAT SINISTER SISTER OF YOURS WILL BE PLEASED. SO EVEN THO I'VE NEVER BEEN TO THE LARGO I'M YOUR FAN. THANKS AGAIN SO MUCH.

WARMEST REGARDS,

Rege

Vincent Price & Peter Lorre
Comedy of Terrors

George Gobel & Beverly
The Apartment House, TV Pilot

Melodyland Theater, Anaheim, CA

Oscar Nominations Seen By Producer

By WINK DeVANE

A film executive is predicting some persons are going to ride the wings of crows and june bugs to bigger and better things.

Harvey Bernhard, executive producer of a movie which is to have its world premiere h e r e tonight, said it could gather at least two Academy Award nominations — one for supporting actress and the other for cinematography.

Beverly Powers, the actress to whom Bernhard was referring, said she's counting on the movie to boost her career upward.

The movie, "Like a Crow on a June Bug," was filmed almost entirely around Lake Park near here and features a large number of area residents as extras. It was co-authored by a former Lowndes County resident, Curtis Taylor, who was one of the prime proponents of having it filmed in his native South Geor-

**BEVERLY POWERS
Nomination Ahead?**

gia.

It stars, in addition to M i s s

Powers, Academy Award winning actress Mercedes McCambridge, John Lozier, Ford Rainey and Maidie Norman. M i s s Powers, Lozier, Bernhard, Taylor and the other author, Jim Lowe of NBC radio's Monitor, are to attend the premiere at the Beverly Theatre here.

Martin Theatres district manager Calvin Brown said they are to arrive about 7:15 p. m. after attending a banquet given by the Valdosta - L o w n d e s County Chamber of Commerce.

Brown said they are to spend about 30 -45 minutes signing autographs and chatting with fans before the curtain goes up on the movie at 8 p. m. The Valdosta High School band is to perform before to the film's intial showing, he added.

The enthusiastic predictions from Bernhard came at a cocktail party - press conference combination sponsored by t h e threatre chain Tuesday night.

"I think she'll get nominated for an Academy Award," Bernhard said refererring to M i s s Powers' performance. "S h e dominates the screen from the

See Oscar — Page 2

Valdosta Daily Times, Valdosta, GA, May 31, 1972

chapter five

THE SEARCH

Things which are not seen are eternal
2 Corinthians 4:18b

The '70s was a decade of disco, paisley, polyester, yellow smiling faces, and curious mood rings. Gone was the social unrest of the last decade with its round peace sign. It was a decade known as the *Me Generation*. A time for soul searching and inner reflection. An era of individuality with focus on self and purpose.

The decade began with me facing my own mortality as I approached a frightening spine operation. I was frightened to death, because this was the same procedure my movie idol, Jeff Chandler, had recently died from! "Oh, that was an accident," the doctors assured me." *Why didn't that make me feel better?*

The surgery was necessary. But, I was terrified. The journey into a second pregnancy played havoc on my already weakened spine. I was hospitalized three times and placed in traction long before our son Darin, named after Bobby Darin, was born. Now, six months later, I was back in the hospital. This time for the dreaded operation. With tribulation I signed the required disclaimer, releasing the doctors and hospital from any responsibility if I were to die. *Yikes! That was certainly a confidence booster!*

When Billy and the boys showed up for a visit the evening before the operation, I calmed down. Billy was good at distracting me. He proudly showed off how Darin had learned to sit up *all by himself,* in just the few days I had been away. Billy had dressed him so cute. I couldn't wait for this ordeal to be over, so I could hold my baby boy in my arms and stroll about, hugging and snuggling him, which I hadn't been able to do since he was born. Hopefully this surgery would be successful and fix whatever needed to be fixed, so I could carry my baby boy in my arms instead of having to sit with him resting on my lap.

Kissing my family goodbye that night made me more determined than ever to face this battle with courage. I was more assured and confident than when Billy had arrived hours earlier. Having him beside me to cheer me on, along with my neurosurgeon named *Dr. Faith*... how could the surgery be a failure?

However, the following two years found me still unable to carry very little, and with a great deal of pain. It was so bad I had to have a nurse to help me out during the day. At night, Billy would come home and tenderly take care of me. After the children were in bed, we would also go to bed. Making love behind locked doors became our preoccupation. It was the one thing we were physically able to do together, and enjoyed immensely. The fringe benefits of having Billy as nighttime nurse held many joys for both of us. His strong tattooed arms held me tight and told of his eternal love for me. I spent this healing process encased in my husband's arms. Eventually I recovered, and the time came to get out of bed and figure out what I would do next.

I obviously couldn't dance any longer. Physically I was limited. But my brain seemed to be okay. Billy and I still owned a four-unit apartment building that we managed--him doing the upkeep and me tending to the paperwork. I began reading books on financial pyramiding, expanding one's wealth. The thought of using our equity as leverage and buying other properties held excitement for me!

I enrolled in a local real estate school and within a short time had my California License, allowing me to participate as both sales and listing agent. My intention was to be both the buyer, and seller, receiving two commissions on one transaction. I was thoroughly enjoying this new role as an investor and had business cards printed up to prove who I was. I listed our four-unit Colfax building and within a month had exchanged it for a spacious nine-unit complex, with a pool and owner's apartment, in Sherman Oaks, the Beverly Hills of the San Fernando Valley. It was a sweet business deal that padded our savings account and gave us stature in the community.

I had completely bought into the illusion that more was better. More stuff meant more happiness, more prestige, and more self-fulfillment. If one car could make a person happy, just think what two could do. So Billy and I began gathering. We gathered apartment buildings. We bought new a car with a matching boat and trailer. A truck and motorcycle for Billy. Furs and diamonds for me. Extravagant vacations for all of us.

Once upon a time, I found happiness through fame and fortune. Now the fame seemed distant, *but* the fortune was still very much intact and growing bigger. Hefty residuals from films made in the 1960s flowed in, along with rental checks from the apartments. We were taking pleasure in the good life. With my newly acquired real-estate license, a healing body and a wonderful family, you can imagine my shock to learn I was being sued. *For fraud*!

What?!? My integrity would never allow me to defraud anyone. I won't cheat you, don't cheat me; that was my motto. Yet, someone was taking me to court, saying I had deliberately defrauded them. If found guilty, I could lose everything I had worked so hard for over the years. It all seemed unreal and unfair, and frightening. They were suing me both as the real estate agent and owner/seller of the apartment complex in question. Apparently termites had been discovered in the crawl space beneath the Colfax building, and the new owners felt I should be held responsible.

This was ridiculous. It wasn't just the possibility of losing large amounts of money, or perhaps even losing my real-estate license that worried me, though they were both of big concern. What really upset me was having my integrity questioned. Memories of the lies and slander I had been forced to endure as a child surfaced. And now, once again, accusations were being hurled at me and my character was being challenged.

The plaintiff's argument was this: how could I *not* have known there were termites under the units? Especially after living there for so many years. The obvious conclusion was, I had to be lying. Anyone who knew me, and the history of my back, knew I'd never worm myself into a crawl space hidden beneath the building to inspect it. Especially since there was never any indication of termites being there in the first place.

It became my word against theirs. I had no witnesses. Yet, somehow they had plenty. People I had never seen came forward and testified to conversations we never had. False witnesses who had just placed their hands on the Holy Bible, swearing an oath to tell the truth, the whole truth, were now lying through their teeth! It was like a *Perry Mason* TV court scene I had once appeared in. But this time I wasn't being cross-examined by Raymond Burr. This was real life, in living color, and I was portraying myself. And, I was scared to death.

Thou shall not bear false witness
Exodus 20:16

My jaw dropped as I listened to the lies being told from the witness stand. One man actually pointed to me and said to the court, "She's the one who prevented me from entering the crawl space. She's the reason the termites weren't found." Under oath, this man testified I had distracted him. This "innocent" inspector, representing the "innocent" termite inspection company, was deflecting his blame onto me! The first day of trial went miserably. I wanted to stand up and shout, "This isn't fair! They're lying!" But, of course, I wasn't allowed to do that. That only happens in the movies. I had to wait my turn. But what could I say? Who was going to believe me? I thought of my stepfather's abuse and what had happened in my youth. I was worried that now, once again, no matter what I said, I would be labeled a liar. I had a lot to lose.

"Dear God, please help me tomorrow," I prayed. I knew the Lord had done it plenty of times before, without my even asking for help. He had saved me from certain death when I was thrown from a car and into the path of another. He could certainly do it again. I needed another miracle and I needed it NOW. But this time, I needed His invisible hand in the courtroom and not in the street.

"Please be with me Heavenly Father," I pleaded. "I need You so much. Shine Your light on this awful mess." I needed His presence in the courtroom or I was sure I would lose. I fell asleep in Billy's arms, tears soaking his shoulder. I woke early the next morning, showered, and put on my most conservative outfit, the one with the Peter Pan collar. I painted my lips a soft pink and wore no other makeup. I felt I was hallucinating as I stepped up to the witness stand to be sworn in. The clerk's voice seemed muffled and distant. The courtroom foggy. Voices and faces seemed distant and obscure.

"Speak up young lady," the judge shouted. "We can't hear you."

"I'm sorry, your Honor," I mumbled, hardly recognizing my own voice. A hazy beam of light shined down from the skylight. I could see tiny particles floating in the air. The atmosphere reminded me of the bar scene I did with Audrey Hepburn and George Peppard in *Breakfast at Tiffany's*, where wiggly molecules floated in the air. It was so bright, and I could barely make out the faces in the courtroom, but I could still hear them perfectly.

"Are you trying to tell the court," the prosecuting attorney asked, "that even though you lived in the building for nine years, you never knew the termites were there?"

"Yes."

"Can you prove that?"

"No," I mumbled.

"We can't hear you," he said, repeating the question.

"No, I can't prove it," I cried. Then turning to the judge, I said, "Your Honor I'm telling the truth. Honest to God."

Amazingly, after only a brief recess, the court returned a verdict of "not guilty!" They had ruled in my favor. The judge had believed me! That night as I lay in bed, I wept again in Billy's arms. This time out of sheer relief and joy.

"I was so scared. I looked for you in the courtroom but couldn't even see you. Everything was so blurry." I sat up, wiped my eyes, and blew my nose.

"What do you mean?"

"The light. After I got on the stand I could barely see anything because of the filtered light coming in, making everything look cloudy."

"What are you talking about?" Billy asked. I explained about the column of sunrays shining through the skylight.

"Beverly, are you nuts?" he said, sitting up in bed. "There's no skylight in that courtroom, Honey. That's a six-story building and we were on the fourth floor." *What was he saying? That couldn't be right.*

The next day after Billy went to work, I drove back to the courthouse to see for myself. Sure enough, it was as he had said. Six floors with fluorescent ceiling lights in all the courtrooms. And, no skylights! Suddenly I felt queasy. The floor began to shake. My head was spinning. "Lady, are you all right?" someone asked. *No, I wasn't.*

I managed to make it to the ladies room before my emotions exploded. What had happened? Had I actually experienced the presence of God again? I remembered my first car accident, when a speeding car raced towards my head and collided with an unexplained, invisible barrier. I had been sure back then that God had saved me. Had it happened again? Had God shown up, this time, disguised as a column of filtered light?

I couldn't convince anyone what I had seen, not even Billy. But I had no doubt that once again, I had been saved by the hand of God. Not as an invisible wall as before, but God had been with me in the court, and had shown himself to me as a misty pillar of golden light.

Suddenly a great light from heaven shown around me
Acts 22:6

After my courtroom experience, my world of making money and collecting things that once seemed full now felt empty. Burt Bacharach's song, *What's it all about, Alfie?* rang in my ears. I tried going to community college and took philosophy and other self-help classes. I also began taking a journalism class. At first, my writings professed of my love for Billy and the boys. But later, the writings began revealing another side of me that I didn't know was there, that no one knew about, including myself. Writings of discontentment. Writings filled with questions. Curiosities about life's purpose and why I existed. And, why the miracles? I wanted to know why. Did it mean I was supposed to be doing something that I wasn't? Or, was there some other mysterious meaning?

I needed a hobby! That was it. I had always enjoyed art, so I applied to the Otis Art Institute in Los Angeles. To my amazement, I was accepted. I loved it, and so did Billy, who warmed up to the idea the first time I came home with an assignment that needed a nude model to sketch. Many afternoons were spent with Billy as my gorgeous model, as we both enjoyed ourselves doing my homework together before the children got home from school and needed help with theirs.

I took classes in etchings, oils, and lino-cuts at Pepperdine College in Malibu. Then, with the encouragement of my teachers, I began entering art contests, and I even won a few awards. Our trip to San Francisco for their celebrated *Arts & Crafts Street Festival* was a true highlight for me. I was doing well and was being accepted as a legitimate artist. Yet, even with all the fanfare and fun, I still felt the twinge of emptiness. I couldn't describe it, but titles from several of my art pieces should have been a clue that something may have been amiss.

Abandonment was a grissaille painting of two children looking forlorn through a glass window pane. I painted it after recalling a time when I had felt the sting of Mother's betrayal. After my spine operation, I had cried out for help—something I rarely did—but I needed help… I was unable to lift my infant son and needed someone to care for him so I could to go to my post-operative doctor's appointment. But Mother said, "No. I didn't raise you so I could be your baby sitter." It was right then and there I swore I would never ask her for another favor. The day I painted *Abandonment* and watched the images of the small children in the window emerge, it released emotions within me I thought had been long forgotten. Now, years later, the memories surfaced and ended up on my canvas as a haunting, monochromatic oil painting that now haunted others.

"Who are the children?" viewers asked. "Are they on the inside looking out... or, on the outside looking in?"

"Good question," I'd shrug, unsure myself.

Barriers, another piece inspired by Mother, won several awards. The etching, printed on satin, is an extreme close-up view of a chain-link fence, with an oasis of mountains, swaying palm trees, and streams seen in the distance. As with *Abandonment*, it became the center of discussion at many art shows. Was the chain-link fence really a cage the viewer was trapped in, keeping them from reaching paradise? Or, was the safe haven a restricted area with a chain-link fence barrier surrounding it?

Earlier in the day, before sketching *Barriers*, I had received a phone call from Mother. Our conversation made me so irate I could barely contain myself. It was either sketch my feelings down on paper, or go over to her house and strangle her. The first choice appeared to be the best option.

In 1976, the San Fernando Valley was in the midst of a water shortage and every home was being rationed. Mamo, being nearly crippled, was unable to bathe at home because of the difficulty getting in and out of the bathtub. She was in dire need of assistance. Mother was the only family member with a walk-in shower on the ground floor, where Mamo could bathe without having to bend nor climb any stairs. I knew we could obtain permission from the county for any extra water Mamo would use.

When I asked Mother's permission to bring Mamo over for a once-a-week shower, it never occurred to me she would say "No." But she did. She refused to help her daughter and her own mother. What made matters worse, I had already told Mamo that I was going to ask Mother! If I had waited until after I had asked, Mamo would never have needed to know.

I tried to make excuses for Mother's refusal, but I knew it hurt Mamo. She never said a word other than to quote her favorite adage, "Remember, Beverly Jean, if ya mother could do better, she would." I could see the sadness in her eyes. Nothing I said or did could wash away the pain in her heart. That day I promised myself I would drive the ninety-mile round-trip each week to Mamo's house and give her the best sponge bath I knew how.

Mamo's baths played havoc with my spine, though I didn't say anything. But, it was the havoc between Mother and me that seemed impossible that it would ever heal. There was nothing Mother could say to justify her actions. She didn't have a clue what she had done! To her, she had done nothing wrong. To me, it was unforgivable. Mother and I got along when I was in the limelight. She loved to brag how she was the mother of Miss Beverly Hills. But when I retired from the stage lights, the lights between us also seemed to dim. To me, Mother had hit rock bottom.

But out of Mother's bitter lemons, God had made lemonade. From that moment on, every Wednesday, I'd drive up to Mamo's. After giving her an "army bath," I'd bring her back to my house, where she'd spend the night with Billy, the boys, and me, having dinner and enjoying ourselves. Even Billy's mother would come over, with her famous homemade apple pie in hand, and we'd spend quality time making memories together. Mother's refusal to allow Mamo to shower once a week had become a weekly slice of heaven!

Why do you weep my love?
I weep because of the injustices man has caused another.
And, for the blindness that spurs it on.
B. J. P.

I became an insatiable reader. History books about injustices done during World War II and the Holocaust were my main topics of choice. Books and novels written of the brave ordinary people who had achieved extraordinary feats intrigued me. Anne Frank and her diary; Corrie ten Boom and those other courageous women in *The Hiding Place.*

Exodus by Leon Uris made my heart soar. In it I read about the founding of Israel. How young men and women fought courageously for their country during the 1940s. I lived vicariously through their stories. I couldn't read enough about their bravery. I wanted to be like them, in the midst of battle, fighting evil and oppression. But the war was over. And how could that ever happen now anyway? I was a married woman with a husband and two children. That left little opportunity for me to join the Peace Corps.

The memory of my courtroom experience with its beam of light left me with many unanswered questions. What was life really about? Chance? Luck? What was its purpose? Where did God fit in? And, how did I, specifically, fit into the scheme of things, especially given my past? A thirst had come over me that I couldn't quench. Was I missing the limelight of Hollywood? Maybe, the cameras? The excitement? The applause? Maybe it was the adrenaline that came from being backstage before the curtain went up, and the announcer shouting, "Ladies and Gentlemen. It's show time!"

I craved for something, but what? I should have been happy. I had everything: a handsome adoring husband, two magnificent children, and a fabulous apartment with a heated swimming pool! What more could a girl want? Yet the deep desire within, that had began in that courtroom, wouldn't go away. It followed me. Haunted me. Hidden for a time, as I busily attended to life's daily routine, then appearing again with that same familiar longing. But a longing for what? Nothing I did seemed to satisfy its wanting. Being a mother came closest. Wife was next. But then what?

When I tried explaining to Billy how I felt and asked, "What's wrong with me?" I sounded like I was complaining, unhappy with him and our marriage. He was kind, but he also didn't understand. I tried talking to Mamo, and again found myself sounding shallow and ungrateful. Eventually, I decided to not bring it up again. But within me the visitations of unrest were relentless. I began writing them down, hoping to gain some understanding. The majority of my writings occurred at night. I would awaken around two in the morning, with a verse or line flooding my mind, repeating itself over and over, until finally, unable to go back to sleep, I would get up and jot down on paper the thought that had awakened me.

Early one morning, I awoke with a question running through my head that I couldn't shake. Half-asleep, I found my tablet beside my bed and scribbled down the persistent thought. It wasn't until later the next day I read the scribble.

"What's my purpose here and what am I to do?" it began, "am I to go through life wondering why I'm not like you...?"

I couldn't comprehend why I didn't feel satisfied when I appeared to have everything. I couldn't make sense of it, nor the beam of light I'd seen in the courtroom. I busied myself with school and the children. Billy enrolled in night school, earning him a new position as supervisor for the city's Street Tree Division. He delighted in climbing trees and was good at it. His civil job offered us security. It didn't matter how our economy was, whether our apartments were empty or full, or whether my agents found me any new roles; there would always be food on the table. Life was good. The boys attended a private school learning about Jesus and God, and on weekends Billy and I went to dinner and a movie.

Films such as *The Exorcist* and *Rosemary's Baby*, purporting devil worship and life in the unknown, were all the rage. Disaster films such as *The Towering Inferno*, *Airport*, and *Earthquake* splashed across the movie screens promoting catastrophe. At the same time, the musical *Jesus Christ Superstar* sang of hope and lifted our spirits.

The thought of dying young in a catastrophe before discovering my purpose spurred additional urgency to my quest. I began reading paranormal books, attending psychic house parties, and dabbling in ESP. It appeared I was quite good at it! My sister who lived in the

Bahamas, and I in California, took turns each month trying to send mental telepathy messages to each other at appointed times. To our surprise, all too often we were extremely accurate, which only fed my infatuation with the paranormal.

When I learned of Werner Erhard and his est training, I was ready to sign up for his program. It offered instant enlightenment, promising to turn a caterpillar into a butterfly. Ugly ducklings, with all the mud gathered over a lifetime, turned into beautiful swans. I couldn't wait to experience this transformation that could strip away years of dirt, revealing a shining gem beneath the soil. The real me, just dying to get out. And, the *transformation* occurred in just two weekends! That was for me—a quick fix to a lengthy search.

I took to the training immediately. A person's title in life was of little importance. Only first names were used. Your word was all that mattered. The purpose of the training was to assist in breaking through any personal barriers in achieving a person's life's goals. It was a chance to look inside yourself and see things as they really were, not the way we hoped they would be, or wished they had been. It was about taking responsibility for one's life. They promised, "You'll either have results in life or the reasons why you don't. It's your choice. It's up to you."

I recognized how blaming others was absurd. As a child, my parents undermined me, but today I was an adult and needed to get beyond the hidden shackles that hindered my walk. Once again, it was my choice, which according to est was everything. The training took off my blinders. Mental filters were removed that once tainted my vision. Every choice, the good and the bad, came from an accumulation of my life's experiences. By shifting my perspective, the world looked entirely different, and wonderful.

At first, Billy was lukewarm but soon warmed up, and attended the endless seminar classes with me. When they began soliciting volunteers, I was the first in line. Billy said, "Go on, I'll watch the boys." So off I went. I felt this was an opportunity for me to really see who I was by placing myself in a subservient role, serving others. It was something I hadn't done, and I found the adventure exciting.

Within six months, I was so enthralled at the transformation I was seeing in myself, and others, I entered est's training program and became a guest seminar leader, sharing with hundreds of people why they, too, should enroll in the est training. Sometimes I volunteered thirty hours a week, holding events as a team captain at the Forum, Hollywood Palladium, and other large convention centers.

Soon, Billy, the boys and I were volunteering as a family. We visited local hospitals, senior citizen homes, and ironically a forestry camp that I had visited as a teenager during a beauty contest, winning the title *Miss Forestry Camp #17*. Now here I was returning to the same camp, as an adult with my family, bearing gifts of love, packaged differently than the bathing suit I wore back then.

> *I don't know what your destiny will be,*
> *but one thing I know:*
> *The only ones among you who will be truly happy*
> *are those who sought and found how to serve.*
> Albert Schweitzer

We joined the *Holiday Project* and visited the veterans' hospitals, offering our Christmas Day to visit the patients. Along with others, we tried to deliver cheer to everyone we came near. Paired up in groups, we wandered the hospital floors, softly singing Christmas Carols that echoed through the hallways. We would enter a room, stand at the foot of a patient's bed and gently serenade him. Then off to another room we would go until everyone had been serenaded.

Most of the veterans were awake and filled with gratitude, even when we sang off-key. I remember Mamo saying, "The Bible doesn't say anythin' about havin' to sing on key, Beverly Jean. It jest says yuz to sing with a joyful heart." And that is what we were doing that Christmas, when a small group of us entered an elderly man's room on the third floor. His eyes were closed. Tubes ran out of him from everywhere.

I went up to the side of his bed and gently placed my hand on his. His eyes remained closed as if in a coma. Softly, we finished singing *Silent Night* and everyone began to leave the room. I lingered for a moment and gently squeezed his hand, careful not to disturb the tubes, when I saw a tear stream down his cheek. He was awake. *His eyes had been shut but his soul had been opened.* He had heard the lyrics of God's wondrous *Silent Night*.

Later that day, as we sat in Bob's Big Boy restaurant eating the familiar french fries and hamburgers for our holiday dinner, I knew this had been the best Christmas I had ever spent. I had given the gift of myself, and, I wanted to do it again and again. Not just on holidays. I wanted to find other ways that I could make a difference. My heart was sincere. My soul ripe. I was ready to roll up my sleeves and get to work.

After the holidays, I went down to our local bank and took out a second mortgage on our nine-unit apartment building, located in the swanky part of town, and purchased a six-unit fixer-upper in the raunchy part of town. Buying and refurbishing this building, even for a good cause, left Billy stone-cold. "You can leave me out of this," he told me shortly after we closed escrow. I didn't know what I was going to do. I hadn't expected him to react like that. "I wish I could come an help ya out," Mamo said when I told her of my predicament. "Jest remembe' child, God'll gives ya all da strength yuz need." So, with Mamo's prayers and my fierce determination, I became the contractor, painter and wallpaper hanger. I would come home at night covered with wall paint, instead of the stage paint I use to come home wearing.

Once the building was renovated, I found myself renting to single women with children. Women, struggling on their own. Women who needed a haven and a helping hand. A safe place for them and their children. A place with charm at a reasonable rate. I hired an African-American woman with two small children to be my resident manager. Within a few weeks, the six-unit, two-bedroom apartment complex was completely filled... and even had a waiting list. I nicknamed the building *My Mt. Everest*. It was the hardest thing I had ever conquered, especially on my own. I had never been happier. Yet, by making other families happy, I had become distracted, and sadly didn't notice how unhappy my own family had become.

###

chapter six

THE SORROW

Sorrow dances before him
Job 41:22

I was grateful for Billy's love during my search for purpose and meaning. He remained my rock. Faithful. Loyal. And, ever so handsome! It had been nearly twenty years since our wedding, yet my poetry still spoke of my love for him. Oh, how I ached when we were apart. Except for those occasional haunting feelings of emptiness that still visited me, I loved my life. There was a comfortableness to it. Billy. The boys. Our routine. A TV appearance here and there. A nice income. Opportunities to volunteer--to help out and try to make a difference. Then, one fateful night, Billy and I began trying different things in the bedroom.

I had always thought what went on behind closed doors between Billy and me was no one's business but our own. But it was then when our marriage began its slow descent into mire... eventually claiming everything we held dear. We had let the demon of deception into our bedroom, and no matter how ignorant and innocent our actions may have been, by bringing marijuana and soft porn into our amber lit retreat, we had invited the devil to enter our union. It wasn't long before rips and tears were unraveling our wedding tapestry. The holy part of our matrimony had been removed.

Billy's mother had passed away. Everyone mourned her loss. It was Billy who took it the worst. He was her baby boy, the apple of her eye. When she died, something within him seemed to die with her. He began drinking. It wasn't the occasional beer at night that I disliked. It was the six-pack that followed. Especially when it became nearly *two* six-packs. Mother Powers' baby boy was beginning to behave badly. He began drinking, resembling the father I had only heard stories of. Stumbling in late after work, bringing havoc to his home and shame to himself. Here was my beloved Billy, drinking and behaving just like the father he had said he hated and never wanted to resemble.

My husband had become a functioning alcoholic. Working by day, senseless most nights. His personality changed. He became mean and verbally abusive. In turn, I retaliated by yelling. Crying. Pleading. Threatening.

"I'm going to leave you if you don't stop this!"

He promised he would. But he didn't. So, I'd yell some more. But, nothing worked. The Erhard Seminars didn't *help either.* In fact, it seemed to make it worse, putting a wedge between us, pitting one against the other. The only thing our sons heard anymore were arguments and quarrels. I had become a nag and hated myself for it. I hated what Billy had become even more. He wasn't my Billy; he was a stranger I didn't know, and didn't like. But, the more I resisted, the more he persisted. Neither of us were able to stop the destructive cycle we were on. Ranting and raving didn't help. Neither did the silent treatment. Where had my beloved Billy gone?

Come to [your] senses and escape the snare of the devil
2 Timothy 2:26

Several years passed. We became adept at sweeping our problems under the rug. Only a few people knew of our marriage turmoil. Then one afternoon Billy came home from work with a problem we couldn't sweep under the rug. He was having chest pains and difficulty breathing. Immediately, an ambulance was called and he was rushed to the hospital. Thankfully, he wasn't having a heart attack. Rather, he was having an acute emphysema attack! We hadn't even known he had the disease! His heavy cigarette smoking over the years, along with the Los Angeles' smog, had taken their toll on his lungs. My Billy was ill.

It was too familiar. Six weeks earlier, one of my son Derek's lungs had collapsed during what was to be a fun-filled hiking trip with friends. He was rushed to the nearest hospital. The doctors blamed his problem on Los Angeles' smog as well. That was it! We had no other choice. We had to move. My family was sick.

So the first weekend Billy felt well, we drove up the coast and found ourselves in Ventura, a small beach side community, approximately sixty miles north from where we now lived. To our surprise, we fell in love with the first place we saw and bought it on the spot. It was perfect. My family would be safe. The condo sat on the ridge of a magnificent dry riverbed, filled with sage, mature trees, and sandy paths that stretched from the Pacific Ocean to the Canejo Mountains, that passed right in front of our house. Even though school had started, both boys were willing to move, which made me proud of them. Especially Derek, because this was his senior year and he would be forced to graduate with a class he barely knew. But, he said he was ready for the adventure. The riverbed was was perfect for dirt bikes, which made it easy to excite the boys about changing schools.

We threw caution to the wind and sold our properties, offering a good purchase for the buyers while making a large profit for us. Three months later, escrow closed. It was on the day I finished shooting my last contract for Columbia Pictures, playing in *Fantasy Island* with Ricardo Montalban and that week's guest star, Sonny Bono. We were headed to our new life.

Years earlier, Billy had been willing to start a new life after I nearly destroyed our marriage with my affair. Now it was my turn to make a sacrifice. I would give up my show-biz career and settle down to be a full-time wife and mother. I knew this was the answer for all our problems. The solution. The start of a new beginning for us.

The date we moved into our new condo was on our twenty-fourth wedding anniversary. That *had* to be a good omen.

It was the first real home Billy and I had ever owned. We had always lived in apartments, mostly as owners/managers. Now, for the first time, we had our own house without the constant interruptions of tenants calling all hours of the day and night in need of help. At first it felt like a dream come true, but our dream became a nightmare. Without the interruptions from our renters, we were truly left alone with only each other, and our children were caught in the middle.

Billy stopped coming home after work. When he did, he usually smelled of beer. Once, I thought I detected perfume, but it must have been something else. Billy would never cheat on me. Not him. He had always been faithful and loyal. He had a drinking problem, that's all. One morning when I was looking for some wire to hang a picture frame, I discovered a jar of "uppers" in the storage room. At that moment, I realized I didn't know who he was anymore, or what he was capable of.

When Billy got home from work that day, I confronted him with the empty jar of amphetamines. I was outraged. But not nearly as outraged as he was when he learned I had flushed the pills down the toilet. That's when the verbal abuse really turned foul. He shouted names at me that would have made Lenny Bruce blush. I tried talking to him. Pleading with him. "Don't you see what you're doing? You're tearing our family apart," I cried. Nothing worked.

Finally, one night in desperation, I cried out to Mamo over the telephone. "Sweetpea, Billy's not himself," she said, "Yuz gonna have ta convince him ta see a doctor who can help." Easier said than done. Our families believed only crazy people sought help from counselors. However, I saw a glimmer of hope when Billy finally agreed to go. The first appointment we went together. After that we were each to have a private session, and then return together for our last visit. But it didn't turn out that way.

Who can survive the destructiveness of jealousy?
Proverb 27:4 NLT

It was the week of my high school's twenty-fifth class reunion. I hadn't seen Billy in days. I hoped he would show up before the gala event. But by the week's end, he was still a no-show. On the coaxing of friends, insisting I attend, I went to the formal event without him. Billy and I had been a twosome since Junior High, so everyone would be expecting to see him beside me. I needed an excuse. I told people that an illness had come upon him. It worked; everyone accepted the lie and hoped he would "get well" soon. Then, halfway through the evening, there was a raucous commotion at the door. I turned to see what the fuss was about, when I spotted him. Billy, disheveled and disgustingly drunk, with some floozie on his arm, equally as intoxicated. I was mortified. I ran from the banquet room, managing somehow to make it to my car before the floodgates of emotions exploded.

"How could he?" I screamed. "No, no, no! This can't be happening!" I could barely see the freeway through my tears as I drove home. It was one thing to suffer because of what life throws at us. But, it's quite another when the someone we love deliberately sets out to hurt us. And hurt me he did. Billy had broken my heart.

"Beverly Jean, how long are ya gonna put up with dis?" Mamo pleaded over the phone. "Child, I love Billy too, but dis isn't good fer you or yer boys. Sweetpea, please..." her voice drifted off.

It took days for me to climb out of bed. But I just had to see him. To find out what was he thinking. Was he really willing to throw everything away? By Wednesday, when I still had not heard from him, I decided to drive down to the Valley and see if I could locate him. I called his work and learned his whereabouts. I didn't have a plan. I just knew I had to speak with him. To plead with him to come home. Everything would be forgiven. We'd start anew. I needed him, and his boys needed him. But, I had to hurry, it was nearly his lunch time. I just had to find him.

Approaching the location given me, I saw his yellow city truck rounding the corner, entering the alley adjacent to the Milbank building. *Where we had lived for nearly ten years,* I thought to myself. I raced to catch up with him. He was in the driver's seat. But he wasn't alone. There was also a silhouette of someone sitting close to him—with their arm around his neck! "Oh sweet Jesus… it's Floozie!" My heart sank. I couldn't believe my eyes. Had he entirely lost his mind? Civilians weren't allowed in city trucks! Was he really willing to lose his job of nearly twenty years, along with his wife of twenty-five?

I pulled up behind him as he waited for the traffic to clear so he could turn left. He had not yet seen me. Suddenly, a calm swept over me as I tooted the horn of my car, waved and smiled sweetly.

"Oh… yoo-hoo."

Billy looked in his rearview mirror. He must have said something because Floozie turned around, and suddenly we were staring at each another. Me with a plastered smile on my face. Hers a look of terror.

"Hi," I waved again.

Without warning, Billy turned left onto the center lane of the boulevard in an attempt to get away. Without thinking, I also turned left and pulled alongside him. I was now driving down the wrong side of the street heading toward oncoming traffic. Immediately Billy slammed on his brakes, which allowed me to pull in front of him and avoid a head-on collision. But as I did, I too slammed on my brakes, and for a second we each sat there frozen in time. In my rearview mirror I could see the horror in Billy's face. Then he turned and cautiously began trying to back up without hitting the oncoming traffic. He was trying to get around me! No way was I going to let that happen. Rage exploded within me. And without thought or reason, I shoved my Volvo in reverse and floored the accelerator. The car went flying backwards with such force it surprised even me.

The collision was explosive, shattering my rear window and causing people on the sidewalk to stop and turn. City workers, riding in the back of Billy's truck, jumped out and ran for safety.

"Oh, yoo-hoo," I smiled again, leaning out my driver's window. "It seems you've been in an accident. You better pull over."

Again, Billy tried to back up to get around me. But again, I floored the pedal and rammed his truck. Then he tried again. And again. And again. Down the street we went, leaping backwards as we littered the street with his headlights and my taillights, and our tires squealing halt all the way.

It reminded me of the bumper-car games we use to play at the amusement park when we were teens. But this time, we weren't teens... and I wasn't amused. There were no smiles, just a deliberate calm, hidden under the adrenaline, as I continued ramming his truck over and over again.

Smoke billowed from the rear of my Volvo. The smell of rubber from our tires filled the air as we inched our way toward the oncoming traffic. Cars honked and screeched to a halt in an attempt to not collide with us. My back bumper lay tragically coiled in the middle of the street. Neighbors we had once known ran out to watch the "bumper-car show" traveling down the street backwards, the entire length of the city block.

Somehow Billy managed to maneuver around me, and he drove off. It had gone too far; there was no way he was escaping. As he sped through red lights, so did I. Thinking only of ourselves, we zipped in and out of streets until we were back where we started, in front of Floozie's apartment.

He slowed down and she jumped out of the truck. Instead of running for cover she stood in the middle of the street, frozen. Her eyes looked like a deer's caught in headlights. I was only thirty feet from her. I could have easily taken her out. I wanted to. But then, without warning, my car suddenly swerved around her and I was speeding down the street, my left wheel screeching and smoking as I sped away. At the end of the block, Billy turned one way, I the other. A burst of tears tore from my soul. My lungs gasped for air. I limped home, smoke billowing from the fender and the tire that wrapped around it. I immediately called a lawyer the following morning. I could have killed Billy. Not to mention Floozie.

The attorneys called it a *Legal Separation*. A maneuver used to protect us from any further shenanigans. Obviously we were both out of control. Neither of us could be trusted. I was shocked at what I was capable of. I had gone off the deep end. We both needed protection. Papers were filed to protect us from losing what we had spent years accumulating. But, Billy didn't see it that way. It enraged him. So, with Floozie, his drinking buddy by his side, and a slick weasel for an attorney, Billy waged war, and he fought the way he was brought up—dirty.

His lawyer had an unscrupulous reputation. Every month I found myself in court over one issue or another. Eventually, our assets were frozen, as our attorneys continued to battle. The accumulation Billy and I had earned and saved during our marriage was nearly gone. Attorney fees had eaten away our nest egg.

When the dust finally settled, I wound up with my credit destroyed, a heavily mortgaged condo, and he got the land contract from the sale of the Nagle Building, my *Mt. Everest* that I had worked so feverishly on. The lawyers got all the rest. Everything we spent a lifetime achieving together was wiped out. I felt my life was over. I wanted to die.

> *The Lord's loved ones are precious to him;*
> *it grieves him when they die*
> Psalm 116:15

I didn't think my heart could take any more pain until I received that horrendous phone call. My Mamo was dying.

"Please, dear Jesus. She can't leave now. I need her too much!" I cried. But as I neared her hospital bed later that night and saw her lying there with tubes coming out from everywhere, I knew it was true. My Mamo was sick. I went up to her bed and gently touched her upper arm. The underpart was always so soft.

"Is thet you, Beverly Jean?" she whispered.

"Yes Mamo, it's me," I whispered back, wiping away my tears. Her eyes sparkled as they opened and focused on me. Tears strolled down her cheeks.

"It's okay Mamo... I'm here." There she was, the greatest woman I ever met, the woman who had always cared for me when no one else did. I didn't know what to say.

"Are you in pain?"

"No child," she paused. "I feel bad though 'cause I can't finish my prayers. I start 'em," she looked up at me. "But before I knows it, I's asleep."

"Oh, Mamo, that's okay. I'll finish your prayers for you. You just fall back to sleep and I'll take care of everything." She smiled ever so slightly. She seemed grateful. Almost relieved.

That began my first prayer vigil with my Mamo. Each day I would visit, lean over and snuggle into the pillow she was lying on, being careful not to touch the tubes that surrounded her, and whisper prayers of love into her ear. The day before passing, she asked if I would pray that God would take her home.

"Tell Him, I'm surely ready." I promised I would. As much as I wanted her to stay, I knew her freedom to be with God was more important. That night she died. But not before speaking one last time. She had been in a deep sleep when suddenly she awoke. She was excited. And very happy. She appeared to be in a state of amazement. She spoke as a child with awe and wonder.

"I knew it," she murmured. "I jus' knew it all along." Her face glowed. Weakly, she raised a finger and gestured upward. "It was always about love..." she whispered, "...Jesus' love." Then, she closed her eyes and was gone. I knew I had just lost the kindest and wisest woman I would ever meet. Obviously, many others felt the same way.

The *Church of the Recessional* at Forest Lawn was filled with people from all walks of life. They were there for only one reason: to pay their respects to a woman who had lived as a housemaid. There were her friends and coworkers. Ladies draped in mink coats wearing diamonds, arriving in chauffeur-driven limousines. There were so many guests that a third of them had to stand outdoors and listen to the service over the sound system. Together everyone watched as her casket was carried to the black hearse, ready to carry her away to her final resting place. This quiet handmaiden of God was finally home. I couldn't imagine having a life without her. Would anyone ever love me as much as my Mamo?

###

chapter seven

THE SURRENDER

Whoever desires to save his life will lose it,
but whoever loses his life for My sake will save it
Luke 9:24

The '80s was a decade of darkness and sorrow. Mamo's death. Billy's mother. And, the senseless death of John Lennon, an icon and advocate for peace... tragically murdered. I, too, was a victim of a senseless death. The death of my marriage. My family broken, torn asunder. How had our life gotten so far out of control? What happened to that beacon of love Billy and I once proclaimed? When had its lights gone out? Why hadn't our love been enough? Those questions and more haunted me as I moved through the second half of the '80s as if in slow motion.

Alone. For the first time in my life, I was completely on my own. Mamo was gone. Mother was useless. Billy had left and convinced Derek to do the same. He had moved back to the Valley to be with his father and Floozie. Forfeiting college. Even forfeiting a relationship with me, or his brother. It broke my heart. They had returned to the San Fernando Valley, where we once lived together so many years before. Darin and I stayed in our new home on the Santa Clara River, living in the 2,100-square-foot condo I inherited after the costly divorce.

I was a single mother with a young son. The mother of a son who loved to dirt bike in the dry riverbed below our home. Stability was imperative. I had to try and keep things as normal as I could for my younger son's sake, and maybe, just maybe, the other half of our family would return. Staying in Ventura was a costly decision, and soon I had a second mortgage, and then a third.

The rental properties Billy and I once owned had been pilfered and divided with the divorce lawyers. There was no money coming in. I needed a job and I needed it soon! I couldn't go back to Hollywood. The thought of trying to resurrect my show-biz career seemed daunting, at best. Plus, where would Darin and I live? It became obvious I had no choice. I had to get a job where I could excel and make some money.

I discovered A.L.Williams, a financial marketing corporation, through a close friend who knew my predicament and my love for figures. ALW was listed in the Fortune 500 magazine as one of the rising companies of the decade, and offered a place to excel. I applied for a sales position and was accepted. I now worked on commission. They seemed to be exactly what I was looking for. And, I was right. Within a few years, I had risen to the rank of Regional Vice President, with an office of my own and dozens of licensed agents working for me, bringing in extra income each month with overrides and commissions. I named my sales team The Prophets, in a company that promoted P-R-O-F-I-T-S. And once again, I appeared to be successful. People looked up to me. Respected me. Yet, inside, I felt like I was sleep walking. Empty. Lonely. Forsaken. I longed for Mamo. To talk with and hear her words of encouragement.

Darin had joined the Army Reserve and was out of the house. Derek was nowhere to be found. I rarely heard from him or his father, except when they came bearing trouble. After the bumper-car episode, they both became scarce, and I was now referred to as *Lead Foot*.

No matter how hard I tried, how much money I earned, how many sale contests I won at work, or degrees I achieved, I was still broken on the inside, but outwardly looking like I had it all together. My "happily ever after" dreams had been shattered. The embroidered linens Mamo had given us as a wedding present sat dormant in the bottom drawer of my chest. What would she have thought had she known? Did she have an inkling where we were headed when she left?

Out of a desperate need to find comfort, I began attending a local church with a New Age philosophy that was empowering to a growing number of followers. They taught we were all God in our universe, created in His image (Gen. 1:27). The way a wave has all the components of the ocean.

"The Father and I are one," they would have us repeat. "You are co-creators with God. What you have in your life is what you created. No one is to blame for your unhappiness, except you."

I didn't quite understand how I created the way my life had turned out, knowing how hard I had worked at trying to keep my marriage together. I certainly didn't think I was to blame for Billy's drinking. Yet, I found solace in learning I'd get another chance to make things right. That I would return again and again in other lifetimes, until my purpose and lesson was realized and accomplished! I was hoping to get it right this time around... and, with the family I was given. The new thought of reincarnation comforted my aching soul and satisfied my intellect. It offered me a purpose for my journey... for this cycle of life, where I was promised I would eventually end up in Nirvana.

I took every class I could find on the subject. Evening classes. Weekend seminars. I volunteered long hours and soon became known as the *Sunshine Lady*, the official Greeter for the Sunday morning worship service. I also took over as the Sunday School teacher for the children. I didn't know which assignment I loved most.

Yet with all their teaching, I was still unhappy. The social mask I wore led people to think I was over Billy and our divorce. But it was a facade. I still ached inside. I mulled the question over and over: why hadn't our love been enough? Had I really created this terrible mess like the church claimed? Was I really God in my universe? If so, I was doing a lousy job.

I began noticing innuendos coming from certain people at church. Eventually these became outright accusations, about who was the real culprit for my pain. The answer was: ME. I felt judged and betrayed.

I had hoped the church would bring me closer to the answers I craved. But as in childhood, all I received was confusion. I was reminded of the time when Ruth from the church had broken the trust I had put in her. I was more spiritually confused, and left with a bitter taste in my mouth. When I needed them most, I was given an empty promise of hope. Instead of offering me the Golden Rule of *Do unto others as you would have them do unto you* (Matt. 7:12), I was met with a breach of trust and covert accusations. What I really needed was a hug, but instead I was given directives to take more classes and lectures. The mire I was trapped in was drowning me. I couldn't find peace no matter how hard I tried.

Old questions began invalidating my existence. *Why am I here? What is my purpose?* My current inability to overcome my situation was paramount. I just wished the world would open up and swallow me whole. I had done everything I could think of to put joy back into my life, to feel some semblance of happiness. Nothing worked. When it did, the feeling was there for only a fleeting moment. Then it was gone. And I would wake the following morning still caught in the *Bondage of Sorrow* that held me captive, and the pile of bills I couldn't free myself from.

Beware of false prophets
Matthew 7:15

"Please, dear God," I mumbled as I entered the house. My beautiful condo sat on the bank of the dry Santa Clara riverbed; where dreams had once lived, and hopes had been spoken. Where a marriage had been torn apart and the children separated. Where light had once shone and only darkness now resided. Where years later I still remained, returning each day to an empty house that haunted me. I hoped and prayed the family I longed for would someday return. However, after years of waiting, sorrow squelched any hope of Humpty Dumpty ever being put back together again.

Glancing around the family room, I placed my purse and briefcase on the table, tossing my jacket over the chair. I kicked off my heels, went to the fridge and grabbed a soda. I was exhausted. It had been a long Sunday morning. My office team had won first place in a recent contest. *The Prophets* had made *Profits* for the company. It was a time to celebrate, with everyone receiving an award for a job well done. I left the victory brunch amongst hugs and cheers.

By the time I got home, I was worn out and drained. All I wanted to do was watch some television. I walked over to my recliner and plopped down, reaching for the remote control and clicking it on. I could see the white-haired man on the TV screen before I could hear him. He appeared to be looking right at me. Slowly, his words followed.

"Do you know why you're so unhappy?" the old man asked.

Did he say my name?

"Because you've been looking for answers in all the wrong places. All paths don't lead to the Creator." He began waving a Bible in the air. I looked around for the remote I had laid down. "There's only one answer for your dilemma, and that's found... in this book!"

"Boy, I don't need this right now," I muttered as I reached for the TV control, accidentally knocking over my canned soda. I immediately jumped up to grab a towel as the man continued talking. He wouldn't shut up.

"Either the Bible is fact or fiction. It can't be both. Which is it to you?"

"Boy I hated this stuff," I grumbled, as I sopped up my mess.

"Ask yourself," the man rambled on. "If the Bible is true, then we would be wise to believe what it says. When God says there's only one way to reach Him, He's not kidding." The soda had run under the table, and I needed another towel.

"Not all roads lead to His house. Only His Son, Jesus Christ, can open that door and let us in."

"That's it," I said, tossing the soaked towels aside. I found the remote control as the man pressed on. "You're only gonna get one chance at life to get things right." I clicked the TV off and headed upstairs for a much-needed hot shower.

> *Jesus is not many ways to approach God*
> *nor is He the best of several ways;*
> *He is the only way.*
> A.W. Tozer

People like that drive me nuts. How could anyone preach about a loving God who only gives His children one way to reach Him? And with only one life to do it in!

"That's crazy," I muttered as I began undressing for the shower. But, the Preacher's words followed me. *What if... what if you're wrong? Are you willing to take that chance?* The questions echoed in my head as I stepped into the shower and turned on the faucet. As a child at church camp, hadn't I asked Jesus to come into my heart? *So, what's the problem?* The warm water felt good on my skin. Soothing. But the man's words wouldn't stop. *What if? What if this is the only chance you get?* "I wish he'd shut up," I muttered, as I began to ferociously lather my hair. The scrubbing was stimulating. I began to sing the hit song from *South Pacific*. "I'm gonna wash that man right out of my hair—I'm gonna—I'm gonna..."

But, what if I am wrong? What if I don't get another chance? Would I be living my life any differently than now? The questions felt intrusive. Suddenly, I wasn't feeling well. My head began to spin. My stomach churned. The shower was too hot. The words too scalding. I gulped for air.

What if you're wrong... what if... what if... what if!? The words reverberated in my head. *Why wouldn't they shut up?* I felt faint.

"Please, dear Lord." Fear gripped me. I groped for the faucet to turn the water off when I began violently retching. Green bile shot out of my mouth, spraying the white tiles a putrid color.

I vaguely remember stumbling out of the shower and collapsing on the carpet. When I awoke hours later, the afternoon sun was streaming through the bathroom window, bathing my naked body with light. I was shivering. Somehow I managed to stumble into bed. The following morning, Gabriel, my loyal doberman-pinscher, began nudging me with her wet nose, informing me of the urgency of the morning wake-up call. She was adamant about getting my attention. A leash hung from her mouth.

Instinctively I rolled out of bed, jumped into my jogging outfit, grabbed my keys, and opened the front door. Gabriel pushed passed me in dire desperation. She was thrilled to be outside. Soon she was chasing the morning birds in her futile attempt to catch one. I watched her prance off in joyful glee as I tried keeping up with her.

The morning breeze felt soothing against my face as I jogged along the path behind her. The air was fragrant with orange blossoms coming from the orchard that skirted the dry river beside my condo. A group of orchard workers were in the dry river bed below, sitting beneath one of the trees. They seemed to be enjoying the outdoors as much as Gabriel.

I let her run on as I stopped and began my morning stretches. My body groaned when I asked it to stretch. Soon, my mind began to fill with memories from the day before; of me having breakfast with my office team; returning home depressed instead of happy, but proud our team won first place; coming home and seeing the white-haired man on TV; the gross scenario in the shower that followed; waking up on the floor and stumbling into bed. Finally being awakened by Gabriel this morning.

I looked around to see where she had run off to, and noticed the men below still enjoying themselves. They resembled Jesus and his disciples gathered under a tree, visiting.

Gabriel came running as I stood up, then galloped off again when I resumed my stretches. I could hear the wind whistling through the eucalyptus trees, in tempo to the breeze. It seemed to be chanting. "What if? What if? What if the Bible is true? What then?"

Did I hear Mamo? "Child, ya only gonna get one chance." The statement pierced my heart. I straightened up and looked around. The wind seemed to echo her words. A panic button within me went off. If I really believed I was going to get another chance then learned after I died that I was wrong, I'd be in BIG TROUBLE! My head began to spin as it had the day before. "Oh please, dear God, not here."

"Oh please, sweet Jesus. Please." Tears streamed down my face. I tried gulping back the erupting sobs. I lowered my head and began to weep. "Jesus," I said, "If You really are who You say, You will take away my pain—my emptiness—this cup of hidden suffering. I can't take it anymore," I pleaded. The tears wouldn't stop.

"If You'll take away this heartbreak, and forgive my sins, I'll...," I hesitated. "I'll give You the rest of my life." I fell on my knees there on the trodden path. Years of shame and anguish gushed from me. "Please, please, Heavenly Father," I begged, "I'll do anything."

That's when I heard another voice. "Sell your home," it whispered. At first, I wasn't sure I had really heard it.

"Sell your home," the voice repeated. This time it was louder.

Sell my home? What a stupid thought. I couldn't believe at the most crucial moment of my life God would ask me to sell my home. He knew I needed that home, a place where my family could someday be reunited. Surely, God would not ask me to give up my security blanket where a light hung in the window that read, "Welcome Home."

"*SELL YOUR HOME.*" As the wind grew stronger, so did the voice. I looked around, but I couldn't see anyone. Even the men below had left. Dazed, I stood up.

"Sell my home?" I shook my head. *No. No. No.*

Just then, Gabriel trotted up to me, her gait enthusiastic. She weaved in and out of the foliage as we headed home. My mind raced. I couldn't ignore what was happening. If this was really God's voice telling me what to do and not my imagination, how could I say no? *I was afraid to take that chance.* The thought spurred me into action. Was Mamo's promise that God had a plan for me beginning to come true?

Here I am in Your hand.
Do with me as seems good and proper to You
Jeremiah 26:14

To my surprise, my condo sold within three days, receiving the highest sales price in our neighborhood. I wasn't expecting such a quick response. But, it was obvious I was doing the right thing. God was in charge, and He clearly wanted me to evacuate right away. I was given a thirty-day escrow as part of the deal. There was much to be done. Inside my home sat a lifetime of precious memories—items collected from twenty-five years of marriage, and children who had left the nest.

It was agony as I sorted through the 2,100 square feet of memories. What should I save? What should I let go of? After four weeks, and two emotionally charged garage sales, I sold or gave away nearly everything I owned. Furniture. Dishes. Souvenir keepsakes. The remainder of my belongings I placed in storage. I rented a room at a local bed and breakfast that allowed pets, and Gabriel and I moved in and began our wait to see what the next chapter of our lives would bring. I could never have imagined the future God had in store for me.

###

FAITH

Faith... more precious than gold... tested by fire...
1 Peter 1:7

chapter eight

THE MOVE

In You I put my trust
Psalm 16:15

Forty days after giving God the green-light to do with me as He chose, I was living in a Christian Bed & Breakfast that allowed me to keep Gabriel. I referred to the *sanctuary* of the B & B as the bridge God built between my old life and my new. My life appeared upside down. I was forty-eight with two grown sons. Thirty years had passed since Billy and I were married. Five years since my divorce and I was starting over, heading into the second half of my life. It was both exciting and frightening.

Trust in your money and down you go!
Proverb 11:28 NLT

After the sale of my condo, I received a substantial amount of money. It needed to be protected until I could figure out what I was supposed to do. Through my financial training, I knew diversified mutual funds were a safe investment. It never dawned on me to pray about it.

All day I wrestled with busy telephone lines trying to transfer all my money into the stock market. With one last ditch effort, I finally got through to a brokerage firm. They acted surprised to hear from me at such a late hour. After some squabbling, I finally convinced them to take my order over the phone. I went to bed proud of myself, knowing I had secured my future. I wrote in my journal that evening, "I shall never forget this moment." It was dated, October 18, 1987. The day Wall Street would later label as *Black Monday*! The second worst day in the history of the American Stock Market.

In one day, I lost nearly everything I had spent a lifetime striving for. One minute I was on top of the world (foot loose and fancy free, so they say), and the next I was in a dark, bottomless pit. It had been a long while since I had felt such fear. It wouldn't be the last.

If *Black Monday* wasn't black enough, it paled in significance to Tuesday morning's news. It began with a phone call. It was from my youngest son, Darin. He was calling from Hawaii, where he went after graduating high school. He wanted to visit Billy and his brother, who both lived in Maui. The *Demon of Divorce* had conquered and divided my family—Derek with Billy, Darin with me. Darin's vacation was to be a time of bonding for the Powers' men. The plan was for me to continue looking for a new residence while he was gone, and when Darin came back, we would have a place to begin a new life together. However, God obviously had other plans. Darin wasn't coming home. He was staying in Maui.

"Oh, dear God...," I whispered. My knees felt weak. I was devastated. Nothing I said could convince him to reconsider. His mind was made up. His feet dug in. He wanted to be near his brother and father whom he had been estranged from for so many years. There was no negotiating. He was a young man and could do what he wanted; there wasn't a thing I could do about it.

Years earlier, I lost Derek to the island. Shortly after he graduated from high school, he wanted to spend a summer on Maui. He promised to return in time to start college, but he never did. The Valley Isle had captured him. And now, history was repeating itself. I was losing another son to the same island!

Peace and rest escaped me that day and throughout that night. My bed, and the surrounding carpet, were covered with soggy tissues damp from hours and hours of tears. By 4 a.m., I had worked myself into a frenzy, vomiting over the thought of losing the only thing that mattered most to me—my two sons. What if neither of my boys ever came back to California? The realization left me feeling devastated.

Then, somewhere in the wee hours of the morning, before the first chirp of the sparrows or glimmer of the dawn's early light, I remembered the words of a wise man who once said, "To abandon your grown children after they are raised is to leave them to a life of doom."[1]

Wow! I knew I didn't want to be like my mother, who had told me, "Once you're out of the house, you're out for good. I did my job. Don't look to come back."

I promised myself I would never raise my boys only to toss them aside like some completed project after they were grown. They had been damaged during the divorce just like me. We all had scars. There was no way I was going to let Darin, a non-smoker, non-drinking, Christian teenager, be influenced by the shenanigans of Billy or Derek. No. If my boys wouldn't come to Momma, then Momma would have to come to them.

I was anxious for the travel agent to open her office the following morning so I could purchase my plane ticket to Maui. Now that I had decided to go, there was much to do. I needed to write the A.L. Williams home office of my intentions. I needed their permission to expand into another state. I was given six months to relocate and get the licenses needed to open my intended satellite office. While I was in Hawaii, I would continue receiving overrides from security and insurance sales made by my California licensed agents. Calculating my commission checks, along with the money left over from *Black Monday* and subtracting moving expenses, I estimated I should be able to support myself for six months. I would be near my sons and maybe even be able to stay longer if I lived frugally.

A friend suggested I earn some extra money while attending school for the licenses required by working at one of the swanky hotels—as a bartender!

"What?" She had to be kidding.

"No, listen," she went on, "the ad could read, 'Now appearing behind the bar: Miss Beverly Hills.' The people will love it."

"Give me a break." She knew I knew nothing about liquor, other than I didn't like the taste. I hated to be around it.

"Why not? You could make money and at the same time meet some people. It might even help you get leads for ALW."

That peaked my interest. The idea began looking rather attractive. Even adventurous. What harm could it do? I didn't drink. The fact that I didn't know the difference between scotch and bourbon didn't seem to matter. So, without giving it another thought, I telephoned and enrolled myself in a mixology school that offered at the end of the two-week course a *Certificate of Completion.*

All I could think about were Mother's words, "Don't ever forget: A lady can be a lady anywhere." The motto had worked in front of the bar as a dancer. Why not behind it?

So a few weeks later, I was sitting at a red-light heading home after my two-week stay in Orange County, admiring the *Certificate of Completion* that lay on the seat next to me. I had just picked up my plane ticket to Maui. I was filled with excitement. However, everything changed a moment later when my car and I were sent flying through the air. I had just been rear-ended by a drunk.

There was no warning. One minute I was fine; the next minute I wasn't. There were no outside appearances of injury, but my spine, weakened over years of injury, had been severely traumatized. The speeding drunk driver was arrested immediately, and I was rushed to the emergency room, where I was told I needed to be admitted. I told them they were sadly mistaken, adding, "Please return me to my car." They released me, and I was taken back to my car, which by now had been moved to the side of the road. The rear end was smashed, but it was still drivable. Once inside, I slowly and carefully drove home.

"There's no way I'm gonna cancel this trip!" my soul screamed. I had to see my sons! My body could heal as well in Hawaii as it could in California. All I had to do was hang onto my belief that I was doing the right thing. I prayed I'd be able to make it, no matter what. No one on Maui knew I was coming and wouldn't be disappointed if I hadn't shown up. But, *I* would have been disappointed. No way was I going to cancel this trip! Do or die, I was going to be on that DC 747 come December 21. And now I only had fourteen days left to get ready.

The big day arrived. With the help of a friend, I shipped my damaged car ahead of me to be repaired on Maui. It would be ready when I arrived. The owner of the B&B said she would keep Gabriel, my precious Doberman. I armed myself with folded dollar bills to tip the porters, and stashed muscle relaxers and pain pills into my purse, praying they'd be enough to tide me over until I could locate a doctor on Maui. Then slowly, ever so slowly, I limped my way onto the airplane, with fear in one hand and blind faith in the other, ready to begin my new life.

As the DC plane touched down in Hawaii, my heart exploded with excitement. It was like being in another Elvis Presley movie— swaying palm trees, young island women adorned with flowers in their thick black hair, greeting passengers with floral leis and singing "Aloha." No one was there to greet me, of course, since no one knew of my arrival. But they'd find out soon enough.

The main thing was, after months of planning, I had arrived! I didn't have a clue what my future held, but I had faith. Even if it was as small as a mustard seed (Mt. 17:20), it was enough to empower me to enter uncharted waters, trusting God would take care of everything. I suspected my arrival would make a ripple. In fact, just showing up could possibly create a storm for my family. Had I known what I was getting myself into, I may have had second thoughts. But at the moment, all I could see was how I had become a feather in God's hands.

Even before the divorce, Derek and I had been on the outs. He believed his father and I should stay together despite Billy's drinking, lying, and cheating, all because he loved me. Derek believed love should be enough. The pain Billy and I brought one another seemed immaterial to him. A wedge had been driven between my son and I.

I was hopeful that my visit to Maui would be a chance for a fresh start, a new beginning. The fact that Billy now lived with both boys greatly reduced the odds of Derek and me becoming close right away. But, peace had to start somewhere. So, why not here and now? Derek's twenty-sixth birthday present was meant to be a gift for both of us... prayerfully a healing between mother and son.

After arriving, I only had two days to prepare for Derek's birthday, four days 'til Christmas. The clock was ticking. There was much to do. As a surprise, I prepared a photo album for him, after learning he had lost everything in a fire earlier that year. All his mementos and photographs had gone up in smoke.

Diligently, I gathered, xeroxed, and reprinted photos I had found depicting Derek's early life, and bound them in a leather album for him, which was to be delivered to his residence the day after I arrived. The gift was unwrapped, with only a white bow and a small handmade truce-flag taped to a birthday card, showing a girl riding a dolphin toward a brilliant light with the enclosed message: "Let there be peace on earth and let it begin with me."

Inside I wrote, "Dear Derek, I want to do whatever it takes to rebuild my relationship with you... because you are worth it. I only have one oldest son and I love him very much. Have a beautiful day and enjoy the photographs. Happy Birthday Son! Love, Moms. P.S. On Christmas morning, look in the personal section of The Maui News to locate your Christmas present."

I awoke early that first morning, did my devotions, and rushed off to pick up my newly repaired car. Excitement was exploding within me. So much to do. The delivery service was first on my list of people to contact. They promised to hand-deliver Derek's unwrapped birthday gift to him, promising to not divulge where the parcel came from. Then I called The Maui News and placed an ad for Christmas morning:

MERRY CHRISTMAS TO MY TWO WONDERFUL SONS.
God loves you & so do I.
A phone call at 11 this morning will tell you
where you can find your surprise.
Love, Moms

After grabbing a quick breakfast, I headed toward West Maui in search of a place to stay. The Pali Coastline was as beautiful as people had said. The ocean view from *Scenic Point* was magnificent. I could actually see the curve of the horizon! I felt I had died and gone to heaven. By the time I returned to my hotel later that day, I wasn't so sure. I was discouraged, unbearably hot, and my body was writhing in pain.

I had spent most of the day traveling up and down the Lower Honoapiilani Road looking for a condo that would prayerfully be close to my boys. I didn't know the name of their condominium, but I knew I was on the right street. I left their actual address back at the hotel. But it didn't matter because there were no vacancies anywhere. It was Christmas and everything was booked up. I started to worry. My body was throbbing. All I wanted to do was to lie down and rest, but I didn't have time to relax. My reservation at The Maui Palms was only good until the morning of the 26th. Then I'd have to leave. Then what? The prospect frightened me. I had assumed I would have found a place by now when I booked my reservations. But, so far, there was nothing. What would happen if I couldn't find a place?

Tomorrow was Christmas Eve. My personal ad in The Maui News didn't say where the boys could find their Christmas present... which of course was me. I had left out that bit of information, because I wasn't sure at the time where I would be, but figured I'd know by the end of the day. But I still didn't, and I could feel the pressure inside me mounting. I knew Derek would never drive to the other side of the island on Christmas morning, present or no present. Maybe some other day, but not on Christmas day. "Oh Heavenly Father, please help me."

Crawling into bed, I reached for my Bible. It opened to Philippians 1:6. "Be confident of this very thing, that He who has begun a good work in you will complete it." I hoped so.

The following morning, I was jolted awake by the ringing of the telephone. It was a realtor. He had heard from the delivery person that a woman from out of state was here to surprise her sons for Christmas, and needed temporary accommodations for the holidays.

"Are you still looking for a place?"

"Yes," I said, glancing at the clock. 7:25 a.m.

"Well, I have clients who had to cancel their vacation, so a condo has become available for the next three weeks in West Maui if you want it. I don't know if it's close to where your sons live, but half the rent has already been paid. You can pay the other half at the office after the holidays. What do you think?"

"What do I think? I think you must be an angel! When can I move in?"

"Right away, if you want." I squealed with joy. He chuckled.

"I hope it works out for you, Ma'am." I assured him it would, remembering the Bible verse from the night before.

"By the way, the name of the complex is The Kuleana. It's located at 3959 Lower Honoapiilani Road. The unit number is 312. A key will be under the mat."

"God bless you," I said as I hung up, excitement jumping out of me in all directions. Tears of gratitude streamed down my face. "Oh thank you, dear Lord. Thank you. Thank you. Thank you!" I quickly gathered my things together and began scribbling down my to-do list.

After the porter had placed my suitcases in my car, I went back inside the hotel room to scan one last time if I was forgetting anything. I glanced around the room. As I picked up my purse on the night stand, I glanced at the pillow that had been so comfortable during my short stay. I hadn't had such rest in weeks. Without a thought, I grabbed the pillow, threw it under my arm and headed for my car. I didn't think anything about it. Hotels always factored in souvenirs for tourists to take. I knew it would be okay. It wasn't like I was stealing or anything. I always left a tip in my hotel room when checking out. I knew the tip I left inside the room was more than the cost of the pillow.

As I opened the trunk and tossed the pillow inside, I heard a voice within say, *put it back.*

I stopped for a moment, listened, then closed the trunk. I walked around the car, slid behind the wheel and started up the engine when I heard the voice again. *Put the pillow back*, it whispered.

"It's only a pillow," I said to myself as I began backing out of the driveway. "Washcloths. Shampoo. What's the difference?"

PUT THE PILLOW BACK! the voice screamed. *That's not a pillow. That's your life!*

I slammed on the brakes. I sat there for a moment, not moving. Then, after thinking it over, I put the car in drive and edged forward towards my recently vacated room. I tiptoed back to the room and was relieved to find the door unlocked. Once inside, I replaced the precious pillow on the bed, knowing no one would be the wiser... except for God.

How foolish. I knew better. Stealing was stealing, no matter how big or little. In God's Kingdom, there are no gray areas. If I wanted God to help me on this adventure, then I would have to play by His rules (Ex. 20:1-17). And, to always remember it is God who gives me my rest... not the pillow. I figured I had just been given a test (Ex. 20:22). I hoped I passed.

I needed to purchase a Christmas dinner and find a small tree, and perhaps a few lights. I had wrapped and brought with me Christmas ornaments that Derek and Darin had made as children, along with a few other favorite items from their past. It was imperative that our first Christmas together, after so many years, be extra special.

Once again, as the day before, all I could see as I drove through the winding curves of the Pali coastline was God's magnificent creation. The expansive sky and cobalt blue sea blended into one. The image was framed with thick white clouds high above and the whitewater coastline below. I had never seen anything as beautiful. It was difficult to stay focused on the winding road.

I could smell the saltwater, as the Pali straightened out and sidled up to the crashing surf. I wanted to pull over. Tears filled my eyes. "Thank you, Heavenly Father. Thank you, thank you, thank you," was all I could say.

My map indicated I had stopped at Thousand Peaks. I located the Kuleana Condominiums. They appeared to be about twenty miles away. I wondered how close that was to where Derek and Darin lived. I dug through my purse looking for their address. I figured it had to be near.

I was shocked when I discovered their street address and compared it to the one given me by the realtor. I couldn't believe my eyes. The addresses were the same! This had to be a mistake. I looked again, but it wasn't a mistake. The numbers were the same. Even my rented unit appeared to be in the same building!

"Oh dear God. Please. I can't do this. I can't stay in the same building as Billy." I knew the boys lived with him. We hadn't spoke since his drunken threat that he made years earlier, over the phone. Even if the threat was all talk, I didn't want to take any chances. He was irrational. Defiant. Hostile. And very volatile toward me. I was frightened of him.

I began to cry... beg... plead. "Lord, please. I'll do anything... but not this. Take this away from me. This can't be Your will."

But the numbers didn't lie, and there was no going back. An hour ago, I had checked myself out of the Maui Palms Hotel. I had to go forward... praying God would take care of me.

"Please, sweet Jesus, make me invisible," I prayed as I pulled into the parking space. My car was not easy to hide, with a smashed rear-end and personalized California license plates that read RVP LADY, which stood for Regional Vice President. *Gee, no one will notice me!*

I eventually found my unit. It was located directly above the boys' unit. This was surreal. I could see the boys' surfboards propped up beside their front door. After the property manager helped me with my luggage, I quickly drove off the property, hoping no one had seen me, and headed for the market.

I found a small artificial tree with lights attached and a nice-sized ham, something I always baked at Christmas when we were together. *The boys are gonna love this*, I mused. I purchased some potatoes, a jar of sweet pickles, black olives, rolls, and for dessert, a pumpkin pie with a can of whipped cream.

Returning to the condo, I parked at the far end of the property hoping Darin wouldn't see my car. He and Billy would recognize my license plates immediately. I didn't want anything to ruin my surprise. Then, I transformed my living room into a Christmas wonderland... with the decorations I carefully brought from the Mainland, along with wrapped gifts I had brought. Items the boys had left behind when they moved out so long ago. I even had a gift for Billy. A Zippo lighter my stepfather, Jerry, had given him. I was truly ready for Christmas!

I went outside and sat on the lanai with my Bible. It opened to Jeremiah. Verse 29:11 was highlighted. "I have a plan for you, sayeth the Lord." Boy, I sure wish I knew what that was. Up to this point I had no idea. I was living on blind faith. I just hoped God really did have a plan for me as the Bible said. As the sun set on the horizon, birds began flocking to the trees. They screeched and squabbled for the best branches to spend the night upon as darkness descended. A groundsman appeared lighting the tiki torches that lined the property. I went to bed that night feeling blessed. It was Christmas Eve! I was on Maui! Soon I would see my sons. I was giddy with excitement. I could hardly wait. I felt at peace. Little did I know I was experiencing the calm before the storm.

The following morning, I awoke excited for the day and grateful for a good night sleep. It had been restful, and without the aid of the notorious pillow. I felt I was on an adventure, and all I needed to do was to continue trusting God. And for sure, I was trying. I prayed my Christmas surprise would go off without a hitch, and the future that lay before my sons and me would be filled with nurturing fruit. I knew this was a chance for restoration... an opportunity for our family to be grafted back together again.

I smile at God's timing. After planning my Christmas surprise for months, at long last everything was in place. Down to the last detail. After showering and dressing for the big occasion, I looked at the clock. I was an hour early! The ad in the newspaper said I would call at 11 a.m., and it was only 10. Even so, I went to the phone and tried calling, but their line was busy. Of course. God didn't want me spending that extra hour with them. He had delegated this time just for us. This last hour had been scheduled before my assignment even began. Sixty precious minutes alone with Jesus. Just Him and me. He knew I would need quiet time alone with Him before sending me out into this new chapter of my life. I may not have known what that new life would look like, but God did. The Creator of Heaven and Earth knows everything. My faith in Him was becoming more real each day... and less abstract.

Create some waves; then ride them
Gina Pearson

Darin was the first to come over after my Christmas morning phone call. Derek, I learned, had a job as a waiter and already left for work. He'd be back later. Apparently there had been a discussion the day before concerning the birthday gift which had been delivered to him anonymously. Darin suspected I might be on the island and would do something like this.

"I felt you were here," he said, giving me a big bear hug. He was authentically happy to see me. We visited, opened presents, and waited for Derek, who wasn't as happy to see me.

"Why are you here?" he snapped. "Who invited you?"

I was shocked at his response in seeing me. And his disrespect! I figured he may be upset at me for showing up unannounced. But I certainly didn't expect his rude behavior.

Just then Billy walked in. I could tell he had been drinking. Immediately, I felt nervous. It had been six years since the four of us had been in the same room together. I could feel the tension.

Suddenly, without saying another word, Derek turned and walked out. Then, Billy became belligerent. At one point, he actually lunged at me. Darin quickly interceded and took him outside, still ranting and raving. Shortly after, Derek returned, charging into the condo, furious that his father had been tossed out of my house. He confronted Darin for sticking up for me. Before I could stop them, they were in fisticuffs. I couldn't separate them.

"Stop it! Stop it!" I screamed. Never before had I seen my younger son physically challenge the older. But Darin was now 19 and a farrier for The Rainbow Ranch. He surpassed Derek in size. My surfer son couldn't hold his ground against the likes of his baby brother. He stomped out of the house swearing so loud I'm sure the neighbors could hear him.

I was shaken and very apologetic. "I'm so sorry, Darin. I didn't intend for any of this to happen. I wanted to bring peace, not this." I pointed to the pink button I was wearing on my blouse, "Let there be peace on earth and let it begin with me." Nothing had turned out like I dreamed. Even my Christmas dinner went uneaten. Sorrow filled my heart.

That night during my evening prayers, I was reminded of the adage, *A house must be torn down before it can be rebuilt.* This was a house... it was the Powers' house... a house that God built and obviously where He wanted me to be, at least for the time being. I just had to stay centered. My objective hadn't changed. My goal was still the same, to have my boys back in my life. God had given them to me to be their earthly mother. I had a responsibility, despite my fears. God was giving me a chance. I wasn't going to blow it if I could help it. The first thing I needed to do was get a permanent address. I also needed a doctor's appointment for my ailing body, and another one for my car's ailing body. But, until after the holidays, I would just have to sit back and enjoy myself, tucked away under swaying palm trees. *Gee, I could do that!*

My arrival clearly had made waves, and my fear of Billy's reaction had been confirmed. It turned out to be a Christmas I wanted to forget. Sadly, it wasn't the last. It took several years before Derek began coming around without saying, "This is my island. Why are you here?"

I started answering back, "Because I love you." That seemed to shut him up. He didn't have a response. And although we seldom spoke, God often placed us on the perimeter of each other's lives. West Maui is a small community with only a two-lane highway. It's nearly impossible for us not to see each other while on the road. Though I continued to wear my large pink button proclaiming peace, I began to feel anger within me that I had hidden away toward my son.

I learned after our divorce that Derek had known about Billy's affair with Floozie long before me and had kept it a secret. Even condoning it by sleeping over at her house and offering Billy an alibi by saying he and his father had been together. Which they had... but at her house! I would have never guessed that my husband and son would someday betray me. I tried to excuse it away within myself, but the pain lingered. My resentment toward Derek's current behavior was tainted by the festering wound still inside me.

"Please, dear God, remove this splinter of betrayal from my heart," I prayed. The splinter nestled well with the other splinters in my heart that had accumulated over the years. I thought they had all been forgotten. But, there was quite a bonfire brewing inside. I prayed Derek and my new start wouldn't be tainted by past hurts... that somehow there would be a healing.

"Please Lord, fill me with Your forgiveness. Don't let me explode inside every time Derek is rude or hurts my feelings. Let my response to him be an example of Your love for me. *Love the sinner. Hate the sin.* Isn't that what You want us to do? Please help me. I can't do this alone. Thank you. Amen."

Be confident... He who has begun a good work...
will complete it
Philippians 1:6

###

chapter nine

THE TRAINING

Teach me Your way, O Lord
Psalm 86:11

In God's garden, there is always a time to plant and a time to sow (Ecc. 3:2). And in between, there is a time for pruning, training, plucking, a painful grafting or two, or even a transplant when deemed necessary. In all the years of training with acting teachers Lee Strasberg, Jeff Corey, or Charles Conrad, nothing was as difficult as the training I encountered after arriving on Maui, the Valley Isle.

A month after the Christmas holidays, I landed an interview at one of Kaanapali's hotel bars. As I drove toward the employment office, my Mixology Certificate sat on the seat beside me as it had a month earlier, the night the drunk smashed into the rear of my car damaging both it and me. Now, with the repairs made to both of us, I was ready for a temporary job while I prepared myself for the exams needed to open my new satellite insurance office.

I could hear birds singing in the trees that lined the road as I drove down the street. Then, without warning, a car coming in the opposite direction suddenly turned left, ramming into the side of my car and shoving me sideways across the sidewalk and through a clump of trees. I eventually came to a faltering halt amongst a bunch of bushes. Stunned, and in disbelief, I began to whimper. My body was crouched, slumped over the gear shift and seething in pain. I was afraid to move.

I could smell the alcohol as the woman leaned through the window. "Oh my gosh," she stammered. "Are you okay?" Somehow she managed to open my door. Reaching across me to unfasten my seat buckle, she asked again, "Hey lady, are you okay?" I couldn't answer. I wasn't sure. My head was spinning. *Was I bleeding?*

"I'm so sorry," she kept saying.

Someone yelled, "Call an ambulance!" I began to cry.

"Are you all right?"

No, I wasn't all right! I wanted to yell. What little mending my body had experienced since my last accident obviously was now undone. I had been a victim in two separate auto accidents, and in both cases the drivers said, "I didn't see you." *Were they kidding?* I needed to take a look at this. I didn't believe in coincidences. I had to ask myself, *Why? Why was this happening?* I needed to try and connect the dots, because one minute I was asking God to use me, and the next I was flying through the air. And, in both cases, alcohol was the culprit! It didn't take a rocket scientist to figure this one out.

"What do ya' think, Beverly Jean?" I could hear Mamo's voice as if she was still here. "Maybe God doesn't want ya to be a bartender. Maybe He has better plans for ya."

I prayed all the time. Yet, I never thought to ask God's opinion concerning my new profession. It was only going to be temporary anyway. But then I remembered that day on the Santa Clara River, when I fully surrendered and gave the second half of my life to Him. I remembered giving Him permission to do with me however He pleased. Why should I be surprised at what was happening? Obviously the direction I was headed didn't please Him. He allowed the *accidents* to happen. I didn't believe He caused them. However, I was beginning to see how I had. Once again, I had lost my senses and bamboozled myself into thinking being a bartender would be cool, a way to meet people and make some extra money. Me, a person who hates to be around drinking. Me, who hates the taste of liquor! Not to mention drunks. I went so far as to divorce one! Yet, somehow I had convinced myself into thinking I could get beyond my limitations, and intolerance toward drunks, and become the world's greatest bartender.

I lack common sense
Proverbs 30:2 NLT

Now, all I could do was trust that the God who had brought me this far would carry me the rest of the way, despite my blindness. I couldn't be trusted to make the right decisions. I needed God's wisdom to protect myself *from* myself. I obviously didn't have sense God gave a goose, because I was *still* making bad choices. I needed God's guidance now more then ever.

I tried to keep a positive outlook, believing things were soon going to improve. I thought the insurance companies from the two collisions would each honor their obligation and cover me, the injured party. But as it turned out, each blamed the other for my disability. In the meantime, medical bills were piling up and personal resources were drying up. I desperately tried to fight off my gripping fear.

But, God's light was shining on me, though it was difficult for me to always see it. I certainly recognized it when, on the day after my birthday, 8-8-88, I found a new place to live, and Darin helped me move. It was a miracle for sure. Dawn, a woman who lived at the far end of the Kuleana condos, had recently broken up with an abusive boyfriend and was in dire need of money, and was renting out her bedroom for six months. It seemed the perfect solution. She worked during the day and would sleep on the couch at night. It offered me the days to be alone and time to try and heal myself before my money ran out. And boy did I need this hideaway to heal myself.

My long-term physical pain continued night and day. I had severely injured my lower back where, years earlier, I had weakened it through a series of injuries that ended with me having to undergo spine surgery. Now I was also suffering from whiplash and migraine headaches. Twice I was hospitalized because of the pain that riddled my body.

Nonetheless, I trudged along and prepared for my future. I enrolled myself in the financial classes needed to continue with ALW. I still planned to open a satellite office on Maui before returning to Southern California. Hawaii was not a reciprocal state and required I retake all my financial exams[1] in order to get licensed and begin recruiting. The California tests taken years earlier were brutal, and I was in good health back then. But this time? I couldn't even imagine how I was going to climb this mountain. The accidents had left me so physically weak and mentally unable to concentrate on anything but my pain. I was forced to drop out of the classes. Then, because I was out of compliance with ALW's by-laws, they terminated my contract. The overrides and commissions I had come to depend on immediately came to a halt, as did my health insurance.

I cashed out the money in my retirement plan and sold all my stock. This was it. I had no more hidden rabbits up my sleeve, and I didn't know what I was going to do. Mamo always said our fears would either kill us or help us grow. I hoped she was right, and that I would do some growing! There was nothing left to hang onto except for the little faith I still clung to. I kept running into dead ends. I couldn't draw unemployment because I hadn't paid into it. Couldn't get disability because the insurance claims were still in limbo. And it was the holiday season once again, and Derek's birthday.

My beautiful car with its new rear-end and side paneling had been repossessed. I was now driving what the locals call a Maui Cruiser because of the sad condition it was in, or *not in,* I should say. I named it my *Humility Cruncher.* The trunk was held shut by two bungee-cords crisscrossing the hatch back to keep it from flying off while driving across the island. The floorboards were nearly gone, and the "air conditioning" was the collection of gaping holes that allowed a person to look down and see the road whizzing by underfoot.

For months, both auto insurance companies had promised they would be sending me money. But so far, *nothing*. "The check is in the mail," became their mantra.

"Honest. You'll have it before Christmas." Well, I didn't have it. Not before Christmas nor by Derek's birthday, and I didn't have gifts for either. My rent was due. And the mounting medical bills had become liens.

Driving home empty-handed from the post office, I was despondent. "Okay God," I wept. "Now what? Do You really want me to be homeless?" A shudder swept through my body. I knew if sleeping in my Maui Cruiser would somehow serve the Lord... then I had to do it.

"Okay, I'm willing to be a bag-lady if that be Thy will," I cried. The thought horrified me. I could barely sleep on the proper mattress I had now—much less waking up crippled in the back seat of a jalopy!

Between worry and pain, sleep escaped me. The few Percodan pills and Codeine tablets I had from earlier prescriptions were long gone. I had been gobbling handfuls of over-the-counter-pain-relievers for weeks. And now, those were gone. I hadn't eaten anything substantial in days. The cupboards were bare except for a half-empty bottle of Tequila that the former tenant had left.

Within moments of taking my first swallow from the bottle, I felt the warmth of the Cuervo Gold. I was glad I had found it. The ferocious pain radiating through my body was more than I could bare.

"Dear Lord, I'm sorry," I sobbed as I slipped into my bathing suit, knowing my hidden agenda was to take my own life through a one-way swim toward the island of Molokai. "Forgive me," I repeated, as I reached for another dose of courage from the Tequila. *What's the use?* I thought, remembering Dionne Warwick's song, *What's It All About, Alfie?* I had made a mess of everything. No job, no money, and now my body wasn't working! I didn't want to be a whiny baby and feel sorry for myself, but in truth, I had gone from being a Regional

Vice President in a Fortune 500 company to being an indigent, all in less than fourteen months.

Wow. Good going, Beverly Jean. If your fans could see you now! I recalled Jack Benny's voice the day he phoned my house to congratulate me on the wonderful reviews I had received after an early New York telecast of that week's *Jack Benny Show.* "Wait until your fans see you in this," Benny said. "After tonight you're going to be a star." That's what Lucille Ball also said after I was in one of her TV shows, and compared me to comedian Judy Holiday.

If they could only see me now! I took the last swig from the bottle. I wished I were dead.

O Lord... I am in trouble
Psalm 31:9

I awoke in Maui Memorial Hospital. The nurses told me I had been admitted the night before, suffering from alcohol poisoning. Now I really wanted to die. My overwhelming embarrassment and unrelenting pounding of my head were unbearable.

Derek picked me up at the hospital Christmas morning and was quick to inform me that it was Billy who had found me. He had become suspicious when he didn't see any activity around my place and called the front desk, who let him in and found me lying in the midst of rubble, unconscious, in a bathing-suit with an empty tequila bottle beside me. He called the paramedics.

Arriving home from the hospital, I phoned Billy immediately and thanked him.

"Sam," he said with concern in his voice. The name sounded so familiar. "In your delirium, you kept saying you wanted to go home and you were apologizing to Mamo over and over again, saying how sorry you were. Weird huh?" he asked.

No, not really, I thought. A better question would have been, "What on earth was I thinking? And, why hadn't God stopped this downhill spiral?" By the looks of my house, I had been out of control. I couldn't believe what I had done.

It took days to clean up the mess from my insane rage. Something had snapped within me, and in my drunken stupor, I was able to surpass my physical limitations and trashed my condo. Clutter and upheaval were everywhere. Dressers tossed. All interior doors, louvre and sliding alike, had been torn from their runners and were thrown about. The coffee pot and damp coffee grounds had been thrown across the room. Dark stains splashed across the white drapes. Broken glass was everywhere. Books were scattered, thrown from their shelves. Bookshelves upended. And there on the floor, where Billy had found me, the Holy Bible Ruth had given me years earlier. It was opened to the inscription written on the inside cover: "Proverbs 3:5 & 6, 1951"

Within days of leaving the hospital, I was contacted by social services, who heard of my financial and physical needs and wanted to help. My pride screamed and my shame worsened. I came to Maui to be an asset, not a liability!

I wanted to return to the Mainland. But how? Maybe I could salvage my business career that had been so successful in California. Or, perhaps I could jump start my acting career. Could either be resurrected? Even if it were so, how would I get home? An airplane ticket cost money. Where would I live? Oh, I was so confused.

The first thing I needed to do was to swallow my pride and receive assistance until I got back on my feet. The script of begging was new to me. But I did it, and my food, shelter, and medical expenses would be taken care of while this mess was straightened out. There was nothing for me to do now but concentrate on getting well. Physically, spiritually, and mentally.

The faith and confidence I had before leaving California had almost left me. The accidents had taken their toll. I had very little fight left. It felt like I was caught in a hurricane, and I knew the only safe place to be at that moment was in the eye of the storm. I had to focus on God. The only way I was going to heal my body was to focus on the One who had allowed doors to open that led me here, and had closed others. The One who had provided me with all my needs up to this point, despite *my* interference. In the midst of mire, God had always been there. Right then my heart overflowed with a mixture of shame and gratitude.

I thought of Mamo, the woman with only a third grade education who knew the value of common sense. She would speak of the three-legged milking stool she used to milk the cows when she was a child. "You can't sit on a two-legged stool, Beverly Jean," Mamo would say. "It won't hold you up." I had heard the story enough times to know she was talking about the body, mind and spirit. "If'n one of 'em is broken, life's gonna be real difficult, child."

Mamo was right. I had to get back to basics. Yet, the more I prayed for a physical healing, the more my pain incapacitated me, to the point where all I could do was lay at the ocean's edge, pray, reflect, and read the Bible. My knowledge of the Bible grew stronger. God truly had my attention. Not part of it, or some of it, but all of it.

I thought of Jesus. What had He done when He was tested by life during His forty days in the desert? I had learned the story as a child, how the devil attacked Jesus during His weakest moment (Lk. 4:2). And each time, Christ fended off the darkness with scripture. He always confronted His problem with scripture. *That was it! I needed to learn more scripture.*

> *Trust in the Lord with all your heart,*
> *and lean not on your own understanding;*
> *In all your ways acknowledge Him,*
> *and He shall direct your paths*
> Proverbs 3: 4, 5

"Trust in the Lord." The words given to me by Ruth, my Sunday School Teacher when I was a child. Now grown, I needed to learn the lesson of that scripture. The concept of surrendering and trusting a *Father Knows Best* ideology was very difficult. Neither of my earthly fathers had been trustworthy. Nor had the father of my own children! Trust had become a huge issue, and the concept of letting go and *letting God* felt unnatural. Total surrender to an invisible Heavenly Father, no matter how many times I thought I had seen His handiwork, was truly a test of faith. But I didn't really have much of a choice. "I was in quite a pickle," as Mamo would say. I had to lean on those "everlasting arms" that she used to sing about.

But I couldn't help but wonder, *Why was I on Maui?* Except for my youngest son, no one wanted me here. My body was a wreck. My finances had gone down the tubes faster than flour going through Mamo's sifter. Things looked bad. I knew God was the source of good, but right now my life looked the opposite, which gave me a clue as to who I was fighting: ME! What I didn't know was God had me right where He wanted me, totally at His mercy. I knew if I ever hoped to get out of the mire I was in, it would have to be done through God's grace.

In the past I had trusted myself, and look where it had gotten me. In the end, empty and alone surrounded with real estate, furs, jewelry, and with a certain amount of notoriety. In my twenties, I had sought fame and passion. In my thirties, fortune and possessions. As a child I had trusted my family, and, except for Mamo, all had betrayed me. First my father, then my stepfather, then Mother, then my husband, and finally even my son. I had to believe God would not betray me. Mamo had trusted Him and He never disappointed her. For as long as I remember, she always leaned on the arms of her invisible friend, Jesus.

Looking at my life, Mamo would say, "Common sense is telling you to stick your nose in the Good Book and learn as much as you can to defend yourself." And so began my first reading of the Bible. In the midst of my desert experience, I was looking to God's written word for directions. I knew I had been given another chance. But, I needed answers. So, with nothing to lose, perhaps everything to gain and tons of time on my hands, along with an overwhelming sense of confusion as to what God wanted from me, I began my quest.

I began reading the New Testament and found I enjoyed it so much, I read it again. Then, with insatiable thirst, and wanting to know more, I began reading the Bible through for a third time... this time starting with the Old Testament. I found the stories of Biblical women from long ago fascinating. Deborah, Esther, Ruth, Naomi, Hannah. These were awesome women, who showed me what real faith looked like. In the line of adversity, each of these women rose to an occasion of difficulty that had been set before her. In a time when women were considered chattel, each stepped forward and proved God was a constant. Even without the gifts of Jesus, His Holy Spirit, or the written word, these women from the Old Testament became my heroes.

Like me, they had once been locked into a place called fear. But, they rose above it and became victorious through their phenomenal faith. Faith in a living God that used their personal fear and developed it into a strong faith. Just like Mamo, these women had courage to do whatever was necessary to get the job done, and I wanted to be strong like them.

Each morning, I would go to the ocean's edge and begin my day in prayer and read the Bible as the sun rose behind me. I always began with a prayer of thanksgiving, then asked for guidance and protection for myself and my boys. I made a commitment to pray morning, noon, and night, like Daniel from the Old Testament (Dan. 6:10). The impact of the scripture got me through each day.

I prayed for peace and restoration for myself and family. For purpose and direction. I knew God would not close one door without opening another. If He really wanted me to step out into the unknown, He would either give me something solid to stand on or teach me how to fly. I knew I needed to be faithful and leave the results to Him. I had to trust God.

The One who calls you is faithful
1 Thessalonians 5:24 NIV

One morning I walked outside and sat down at my patio table. My sorrow was overwhelming. "Oh, sweet Jesus, please help me," I sobbed, my head buried in my arms. "I'm so sorry," I cried, "and...I am so confused. Won't You please help me and reveal to me Your will for me... please?"

I must have fallen asleep. I don't remember. However, when I raised up and opened my eyes, I felt I was still sleeping. I rubbed my eyes. "This can't be," I whispered. "I must be dreaming." It was either that or I was hallucinating.

I rubbed my eyes again and looked around. The journal and pen were still on the table as I had left them. The pink bougainvilleas I cut that morning were still in their vase. But, in front of me was the same view I had seen in my dreams more than a dozen times during my lifetime.

I gasped. How could this be? This dream had always been the same; me seated in front of a large pane-glass window busily working at a table outside in my yard. A grassy knoll gently sloping down toward the edge of a lake where an expansive tree loomed overhead. Flowery shrubs and bushes dotting the landscape. And across the lake, two beautiful mountains.

Over the years, this same dream often became the topic of conversation.

"Mamo," Billy would say, "did Beverly tell you she had that dream again?"

"Has she figgered out yet, where it's at?"

"Not yet," was always the reply.

I had visited this place numerous times in my sleep and could never figure out what it meant or why it was always the same. After awhile, I stopped speculating and just enjoyed the afterglow it left me with. However, this time I wasn't feeling its tranquility but rather bewilderment. The sight was unnerving. And bizarre! It frightened me.

The Kuleana was built in 1975. I began having my dreams in '57. Had God known all along that I would some day end up at the Kuleana?

I knew I wasn't dreaming, that I was awake. There was no denying it. The lake in the dream was really the Pacific Ocean in front of me. The two mountains were Maui's nearest islands of Lanai and Molokai. The view had been in front of me all along! I had been living in my dream all this time on Maui and not noticed! Tears gushed down my face as I choked, "Help me, dear Lord, I don't understand! How can this be happening?"

I didn't know the answers to these questions or what I was supposed to do with this prophecy that God had revealed. But I did know Maui was where God wanted me. I didn't know why, but it soon became evident that the Kuleana would be the classroom where God would teach me the lessons needed for my future.

We are [God's] workmanship created... for good works which He prepared beforehand
Ephesians 2:10

I rarely saw Derek. Darin had moved back to the Mainland to work, and I tried avoiding Billy as much as possible since he was still drinking heavily. I had only a few acquaintances on the island. I rarely spoke to anyone. I spent most of my time either receiving physical therapy or reading the Bible.

Over and over again, I repeated God's words, as I huddled alone at the water's edge in the wee hours of the morning. "Let there be peace on earth as it is in Heaven," the words from Matthew stated (6:10). Christ promised we could have Heaven on earth, and even reiterated, "Behold, heaven is at hand (10:7)." However--I figured before I could see Heaven on earth I would first have to get past my tenuous circumstances.

"Child, all it takes is faith the size of a mustard seed," Mamo would have said.

Well, I certainly had that much! I had enough faith to believe the Creator of the universe, who parted the Red Sea, could certainly turn my worrisome experience into one of wonder. I didn't know how it would happen. Or when. I just knew it would.

I related to the story of the apostle Paul and the thorn in his side. Through my weakness I, too, was being made strong. But I also knew that if I were truly healthy and strong, I probably would be frolicking in the surf, instead of propped up on a lounge chair with a Bible on my lap. Paul's story empowered me. Two years went by, and my physical prognosis was finally given: "permanent, partial, disability."

"Now what?" I wanted to know.

"You learn to live with your pain," the doctor had said.

I didn't know if I could do that. Is that what the Master Physician wanted me to do? To suffer and live with this pain? I knew many people did, but I found the news very disturbing. I also became angry—at myself. I couldn't believe I had gotten myself into this mess... a person who had worn many hats in life and knew the sweet smell of success, now barely able to do much of anything.

Do not forget to entertain strangers,
for by so doing some have unwittingly entertained angels
Hebrew 13:2

That's when God sent me my first earth angel. Actually, He sent me a mother of an infant named Angel. The mother asked one day if we could pray together. We began praying about her situation. She was a single mother living on assistance, because the father of the child didn't want the responsibility. Within a short time, our prayers branched out and we began praying not just for ourselves but for others. Soon those *others* that we had been praying for joined us, and on Tuesday nights at the water's edge in front of my condo, us ladies began holding a weekly prayer meeting we named *The Winner's Circle.*

For nearly two years, approximately ten of us gathered together each week and read favorite scriptures, prayed, and studied the plight of others from the Bible. We especially identified with Deborah of the Old Testament and the women who gathered with her to pray under her tree. We loved the telling of Mary, Martha, Mary Magdalene, and the woman at the well who had six husbands, plus all those other women found in the New Testament. All valiant women. All with varied backgrounds and different personalities. Some with much to be forgiven. Some with much to overcome. But all with one thing in common: their love and faith in Jesus Christ. From the beginning, that was the common ground for the prayer circle. And, out of that circle our faith grew. And, so did our spiritual vision as we focused on God's word.

Together we learned the meaning of trust. Trusting one another as well as the One who made us. We watched as God spread His unconditional love over us like a blanket, in a variety of ways, to a variety of women who attended. From the professional harpist; tennis coach; retired nanny with breast cancer; the unwed, unemployed mother trying to do it God's way; the housewife with a cheating husband; the struggling waitress trying to pay rent. All lifestyles were represented from the young to the old. Together, our faith and trust grew hand-in-hand as we witnessed God's omniscient love and power covering each of us and orchestrating results that were often extraordinary.

One of the issues I had been struggling with were the voices that haunted me at night. Voices that chimed in when my eyelids closed—opposing my rest. The *What If's* and *How Comes* filled me with memories and distortions. *Guilt. Shame. Blame.* They were all there taunting me in the darkness. *Sorrow. Regret. Loneliness.* Along with *Lack* and *Limitations.* Often, the voices created within me a vulnerability so deep I'd be nearly paralyzed with fear. They were beginning to take their toll. Sometimes they wouldn't shut up longer than a moment before they'd return, no matter what I tried doing.

My sleep was being deprived. The girls of our weekly prayer circle prayed, and God answered.

Soon those voices were replaced with another that I recognized as *Myrtle,* the name I gave the voice when I was young. The voice that sounded very much like the one that told me to "Sell my home." The one that told me to "Put the pillow back." It was now saying, "Take a picture of me."

More than once, as I traveled across the island for my weekly doctor's appointment, I would see breathtaking sights that would move me to tears, the view was so beautiful. And within seconds, I'd hear that familiar voice saying, "Take a picture of me." *Was it kidding?* My body was killing me... plus all I owned was a cheap Instamatic camera. How could I ever capture such a *Hallmark moment?*

I tried ignoring the voice, but it only became more persistent. I decided to share it with the circle and asked for prayer. Within a short period of time, God sent us my answer: Another angel. This time his name was Terry. He came bearing a gift of a 35mm camera with a zoom lens. And he wanted to lend it to me. He was offering me the opportunity to capture those images the voice kept directing me to take. But what about my body? That was another story. Obedience is difficult when the heat is sweltering and your body is experiencing excruciating pain. But, the guilt of *not* obeying when it says, "Take a picture of me," is worse than the pain of obedience and doing what it says.

Through my grumbles and groans, when I felt the inspiration hit me, I would obediently make a u-turn and try to find the place where I had originally been inspired. There, the shot would always be, as if waiting for me. I called them *Photos of God.* I recalled a joke of a teacher asking the kindergartner, "What are you doing, Johnny?" she asked.

"Drawing a picture of God."

"But honey, no one knows what God looks like," she said.

"They will when I'm finished," he confidently explained.

I felt the same about my photos. But it soon became apparent the task was going to be difficult for me to drive around, search out the picture, then lug the equipment and try to capture the actual shot. But that's what I felt urged to do. And, I loved doing it. Except for the physical pain.

One day a neighbor named Bert, who lived in the same building, said he often watched me taking pictures of the horizon. As we sat together, gazing out at the expansive display of God's beauty, I began to describe my visions and the words that came with them.

"I see God everywhere. Generally in black and white. Like in the Bible where it says life is either yea or nay with little room for gray (Matt. 5:37). The brilliance of God's light contrasting against the dark sea. A rainbow arching across the sky, silently displaying His promise. The majesty of the West Maui Mountains. Magnificent cloud formations floating quietly by. They all seem like kisses. Kisses from God." I paused for a moment. "If I had my way, I'd do nothing else but take pictures of Him."

"What's stopping you?" Bert asked.

I laughed.

"No, seriously. What's stopping you?"

"Well, my physical condition for one," I explained. "It's exhausting lugging a camera around, not to mention the driving back and forth tracking down the right shot."

"What about me?" he asked.

"What about you?"

"Why can't I be your chauffeur with my jeep as your limo?" He stood up and bowed gracefully as a gentlemen of days gone by.

"Madam, it would be my great pleasure. I've been looking for a way to make brownie points with the Lord. This sounds like the perfect vehicle," he winked. "If you excuse the pun."

Another angel had been sent from God to encourage and help me.

It seemed so simple. All I had to do was show up with my borrowed camera and film. I knew if I was willing to give my best, God would do the rest! He was already proving it by surrounding me with angels. Not only was He sending me physical support and telling me the shots to take, He was now also giving me names to go along with the photos. *The Light. The Vine. The Way. Faith. Behold.* But, the one I couldn't get out of my mind was the telephone pole resembling a cross that bellowed, *Tell Them I'm Alive and Well.* I knew it was a directive. But how? And, to whom?

I began to feel like a puppet with the urgings telling me what to do. Maybe I was. Was I going mad? I didn't think so, because when I was taking photos, often with my sciatic pain registering off the chart, I would feel God's arms wrapping around me... supporting me. And slowly, over time, I began to emerge from the mire I had been living. And the photos? They became a line of black and white greeting cards for a ministry yet to be born.

Tell Them I'm Alive and Well

THE LIGHT

I am the light of the world
John 8:12

chapter ten

THE VOICE

The voice of the Lord is powerful
Psalm 29:4

Occasionally, the haunting voices still visited, stealing me away from the peaceful future I craved. Still concerned about my health and finances, I sometimes wondered, *What's going to happen to me?* I'd scold myself, "Stop it, Beverly Jean! Choose the thoughts that support you. Don't buy into those mental tapes of *What Could Have Been* or *Should Have Been*. Have *faith*, girlfriend!"

When I met Pastor Clarence Kamai, I knew he was another earth angel. He was Chaplain of Maui County Correctional Center (MCCC) in Kahului, and was looking for a second volunteer to assist him on Sunday nights.

When I heard about it, I jumped at the chance. Years earlier, my younger brother Jimmy had been in prison. He had been turned around and saved from falling further into a life of crime by a woman the inmates called Momma. She was a volunteer at the prison, and shared her love, compassion, and wisdom with those who would hear. This was not Jimmy's first conviction. His life was looking dismal. But God sent him Momma, and his life was never the same. With Momma's help, he had found God and turned away from his past. After being released from prison, he met and married a strong Christian woman. Together, they had three wonderful children, two of which ended up as youth pastors.

So, with Momma as my role model, I applied for the volunteer position with the Prison Ministry and was accepted! I was so happy.

I wanted to make a real difference in someone's life like Momma had. However, I soon discovered nothing was like I had imagined.

The novelty of a female lay-minister with a celebrity past soon wore off. In an effort to warm them up to me, I was introduced as an *Albino Hawaiian*, which the inmates found amusing. Soon they were calling me *Rev Bev*. I wasn't sure if my new name was because of my enthusiasm for God, or to shorten the six syllables, to two. Whatever the reason, the name stuck. But there was still a broad chasm between me and the inmates.

I adored Pastor Kamai. He was a wonderful old Hawaiian who loved to tell the story about the Man from Galilee. "Yo," he'd say. "Da only one who can truly set yuz free ain't gonna be da parole board. No. Da only one who's gonna save yuz is Jesus." I loved to listen to him talk about his love for Christ, singing songs of hope to the inmates as he strummed his ukulele. I didn't play an instrument, but as a dancer I had rhythm. Apparently Pastor Kamai noticed, and the following Sunday he showed up with a crescent-shaped tambourine. "It's all yours," he smiled, handing it to me. "Enjoy."

I was touched. But I could barely contain myself from laughing. All I could think about was the expressions on my old press agents' faces if they could see me. Back then I was known as Trudy, the mountaineer Kittyhawk who stalked Elvis Presley in *Kissin' Cousins*. Now here I was, singing and banging away on a tambourine to a bunch of bored inmates, many who were there only because it was two hours of free time spent outside their jail cells.

My main assignment was to give a testimony to the listeners about my personal experience of God, read a passage from the Bible, and hope a heart or two would be moved. But my audience offered back only blank stares. I seemed to be speaking another language. They weren't interested in anything I had to say, or how I said it.

"They don't want to hear from me, Pastor Kamai," I complained. "To them, I'm just an ole haole, a Mainland white person. You're the Hawaiian. You speak their language." I paused. As a wise leader,

Kamai listened intently as I continued releasing my flood of pent-up frustrations. "Their minds are closed. Their hearts hardened. They just don't seem to care... or maybe they just don't like me."

"Dat's not it," he gently assured me. "They care. It's jus' that life has blinded them, and their anger has given the devil a stronghold (Eph. 4:17-19). Our job is to set the captives free, by showing them God's forgiving love." That's what I wanted to do, but I didn't seem to be making any difference, anywhere, or with anyone.

The following week, much to my surprise, Pastor Kamai greeted me with news that he had registered me in a five-day retreat at the *School of Practical Christianity* in Pawling, New York, starting the following month. "I had da feelin' yuz needed to be refreshed," he said, "and, dis is da place that can do jus' dat."

The Pastoral School was founded in 1975 by Norman Vincent Peale to encourage the clergy and those on the front lines of God's Battlefield. It offered fellowship and restoration to those in need of having their spirits lifted and fluffed. Pastor Kamai had seen to everything, both the tuition and airfare. His only instructions were, "You jus' come back filled with God's Light, and we'll be waitin' fer ya."

It was more than I could have dreamed. New England foliage in the Fall was breathtaking. The trees were beautiful shades of reds, yellows, and oranges. One year earlier, I had been frightened for my future. Now, here I was at one of the most prestigious Christian centers in America, with a hundred-and-forty clergy and their spouses gathered together for the 46th Minister's Conference. Pastors, Deacons, Bishops, Ministers, Reverends... and *me*. We all came from various states with various Christian faiths and backgrounds. But, everyone accepted each other and enjoyed the jovial fellowship as we talked, and listened to each other's personal victories and testimonies.

My spirit soared as I strolled the path that circled the private lake. Cottages with chimneys, partially hidden behind trees that were changing their colors for the holidays, dotted the hillside. I had only seen such beauty on calendars. My colleagues appeared as angels sent from God. Each was unique with experiences to share of their encounter with God.

What a privilege to be there! Having traveled the furthest, I won a seat at Mrs. Peale's table for dinner. Dr. Peale was ill and would not be joining us. This turned out to be his last seminar. He died two months later at age ninety-five on Christmas Eve. Dr. Peale had been a mighty ambassador for the Lord[1] and his legacy would live on. How blessed I was to have attended the last retreat while he was alive.

The Maui News picked up the story of my attendance. A picture shows me smiling from ear to ear as I stood beside Mrs. Peale. The photo and story was buried in the back of the newspaper, but my reaction to it was much different than when I had been the darling of Los Angeles and appeared in the front sections. Back then, I picked myself apart and only saw flaws. Today, I saw joy. The person smiling back at me in the photo appeared to be sincerely happy. And she was!

The retreat did what Pastor Kamai said it would. My battery was fully recharged. I returned filled with an eagerness to share my experiences. And I did, for nearly a year.

Eventually it was the stories the prisoners shared that became a problem for me. I began having difficulty sleeping. Every Sunday night, I dealt with the awful trials and tribulations the inmates shared and had gone through in their lives. My sleep began to be affected. I was like an ink blotter, absorbing dark energy from the inmates, but unable to rid myself from the darkness I blotted. Driving home after one of our Sunday night meetings I noticed the lights from oncoming traffic hurt my eyes. I was also becoming concerned that my *Maui Cruiser* may strand me one night on the side of the road. It was a scary thought. I began praying and asking God to lift me out of the prison ministry but still allow me to try and make a difference— somewhere. And He did! In a way I never imagined possible.

I will bless you so you can be a blessing
Genesis 12:2

"Please, sweet Jesus, guide me," I wept as I sat on my patio praying for God's intervention, my head cradled in my folded hands that held scores of moist tissues. That's when I heard her voice.

"Excuse me." I jumped, startled to see someone standing two feet away from me.

"I'm sorry," she quickly said. "I didn't mean to frighten you. I just wanted to know if you are Rev Bev?" Few people knew the nickname the inmates had given me.

"Yes," I nodded, wondering why she was there.

"The condo's front office told me where to find you. I hope you don't mind me barging in on you like this?"

"No," I mumbled, grateful for the sunglasses that prayerfully hid my red eyes.

"My fiancée and I are vacationing from Florida," the smiling sixty-five-year-old woman explained, "and we want to be married while we are here. The lady at the front desk said you were part of Maui's Prison Ministry and may be licensed to marry people."

She was right. I *was* licensed. It was something I had applied for, thinking I needed it in order to assist at the prison. But I was mistaken and filed it away, along with the Federal ID number I received, under the name *The Living Ministry.* It was meant to be a ministry without walls, when I could someday enter prisons on my own, like Momma had.

"I'm sorry. But, I've never performed a wedding," I admitted. "Maybe you can find someone who has," I suggested, "or perhaps call a judge."

"Oh, heavens no!" she quickly responded. "We want a Christian blessing."

Well, I could do that, I thought to myself. I knew where blessings came from and obviously she did too. "But I've never done a wedding ceremony," I repeated.

"That's okay," the spunky woman said matter-of-factly. "Just read a Bible passage, ask God to bless our marriage, then pronounce us husband and wife! That's it! That's all we want." She smiled. "Oh, by the way, Dean and I plan to make a donation to your ministry for your kindness."

I couldn't believe my ears! This couldn't be a coincidence! God had intervened once again in a totally unexpected way! One moment I was crying out to the Lord for help, and the next He's sending me an angel bearing a gift—a gift that got me off Government assistance through performing weddings. God had answered my prayers by exchanging my jailbirds for lovebirds.

Being divinely warned
Matthew 2:12

I was excited to write family and friends about the good things that had been happening in my life. All day I enthusiastically wrote letters on my new computer about my various experiences. Hours passed. Hunger pangs eventually hit me, and I stopped to make a sandwich. For company, I flicked on the TV as I walked back to my desk. Hours later, I heard the ten o'clock news come on.

The sun had disappeared and the dark abyss outside contrasted starkly with the inside, where I sat in my lamp-lit living room. No longer could I see the beautiful blue ocean that lay twenty-five feet beyond. I had been so engrossed in what I was doing I hadn't even thought to close the patio's sliding door, which was still open from earlier in the day.

"I need to get up and shut the door," I mumbled to myself. But it was so hot. I returned to my letters, determined to finish them before going to bed.

A few minutes passed. *Get up and shut the door,* a voice within me whispered.

"I really need to get up and shut that door," I decided. "As soon I finish this page," I promised. I could hear Joe Moore reporting on the news.

Again I heard the voice. *GET UP and SHUT THE DOOR!* I turned to see who was behind me, but no one was there. I moaned and reluctantly got up. "I wish I had a fan."

Walking across the room, I decided I would leave the sliding door partially open so the ocean breeze could enter. I knelt down and slid the two-inch security bolt security bolt into the patio window frame that was installed when I moved in. I went back to my chair and sat down. That's when I heard the gruff voice of a man behind me say, "Don't move!"

I thought it was Derek playing a sick joke. But I was horrified when I turned and saw a masked man with his arm sticking through the small opening, waving a gun at me!

"Don't move," the would-be intruder repeated, as he struggled to open the sliding glass door. I jumped to my feet, knocking over my chair. The gunman was dressed completely in black, including his mask and gloves. His eyes and mouth bulged behind the ski-mask he hid behind. His right arm was completely extended through the six-inch opening I had left ajar, and his revolver was pointed directly at me. Becoming enraged that the patio door wouldn't budge, he began violently shaking it with his left hand, trying to force it to slide open. But the two-inch bolt held fast.

For a moment we both froze. Me in fear. He, apparently in confusion as to why the sliding door wouldn't budge. His eyes widened in a glaze of anger. We stood there facing each other in what seemed an eternity; the gun-barrel only a few feet away, looking like a cannon. I heard myself sob, "Oh please, sweet Jesus."

His eyes darted from my eyes to a small framed picture of Christ I had sitting on the shelf above my computer. Time stood still. Then just as fast as he had looked away, he diverted his fury back towards me, ranting and raving, shaking the door all the harder in an attempt to open it, the gun ferociously waving all over the place but staying generally pointed in my direction.

I crumbled to the floor. Screaming, I began crawling out of the room, terrified a bullet would hit me any second. When I reached my bedroom, I found the revolver I had hidden. The Smith & Wesson was a Powers' family heirloom. I had always kept it wrapped in one of the boy's old, worn-out knee-high socks they used to wear as kids for baseball games. With my gun-barrel protruding through the hole in the toe of the sock, the hammer sticking out through the heel, I crawled back toward the living room with that dirt stained tube-sock pathetically trailing on the floor beside me.

Then I remembered the gun was unloaded! I never kept a loaded gun in the house. The bullets were always stored in a separate place. But I couldn't go back to the bedroom now! I had to keep crawling no matter how frightened I was. I needed to get to the telephone in the living room. So, dragging the sock with my empty six-shooter inside, I continued on. When I arrived back to the living room, the gunman had gone.

I called 911 immediately. The police arrived moments later. The flashing red lights parked in front of my condo brought Derek and Billy to my door.

"Are you all right?" Billy asked. I was surprised to see their genuine concern.

"I'm all right, thanks to God," I answered. But the truth was, I was scared to be alone and asked Billy if he could sleep over.

"I have a couch." I smiled, remembering when we had been married, and I'd make him sleep on the couch. I hadn't been smiling during those times.

"I'll get my pillow," he said.

The culprit was never caught. I knew the face behind the mask was the same face that's behind all evil. Once again, God had protected me.

I wept during my prayers the following morning. "Oh, thank You, Heavenly Father." I was overwhelmed with gratitude. The sound of a dove cooing in the tree above me was soothing, and I sat and listened to it for some time, until it flew off.

I often wondered if the man who terrified me that night ever saw me again. Perhaps in a crowd. Did he recognize me? And if he did, what were his thoughts? Did he regret his actions? I hoped so. I prayed he would eventually find the Omniscient Father who had saved me from his evil deed by using only a two-inch bolt.

God does not slumber
Psalm 121:3

Several weeks after the masked man incident, I was awakened by something in the wee hours of the morning. I looked at the clock. 4:20 a.m. I listened for a moment wondering what had disturbed me but couldn't hear anything. I rolled over to go back to sleep. However, after a few minutes of tossing and turning, I figured I might as well get up. For some reason, I had a strong urge to go outside and pray; something I did nearly every morning. But it was so early!

I glanced through the curtains. It was still dark! A shiver ran through me as I thought of the "uncaught" masked man who was still out there someplace. But the prompting wouldn't leave. Finally I surrendered, slipped on a cozy jumpsuit, grabbed a can of cappuccino and my beach chair, and headed for my favorite spot at the water's edge.

Snuggling into my favorite worship spot next to the water, I suddenly realized I didn't have a clue who, or what, I was supposed to be praying for. I only knew I was supposed to pray.

"Dear God," I began. "I think You're the One who woke me this morning to come outside and pray. So, here I am." I paused and looked around into the darkness. "Won't You surround me, and the person You want me to pray for, with Your protective light? Please send Your band of angels to help this situation."

The scent of the ocean enveloped me. The birds in the trees were beginning their morning ritual of song. Tears filled my eyes as I slipped deep into prayer. I was there for a long while. The birds had quieted and the sun was up. My stomach growled for food. Entering the condo, my telephone was ringing. I glanced at the clock. 9:20 a.m. "Aloha," I answered. It was the hospital. Derek had been in a surfing accident. He was badly injured but was alive! "Thank you, God," I cried. My son had chosen to go out alone into the darkened Maui waters of Paia in the pre-dawn hours to try out his new surfboard and leash. The water was black, but the foamy white surf was visible. It could be heard pounding the shoreline as Derek prepared to enter the water.

"The waves were brutal," he later shared. "Over and over they slammed me." Unsuccessful, he tried again and again to catch that perfect wave that surfers seek in testing new equipment. After awhile, he became tired of the physical battle. Then frustrated. Then angry. Profanity spewed out of his mouth as he cursed at the sea. Suddenly a massive wave rose from the darkened depths below and came crashing down upon him, dragging him below the surface.

The elastic leash was still connected to the six-foot board, which was attached to his ankle. He was tossed to and fro like a fish caught on a hook. Yanking and spinning until he was unable to hold his breath any longer, Derek was suddenly spat out and shot to the surface of the water. As he gasped for air, the tension on the stretched-out leash released itself. His surfboard boomeranged back toward him, its metal fin crashing into his face, knocking him unconscious.

Now is the time to get rid of anger, rage...and dirty language
Colossians 3:8 NLT

No one, not even Derek, figured how he managed to pull himself out of the water and drive himself to the hospital's emergency room. Yet somehow he had. He was covered in blood; his right eye-socket and cheekbone were shattered. It would require a metal plate to surgically replace them both. He would carry a crescent-shaped scar with him forever as a reminder of the miracle Derek experienced on that frightening morning.

"Your son is lucky to be alive," the doctor said.

"Oh my goodness. It's deja vu all over again," I said to myself. I knew luck had nothing to do with Derek's life being saved. I was filled to the core with gratitude that God had spared my son's life. I was also grateful I had obeyed the voice that woke me in the early hours of the morning to pray for someone, not even knowing who it was.

I wondered if Mamo had felt such an urge to pray for someone she thought she didn't know, on the day, at the very moment I was drowning in rage miles away, playing *bumper cars* with Billy.

###

Beverly Performing Wedding Atop "Black Rock"
Sheraton-Maui, HI

Local Church Briefs

October 29, 1993 — THE MAUI NEWS

Powers attends school

KAANAPALI — The Rev. Beverly Powers of The Living Ministry at the Sheraton-Maui Hotel recently attended a four-day school for clergy that was founded by Norman Vincent Peale.

Powers was among the 140 ministers and their spouses who attended the School of Practical Christianity Oct. 6-10 in Pawling, N.Y.

The school was founded in 1975 by Peale and his wife, Ruth Stafford Peale, and is sponsored by the Peale Center for Christian Living.

Powers said: "It was a privilege to be with different pastors from all over the Mainland, representing many different Christian denominations. It was an extra bonus to represent Maui."

Beverly Powers (right) of The Living Ministry at the Sheraton-Maui Hotel meets with Ruth Stafford Peale during a ministers conference this month in Pawling, N.Y. Peale is the wife of Norman Vincent Peale.

Mrs. Ruth Peale and Beverly
The Maui News, Hawaii

chapter eleven

THE DARKNESS

He who walks in darkness
does not know where he is going
John 12:35

Within three weeks, God had wonderfully looked after both Derek and me. My heart was filled with thanksgiving. As I sat at the ocean's edge doing my morning devotion, I prayed. "Thank you, thank you, thank you, Heavenly Father." I shuddered to think of what could have been, had God not intervened. Me, saved from the intruder that visited my home, and Derek, who challenged the danger that lurked in the darkened waters, growing angrier by the minute in his failed attempts to conquer the powerful force before him.

Why was Derek so angry all the time? He was constantly spewing profanity anywhere and at any time. His anger had nearly killed him, and it certainly frightened me, for Derek and his future.

How had he become so volatile? Billy and I had showered him with love. Sent him to the finest religious schools. What was his problem? I secretly wondered if his anger could be deeply rooted in *my* past. The thing that I had done before he was born. Could Derek's defiant attitude be traced back to the sins I committed against my uterus when I was a young woman? The sins I committed in order to cover up my infidelity? Could my angry son have the mark of Cain on him because of my transgressions? Oh dear God!

Blot out my transgressions
Psalm 51:1

I didn't want to believe my sins of yesterday could somehow undermine my son today. I knew that all our actions have consequences. Some actions are irreversible and destructive, reaching far beyond ourselves and harming innocent people. Could this be one of those cases? Over the years, I had successfully suppressed the horrendous memory of my visit to Satan's kitchen-table. Had Derek's spirit been screaming to be born after the assaults made on my uterus? Satan wouldn't let me forget them.

"Remove from my son the stain of my guilt," I prayed. "Remove from him any burden caused by me for shedding blood. Lift 'the sin of my youth' (Ps. 25:7) from my son's spirit so that he will not have to fight this stubborn evil stain that fills him."

I remembered Derek's birth. The broken tailbone from my childhood had been in the way of his delivery, and he arrived with a knot on his head the size of an acorn. He appeared to have been in a fight. He seemed to be saying, "I'm not gonna let anyone get the better of me," as if he had a score to settle. Maybe he did. But now, whatever the reason for his behavior and filthy language, I wanted it to stop. I wished I could wash his mouth out with a bar of *spiritual soap*!

"You also used to swear, Mother dearest," Derek said sarcastically. "Don't try and get righteous with me."

He was right. I once had a mouth on me like that of a truck driver, but being an actress, the superlatives I used were to color the stories I told, and not to display my anger. My tales were enhanced with explicit adjectives that painted my stories, often while holding a long cigarette holder to accentuate the effect. I could see what a poor example I had been when Derek was growing up.

Then one day my swearing began to evaporate. After I gave my life to Jesus, I noticed my foul language began to disappear. And, it just happened, with very little effort on my part. But Derek's foul language wasn't being used to flavor a story. It was used to stir up trouble, and it wasn't going to stop unless he quit defiling himself (Jas. 3:6). He wouldn't listen. My words fell on deaf ears. He reminded me of the inmates Pastor Kamai and I had worked with at MCCC. I started to see how it wasn't an accident God had me spend two years on Sunday nights behind barbed wires. A decade ago, when I surrendered my life to God, giving Him permission to do with me as He pleased, *He did*! And there I was surrounded by a bunch of angry young men. But none of them seemed as angry as my own son!

The tongue is a small thing, but what
enormous damage it can do
James 3:5 NLT

Derek's language was like a boomerang, bringing back to him all the negativity he threw out (Gal. 6:7). No matter how soft or loud my approach, anything I said that opposed his way of thinking caused him to storm out of my condo. Without listening to any form of reason, he'd slam the door behind him on his way out, shouting and calling me filthy names for all the neighbors to hear. My soul screamed.

After he left, I always felt I had been physically assaulted, even though he never had laid a hand on me. It absolutely broke my heart. The profanity was like having manure thrown at me. I desperately wanted to be in Derek's life, but it was so difficult. His behavior was intolerable. When he was a child, I thought I could break the streak of defiance that he appeared to have been born with. I tried everything. Coaxing. Scolding. Banishing. Nothing worked. I appeared to be the devil's advocate, even angering him more.

"I don't want to hear anything you have to say. Don't you get it?"

Yes, I got it. But what good did that do? I couldn't ignore the problem--he was my son and I loved him. I didn't know what to do. I tried to control my emotions, and not react to his aggressive behavior. Sometimes, I was able to hold my tongue. Sometimes not. I couldn't see any way I could get him to stop swearing. I knew that if I ignored it and tolerated it, it would never change. I thought of Mamo's words, "Child, jest remembe', yu'll catch more flies with honey than with vinegar."

Then, God sent me a solution so simple, it was silly. It was childish to the point it broke through Derek's hardened exterior wall. The front line of defense God gave me wasn't a bar of ivory soap, but rather a child's squirt gun!

The following week, Derek dropped by and I was ready for him. Sitting on the table next to me was my loaded water pistol.

When he saw it, he laughed. "What's with the pink dolphin?"

"I've decided from now on," I answered coolly, "every time you swear in my house, I'm gonna shoot you." He thought I was kidding.

I sat back and waited. I had rehearsed this moment many times. Within five minutes, he let the descriptive F-word fly out of his mouth. I grabbed my pink squirt gun and sent a spray of water flying across the room, hitting him square in the chest.

He shot me a look of disbelief.

"I told you so," I smiled, looking away. I had no idea how he would react. Much to my amazement, I heard him chuckle. Then, I began to laugh with him. The tension between us had flown from the room. The squirt gun had been a success!

But, I wasn't fooling myself. I knew Derek hadn't changed. Even though things between us improved, it was only skin deep. He was still that angry young man I had met on that first Christmas on Maui. But, I had done something and made a small step forward with him that I was proud of. And I knew Mamo would have been proud of me too. I had learned to play squirt guns instead of bumper cars.

It was nice discovering what a good shot I was. Derek began visiting more often, and little by little, the son hidden behind the mask of aggression began to emerge. Some of his misconceptions about me, given to him by Billy, were beginning to be laid to rest...

one burial at a time. My pitch fork, horns, and red suit that Derek perceived were starting to melt away. At least I prayed so. However, the mother inside me was still on duty whenever his dark qualities surfaced. It was nearly impossible to keep quiet. As hard as I tried, I rarely was able to stay silent. And so the cycle continued.

You will know them by their fruit
Matthew 7:16

I rarely saw the healthy fruit of "joy, peace, love, kindness, or gentleness" that Mamo often spoke of (Gal. 5:22). Instead I saw thorns in Derek's garden... sour grapes, weeds, crab grass, and lots of spoiled fruit. The parallels between the inmates inside of MCCC, and my son on the outside, were very similar. Neither were receptive. They believed they knew everything and were not interested in anything they perceived to be criticism.

How did I ever think I was going to make a difference in my son's life when I hadn't been able to do it with the men I visited on Sunday nights? And "they" were captive and couldn't run out and slam the door. Those young prisoners had no loyalty or commitment, and were going to fight against anyone who might try to make them think differently by suggesting a set of imposed rules. They were centered on their own value systems of blame and judgment— everyone was wrong except them. The majority were in denial. Everyone had a deaf ear.

I could see that *darkness* was not exclusively locked up behind bars. It's a reality that can permeate anything and show up anywhere. And all it needs is an opening. It festers and starts within a person with a single negative thought, then spreads out like a virus to their family and friends. It grows larger and continues out to society, person to person or over the air waves, until it circles the planet. It can only be stopped on a personal level—a *one on one with God*. To stop the demons of darkness from filling the world, we must be willing to confront them where they begin, within ourselves.

What about my son? I wanted more than anything to make a difference in his life and pass my baton of light to him—that Mamo had passed to me. But how? He had turned into an adult with a *massive attitude*. Insufferable. Impulsive. Rude. Belligerent. *Trouble* following him everywhere he went.

Occasionally he would put his best foot forward and be charming. But all too often, I would learn he just wanted something. During those rare moments of charm, I didn't want to rock the boat. They were moments to be savored. To enjoy. His smile. His laugh. The next time I saw him was not going to be one of those times. I could see the dark cloud that followed him, and this time the cloud smelled like alcohol. I knew that before things got better, they were going to get worse.

I recalled a time when Mamo told me the story of how her husband's brother—and partner-in-crime—had been killed by an outsider over the ownership of a whiskey still. It was then that Mamo, Grandpa, and their three kids, one of them my two-year-old mother, fled Texas and ended up in California. Mamo definitely knew about the dangers of alcohol.

"Child, I want ya to come here for a second," she said one day. "I wanna show ya sumpin." She was standing over a pot of cooled pinto beans she had cooked the day before. Hardened fat from the ham hocks she used for seasoning had floated to the top of the soup, creating a half-inch layer of waste. "Ya' see this?" Mamo asked, cracking a solid piece of lard with her wooden ladle and tossing it into the garbage pail.

"This reminds me of the bootleggin' still yer Grandpa hid in the back woods of our farm." She paused for a moment as she scooped up another spoonful of noxious waste and tossed it in the trash. "The Hatley boys brewed up their malt until it was done. Then they'd scoop the stuff off the top, like I'm doing now. But instead of puttin' it into the garbage, they'd put it in a bottle and sell it. They called it moonshine. Lemme tell ya child, when a tavern sign reads *Spirits*

Sold Here, they're not kiddin'. *Evil spirits* are what they're sellin'!" She turned and looked at me. "Beverly Jean, yer datin' now. And, I want ya to be careful. I've never seen a good girl go bad unless alcohol was involved." She then returned to her next task: the corn bread.

He who walks in darkness
does not know where he is going
John 12:35

I was surprised that Derek had taken up the drinking habits of his father, but hadn't Billy done the same? How was I supposed to stop this cycle of darkness in an adult child who doesn't want my help and thinks he knows it all? A son who had listened to his father's perception of me for so long, I'm sure he only saw the Devil's handiwork. He didn't want to hear anything I had to say.

Derek had been eighty-sixed (tossed out) of most bars in Kaanapali. Drinking and fighting was his norm. He and Billy lived together and were drinking buddies instead of father and son. In their eyes, I was the bad guy. I needed to be careful when I was around Derek. It was off-limits to talk about his father. It was bad enough that Billy had thrown away our life together, but now he was helping our eldest son to do the same. It was the blind leading the blind! Ignorance breeding ignorance.

Ignorance wasn't going to protect Derek from hard knocks anymore than it had me. I knew first-hand the dangers of being spiritually blinded and walking in the gray areas of life. It was bad enough I had passed down to Derek my horrible example of my mouth. But now, Billy was passing him a legacy of drunkenness that could potentially kill him! Well, it wasn't going to happen if I had anything to do with it.

Derek had walked away from the teachings of Jesus he had learned as a child, and had taken up a path of darkness where shadows lurk. Without Jesus' light, Derek wouldn't be able to see where he was going. He wasn't an owl. He couldn't see in the dark. He was an unprotected and vulnerable young man, susceptible to any dark notion that came along.

"Please, dear God," I prayed, "help me to be the mother You want me to be. Let me reflect Your love back out to Derek. Let Your light shine through me. Not so dim that he can't see You, or so bright that I blind him. But just enough to spark a flame of love within him, for You, and himself. Let him know how much we love him. Please, dear Lord. Thank you. Amen."

I knew it wouldn't be easy winning my son back from the clutches of darkness. I figured the enemy wouldn't surrender him without a fight. Derek was too important to me. I was willing to go toe-to-toe with Satan himself if I had to. And before it was over, I would have to do just that.

###

THE WAY

I am the way
John 14:6

chapter twelve

THE FLEECE

By God's special favor and mighty power,
I have been given the wonderful privilege of serving
Him by spreading the Good News.
... I did nothing to deserve it, and though I am
the least deserving... I was chosen
For this special joy of telling... about the endless
treasures available to them in Christ
Ephesians 3:7, 8 NLT

Filtered morning sunlight rose over the West Maui Mountains as dozens of tourists on beach chairs waited for me to begin telling them the greatest story ever told: The story of Jesus Christ. It was Easter morning, 1989.

I could feel the balmy ocean breeze coming from behind, wrapping around me like a warm hug. One of the islands, Lanai, in my reoccurring dreams from years ago sat on the horizon like a jewel showing off her beauty in the early morning light. The ocean was turquoise. Black Rock sat majestically above me, like a watchful tower, caring for the modest open-air church that sat below on the shores of Kaanapali Beach.

I lifted my arms wide as I began, declaring the awesome beauty that God has shown for all of us when, without warning, everyone suddenly shouted in unison, *Oooohh*. A whale had breached behind me not more than a hundred yards offshore, leaving a massive explosion of water in her wake. I was grateful my audio cassette had captured the moment.

How had it happened that I should be so blessed to be a part of such a glorious display of God's majesty? Only a week earlier, I was taking a walk and praying for guidance. And now here I was preaching an Easter Service at one of the most prestigious hotels in the world: The Sheraton Maui Resort. The minister from the Lahaina Baptist Church had seen me walking the week before and pulled to the side of the road and motioned for me. I walked over to his car. "Hi," I said.

He quickly told he was in a rush but was pleased to see me. He then explained, "Our church has had two outreach ministries on the beach at Kaanapali. One at the Marriott Hotel, the other at the Sheraton. The lay person at the Sheraton is leaving the island and we need a replacement. I heard you were free on Sunday mornings and was wondering if you would be interested in taking over?"

I gulped in surprise, thanked him... but politely declined. My contribution to Maui was performing an occasional wedding or blessing. My body was still recuperating from the auto accidents of a couple years earlier. I was still under doctor's care. I couldn't imagine how I could endure an hour-long service each week, not to mention all the work and preparation I suspected it would require.

"Well, give it some thought," the pastor said. "I'm on my way out of town for a few days. Pray on it and give me a call. I'll be back in my office Thursday afternoon. You can tell me then what you've decided." He smiled and drove off toward West Maui's airport.

Wow, I thought as I walked back to my condo. *The Sheraton,* what a compliment! Then I remembered the promise I made to the Lord before leaving Ventura. Shattered by disappointments, I vowed to God if He would take over my life, I'd give Him the rest of it. I promised I'd never make a decision without consulting Him first.

Maybe this is a test, I pondered. *A test of faith.* I knew I'd have to stay focused, keeping myself out of the equation, if I honestly wanted to know His will. But how would I know what God wanted? How would I recognize His voice? It often sounded like mine.

Then I remembered Gideon from the Old Testament (Judg. 6:38-40) and the fleece he put before the Lord when he desperately needed a sign. I felt I already knew what was best for me and my body, but I also felt an urge to use a fleece, something I had never done before, if I really wanted to know what God wanted. So, after returning from my walk, I promptly went into prayer and placed a fleece before the Lord as Gideon had done. The Pastor needed my answer on Thursday—a mere four days away.

Show me a sign
Psalm 86:17

"Lord, if this is something You want me to do, please give me a sign." I hesitated. What kind of sign did I want Him to show me? *What was my fleece to look like?* I knew it had to be something unusual and out of the ordinary. Something I'd recognize as being from Him and couldn't misread. As I continued in prayer, an image began to emerge. An image of a yellow rose. *A yellow rose?* It wasn't my favorite flower. But it certainly was out of the ordinary, especially in Hawaii. So the yellow rose became my fleece... a sign from God.

As I entered the week, I found myself paying special attention to the tropical gardens in the various hotels I visited. At my hair appointment, I flipped through the shop's magazines, looking for a photo of a yellow rose. At home I closely watched TV ads. Everywhere I went, I looked for my fleece. But it was nowhere to be found.

I knew my answer had come in the form of silence. Somehow I was relieved. The thought of having such a large responsibility placed on my shoulders as Pastor of the Sheraton was daunting. Having to give a service every week, no matter how my body felt, was an overwhelming thought. Sunday morning service had to go on, rain or shine, whether I felt up to it or not.

On Thursday morning, the day of his return, the Pastor was expecting an answer from me. I had been scheduled to do a baptism at the Napili Kai Beach Club for a family vacationing from England. The twelve o'clock sun was high in the sky as the blessing closed and I began gathering my belongings to go home.

"Before you leave," the child's mother said, "Could my husband take a picture of you and Joshua?"

As the two-year-old and I posed for the camera, the mother turned and said to the father, "Wait a minute, Honey. I brought something for Josh, remember?" And with that, she reached down into a white plastic bag she had been carrying and pulled out a lei made of yellow roses!

Tears sprang to my eyes. When I asked how she had decided on that specific flower, she answered, "You know, it was the oddest thing. After I called and scheduled you for today's ceremony, I was heading back to my car at the Marriott where I had breakfast, and passed their floral shop. I went in and asked, 'Do you ever make leis for toddlers?'"

"Yes," the clerk answered.

"Do you deliver to other hotels? I'll need it for my son's baptism Thursday morning."

"No problem," he replied. "What kind of flower do you want for your child's lei?"

"I thought for a moment then said, *Yellow Roses*. I don't know why I chose them. They aren't my favorite."

"That's interesting," the man responded. "I just ordered several dozen of them not more than an hour ago. They'll be here Wednesday afternoon," he smiled, "just in time for your child's blessing."

I have spoken
Genesis 28:15

There was no doubt what God wanted me to do. I called the Pastor and told him my answer. Three days later on Easter morning, I was preaching my first sermon. I assumed it would be for only a few Sundays until someone came and replaced me. But I assumed wrong. For the next seven years, with thousands being reached for the Lord, I continued standing in front of travelers from around the world, telling them the same story; the story of our Father's love for His children. I told it in many ways. Sometimes I was effective. Sometimes not. Sometimes we saw whales. And sometimes not. But always we experienced together the wonder of God's beauty and the promise of His words.

I knew on Sunday mornings I was standing in front of people who came for a vacation, but not a vacation from church. They wanted God to be with them while they were away from home, and my modest chapel was there for them. God was a constant in their lives, and in the Bible they are called the saints and faithful brethren of Christ (Col. 1:2).

As I prepared for my sermons, I became obsessed with the reading and studying of the scriptures. On Sundays I would talk about what I had learned and discovered that week. I knew that many of the congregation were well-versed in the Word. It was imperative that I present my Biblical facts correctly. I spent days doing research. What I soon discovered was many of my former beliefs had been based on fiction and not on fact; something I was unaware of until I began my close study of the Bible. Without a middle man to confuse me, I deciphered God's Word for myself, and was able to share my new understanding with the congregation.

The Sheraton Maui became a learning curve. My mind expanded. My strength renewed. Most Sundays I left church feeling invigorated, and not worn out as I had worried about. After several years of preaching and not having a Sunday off, I decided it was time I took a vacation. I took a trip to the Holy Land, the place I preached about. I found a replacement for the two Sundays I would be gone. Arming myself with a suitcase of black and white film, and my camera wrapped around my neck, I flew off to Israel.

I had been asked to participate in a pilgrimage, along with eleven other pastors, to assist in a baptism taking place at the Jordan River.

There would be a group of approximately three-hundred people. It was a once in a lifetime chance! Being from the warm waters of Maui, I was shocked how cold the water was where Jesus had been baptized (Mt. 3:13). It was freezing! But the people were warm and the experience unforgettable. And the photos? Marvelous! I framed the photo of the large woman I baptized who wore a pink shower cap for her submersion! The shower cap obviously didn't work. Her hair was soaked when she rose from the water. But so was mine later that day when I rededicated my life, and was submerged in the chilling water by other ministers. I came up from the water looking like a happy drowned rat.

While in Israel, I took more than 1,200 pictures. One showed me sitting on the hillside alongside others on the pilgrimage, looking healthy, listening intently to the words being recited that Jesus first spoke on the Mount of Olives over two-thousand years earlier. "I have come into the darkened world to bring light," Jesus said (Jn. 12:46). Adding, we were to also be a light in the world for those around us. He had come be an Intercessor between God and us (Rom. 8:27).

I took photos where Jesus had walked on the water as I sailed on the Sea of Galilee. "Do not be afraid," He had told His disciples (Jn. 6:19-20).

I captured photos of men praying at the Wailing Wall where Jesus had taught at the Temple. Where women and men today are still segregated during worship as back in Christ's day.

Goose-bumps rose on my arms at the Mount of Olives, as I listened to Christ's Be-Attitudes being recited from where Jesus had taught (Mt. 5:1). I stood where He had knelt, as He prayed for me and future believers yet to be born (Jn. 17:20).

At the Garden Tomb, I wept where Jesus stood three days after His death. He had appeared to a *woman*! With all the masculine fishermen and followers to choose from, Christ chose to reveal Himself, after His resurrection, to Mary Magdalene, a woman of ill repute! (Mk. 16:9) And that's not all! The Bible tells us the Risen Christ's first assignment was to instruct this woman to go and tell the *men* Jesus was alive. Words to be told to the men who had personally seen Jesus crucified... men who had seen His blood drain from His body.

Mary went and told the disciples that Jesus was alive! A woman was given the first assignment to tell the *good news*. But did she do it without fear? Probably not. And, did the men believe her? *No.* Not at first (Mk. 16:11). But eventually they saw for themselves that Jesus was truly alive. Alive in the Spirit. What none of them realized at the time was, they, too, would soon have Christ's Spirit living inside them. They would become known as Christians: one with Christ (Acts 11:26).

I will pour out My Spirit
Isaiah 44:3

The trip to Israel turned my life around. It was life-changing for me. I returned home *on fire* for the Lord! I had felt God's awesome Spirit while I was there. I realized I had felt Him on Maui, too, but hadn't recognized it. His Spirit is everywhere (Ps. 139:7-10). He's ever-present (Deut. 31:8). For years, I had spoken of Him at church, but the heightened impact of experiencing Him half-way around the world where he had walked was extremely emotional. I learned the difference between *speaking* about the Holy Spirit, versus being *led* and *filled* by Him (Lk 12:12). I saw how hard I had always tried to inspire people using my own gift of gab, instead of leaning on the Holy Spirit.

Many people who visited our church at the Sheraton-Maui returned and shared their experiences of the Holy Spirit. One woman I remember, who appeared happy on the outside, was actually weeping on the inside and desperately in need of a prayer. When she returned the following year, she had a big, genuine smile on her face, instead of the hidden tears I had seen before. She told me she had embraced the Holy Spirit, and her life had changed immediately.

She had been touched by the Holy Spirit, as I had, after surrendering my own life to Christ and moving to Maui.

I knew how the returning visitors felt. Scales had fallen off our eyes. We saw things we had never seen before. Spiritually deaf ears began to hear things we had never heard before. Different choices were being made. The Holy Spirit had kissed away our tears on an individual basis. One by one. Individually. Personally. The Spirit of Healing had touched us all, one way or another. Not as a bandage of false hope, but as a Cure-All.

Beware of false prophets
Matthew 7:15

"What if your *Ladder of Life* is leaning on the wrong wall?" the Evangelist asked. "What if when you reach the top rung of your life, you discover you've placed it against a wall that is lethal—built of false teachings and faulty bricks? A wall made of sand that crumbles at the first sign of a storm?" (Mt. 7:26, 27)

What kind of question was that? Decades after hearing those words the question still haunted me. The thought of anyone dying and discovering, after they're gone, the wall their "Ladder of Beliefs" had been leaning on was made of crumbling cinder block and mortar—a wall built of misconceptions, misinformation, distortions, and deceit. It would be devastating.

Believing our soul returns again and again until we get it right, or that all forms of transportation (religions) end up at the same destination, then learning the truth after we're gone is cruel... has Eternal consequences.

For years I honestly believed the *Father and I were one.* Literally. The phrase was empowering to me until one day, I read the scripture for myself without an interpreter, a middle-man, and learned it was Jesus who spoke those words. He was referring to *Himself* and the Father while in Jerusalem during Hanukkah (Jn. 10:22). "*I* and the Father are one. I am, the son of God" (Jn. 10:30).

In the Hebrew parable, God is described as the Potter and we, as the clay (Jer. 18:6). When I was a child, Mamo told me that story on our bus ride home after working all day in one of those fancy homes she cleaned. I loved to look at the elegant porcelain pitchers that sat throughout the house. Glorious pieces of pottery. Glazed. Shiny. Colorful flowers and designs painted on them and used as vases and decorative urns.

I had always thought that wasn't me. I was a piece of stoneware. Plain. Flawed. With little potential. However, I knew now the heavenly angels were probably chuckling. They had known God's plans for me. To be molded into a cherished vessel of clay that would someday be used for His Banqueting Table (Est. 7:2).

Most of my life I had been seeking God, even if I hadn't known it at the time. I wanted my Ladder of Life to rest on a solid wall of truth. Not on the persuasion of others, or my ignorance, swayed by my own likes and dislikes. Many of my original assumptions were wrong, and not based on Biblical teachings. It made me shudder to think that I might have reached the top rung of my life, and had discovered I had been conned—led away from the right path.

A ladder that leans on a fake storefront, as on the back lot of a Hollywood studio, will fall. The whole purpose for a *facade* is to appear authentic, so that the audience will believe the illusion. It doesn't matter how short or tall, or what the ladder rungs are fashioned from—pain and suffering, ignorance and blindness, failure and false beliefs. If the ladder is leaning on a mirage, it will collapse when you put your weight on it.

I was glad of the new wall to lean on that I had received from God the morning I stood on the dry riverbank in Ventura, with Gabriel dancing around beside me. I was given a victorious wall that promised to never collapse and a new beginning.

Lay up for yourselves treasures in heaven
Matthew 6:20

When the phone rang, I was preparing Sunday's sermon. It was from the spouse of a man named Warren who often attended our beach ministry when he visited Maui on business. I had never met his wife. He once confessed to me that at one time, he had been a severe drunk, and that alcohol had nearly destroyed his marriage. Then... he gave his life to the Lord and began faithfully attending church. His wife was calling to tell me Warren had passed away.

"He had been in a coma for several days," the grieving widow sobbed over the phone. "Then without warning, Warren opened his eyes and began to look about saying, 'Wait a minute. Wait a minute,' as if he was talking to someone. 'You don't understand. It's only me'. He repeated it twice." She paused. "Then Warren closed his eyes and was gone." Her voice broke. Gaining her composure, she asked, "Reverend Powers, do you know what he meant?"

I thought for a moment. "I'm sorry, but I don't." I had no idea what he may have been referring to. I didn't recall any sermons I had given with the words, "It's only me. It's only me."

But, later that night I dreamed of Warren. He was ascending into heaven. The *Pearly Gate Band* was playing. I could see Warren was self-conscious. He was waving, trying to get the music to stop, but the band played on. Well-wishers and family members who had arrived centuries earlier tossed confetti and waved banners that read, "Welcome home!"

Warren believed in Christ. Years earlier, he had received the anointing of forgiveness. However, in my dream, as Warren approached heaven's door, he carried with him a *Bucket of Shame*—of past sins he had been cleansed of (Is. 1:18). Warren had not forgiven himself! And as he walked toward St. Peter, his *regrets* followed.

Amidst all the cheering, open arms, and music, Warren wasn't able to comprehend what was happening. This had to be a mistake. "Wait a minute. Wait a minute. You don't understand. It's only me!" Warren may not have been able to forgive himself but Jesus had, as well as his family. They had demonstrated what God's forgiveness looks like by letting go of the past and extending love to each other.

The people rejoiced
1 Chronicles 29:9

Years later, when Mother became ill, I, too, needed to practice forgiveness. My whole life I felt I had been cheated—robbed. After a lifetime of hearing her deny that Jerry was a pedophile... even after he had been convicted in court for doing the same thing to another child, Mother maintained his innocence. She continued blaming me for what Jerry had done.

I prayed our damaged relationship would someday be healed. That someday I might hear her say, "I'm sorry." But that day never came. Circumstances robbed me of that when Mother slipped into Alzheimer's. Dementia was slowly robbing her of her memories. And, I was to be left with a scar hidden in my heart that only Jesus could heal.

The pain Mother inflicted on me emotionally over the years ran deep. But the Lord's 5th Commandment said I had to honor her, no matter what (Ex. 20:12). Even if I never received an apology! He didn't care if I liked her or not, spent time with her or not. He said I had to *honor* her. So I began each week sending Mother greeting cards to the care-facility where she now lived.

Mamo had named Mother *Dolley Jewel* when she was born. She was to be a doll to hug, and a jewel that sparkled. Sadly it didn't turn out that way. The child born to be a jewel became encrusted with mud, making it difficult for her inner light to shine through the emotional pain of betrayal she *had* experienced as a young woman. Her first husband, my father, a bigamist. The second husband, my step-father, a pedophile. Mother buried her feelings and stayed in denial, She blamed me instead of Jerry, and never admitted any responsibility for her part—going to work and leaving me alone with him at night, even after the accusations. She allowed the darkness to grow by ignoring the problem. Obviously it was easier to blame me rather than acknowledge she had married a pedophile.

Apparently, Mother never saw her own value. I never saw her value either until I came to realize God knew what He was doing when he gave me to Mother. The child would need to be strong. Mother had made a difference in my life, though most of my life I didn't recognize it, and seldom gave her credit. I had been blind to the beauty of God's orchestration (Ps. 139:13).

Her phenomenal work ethic was not lost on me. She taught me if I was going to do something, do it right. And, I better always wear clean underwear because *ya never know when ya might end up in the hospital.* Because of Mother, I have an abhorrence for lying, even though I've done it. I was taught to *mind-my-manners, and cleanliness* is next to *Godliness.*

Shortly after Mother was placed in the Alzheimer's home, I learned she was being ornery. *Sundown Syndrome* is not unusual and can make people mean, especially for someone who has worked their entire life and now must sit around doing nothing. By sundown, the patient is frazzled and often creates trouble.

"Please, dear Lord," I prayed, "show me how to help Mother." She lived in Oregon near my siblings and their families. There was no way I could assist her from Hawaii. I prayed, and the following day, while on the phone with her, I surprised myself by saying, "And mother, don't forget to do your job."

"*My job?*"

"Yes. Your job," I stated. *Oh my, what was her job?*

"Mother your job is... to *make people happy.*"

There was a pause at the other end of the line. Then I heard her say, "Oh. I can do that." And that was that.

Several months later, I visited her in Oregon when one of the nurses came up to me. "Are you Dolley Jewel's daughter from Maui?"

"Yes," I smiled, feeling complimented she knew where I was from.

Reaching out to give me a hug, the nurse exclaimed, "Thank you for giving your mother a job. We've really seen a change in her."

It was so simple. The seed within us yearns to make a difference. Mother had always been ornery. But with God's Grace, I was able to experience what forgiveness felt like. For both Mother and I, God replaced our individual sour memories with sweet new ones. Mother began referring to me as *Beverly Jean*. She now said it with love in her voice. She bragged to the other residents of her new Adult-Care home, saying, "Did you know my daughter is a minister in Hawaii?" My unfulfilled expectations had become unexpected fulfillment.

After years of prayer and counseling, I was eventually able to lay to rest the feelings of betrayal. Betrayal had been a huge part of my life. Mother. Both fathers. My husband. Even Derek, who had known about his father and Floozie's affair. At one time or other, *all* had betrayed me. But hadn't I, also, been a betrayer? Actually, I was probably the biggest of them all, when I asked Jesus into my life, and then placed Him in the back seat of my life's vehicle, calling upon Him only when I needed something. Shame on me.

I had betrayed my main Love. The One who had always been there for me as an Invisible Hand. A Beam of Light. A Voice in the night. He had saved my life more than once even without me asking. I owed Him everything, yet I often behaved as a wayward child. Many people had betrayed me, but I had done worse. I had betrayed the Creator Himself. I begged for His forgiveness.

###

A Gift of Yellow Roses
Bethlehem, Israel

A Group Baptism
Jordan River, Israel

Beverly Preaching Easter Morning Sunrise Service
Kaanapali Beach Hotel, Maui, HI

Royal Hawaiian Ladies Society Visiting KBH Church Service

Beverly and Mother

chapter thirteen

FORGIVENESS

*That what has happened to me has really
served to advance the gospel*
Philippians 1:12 NIV

After returning from the Holy Land, I decided to exchange my
rusty Maui Cruiser (that I lovingly called my *Humility Cruncher*) for
a bright, shiny, new Volkswagen Rabbit. With graying hair tied in a
bow, driving my white little convertible, I resembled *Bam-Bam*, The
Flintstones cartoon character. But, older—*much older!*

To share my love for God, I ordered personalized license plates,
GOD BLS, using the closing words I loved from Red Skelton's weekly
TV show. No longer would there be any doubt about which wall the
ladder in my life leaned upon. People would see my allegiance. And
not just on Sunday. God's Son was behind the steering wheel, and I
was His passenger.

One morning I drove up Honoapiilani Road and was awestruck.
The beauty was magnificent. The tropical blue sky. The ocean
sparkled like an emerald gem. Palm trees swaying. My hair blowing
in the warm sea breeze. My heart was filled with joy as I approached *S
Turns*, aptly named for the shape in the road. Because of the rise in the
road, for a brief moment as I entered the curve, I couldn't see the road
ahead. As my car came over the knoll, my mood instantly changed.
There, lying in the middle of the street directly in front of me, was a
man whose moped had tipped over in the middle of the road.

I screeched to a halt only feet from him. The frightened man
looked up. Terror written all over his face. "Oh, sweet Jesus! *It's*

Billy." I had nearly ran over my ex-husband! Our eyes met. For an instant, we both froze. Unhurt, frantically he began to upright his bike as he fumbled to retrieve the beer cans scattered from the twelve-pack carton he had been holding under his arm. Then clutching his *spoils,* he clumsily rode off toward the small condo where he lived.

The image of Billy lying in the road was extremely disturbing. I wasn't able to sleep for nights. The constant replay of nearly running over him was haunting. What were the chances of him falling at the very moment I was driving by? This was far more than coincidental.

"Please, Heavenly Father, help me," I prayed. Billy was in trouble and I didn't know how to help. This couldn't be an accident. Him falling in the direct path of a car with license plates that reads *GOD BLS!* Those words were meant to bless people, not harm them. Obviously, God wanted to get our attention, and He sure did!

The following Sunday after church, I found myself driving to the apartment complex where I heard Billy lived. I sat in the parking lot for awhile, uncertain why I was there. Finally, I got up the nerve, got out of the car and headed to the unit I believed was his. We were both surprised when he opened the door. He was not expecting me, and I didn't expect an open can of beer in his hand at ten in the morning.

"May I come in?" I asked.

He offered me a chair. I politely declined and said, "I'm only gonna stay for a minute." We stood there facing each other, feeling awkward, neither of us knowing why I was there. I began to mumble something about being concerned for him when, without warning, I dropped to my knees. His look of surprise equaled mine when suddenly, without warning, I hugged his legs and began to cry.

"Oh Billy," I mumbled. "I love you so much. We've been together almost our entire lives, and when I die I'm not willing to spend eternity without you." I stopped talking for a moment and looked up. He appeared dumbfounded. "What's going to happen when one of us dies?" I sobbed. He still had a puzzled expression on his face, not having a clue what I was about to do next. I was still hugging his knees. He reached for the wall in an attempt to brace himself from falling.

"Billy, eternity is forever," I choked. "The thought of my going to heaven and you not being there is frightening." Neither of us moved. Then, slowly I let go of his legs and got up from the floor.

"Oh, Billy. Please come back to church."

I knew if Billy's life was ever going to improve for the better, it would come from the inside out. He and Derek had attended the church when I first began preaching at The Sheraton. They would paddle their glass bottom canoe around Black Rock and pull onto the beach where the church service was held. Nanuk, one of Derek's mixed wolves, always sat in the front of the canoe beside Billy as Derek paddled. All three would sit on the lawn listening as they leaned against the palm trees that dotted the landscape. When the service was over, they would paddle back home again. But after awhile, they stopped coming.

When Billy's moped fell directly in front of my car on that fateful day, it was divinely orchestrated. The fact I didn't run over him was a miracle. He must have known it too, because a couple weeks later, the real miracle began when Billy started attending Kumulani Chapel, a large Bible-based church not far from where he lived. I was seeing God's handiwork.

That year, Halloween fell on a Sunday. I had just arrived home when there was a knock at the door. It was Billy. He couldn't wait to tell me what had happened to him at his church that morning. During the Altar Call, he gave his life to the Lord!

"Sam, it was so weird," he said, plopping down on my sofa. "At the end of the service, the Pastor asked if anyone in the congregation would like to ask Jesus into their hearts, asking to be forgiven for anything they may have done in their lives. "Sam, I couldn't believe it. My hand raised in the air as if it was attached to a string." He shook his head as if in disbelief. "Then, if that wasn't bad enough, the Pastor then asked those who raised their hands to stand up!"

Billy looked at me in astonishment. "Hon, there was no way I was going to stand up. But then, I can't believe it, I shot out of my chair like someone had goosed me. I was so embarrassed, I thought I'd die." I knew he was telling the truth. Billy would never bring attention to himself like that—standing in front of a church filled with people, with only four others doing the same thing? He had always hated the spotlight and preferred to remain hidden in the background. This was totally unlike him. God definitely works in mysterious ways.

As Billy told the story of his outrageous experience in church that morning, my heart soared. Goose bumps ran up my arms as I raced over to the couch and gave him a massive hug of congratulations. What had started out years earlier, as a long and difficult separation, was turning into something neither of us could have imagined. After lying dormant for so many years, my arch-enemy was gone and my long lost friend had returned.

If anyone is in Christ, he is a new creation;
old things have passed away; behold, all things have become new
2 Corinthians 5:17

As happy as I was, I secretly wondered if I could ever completely forgive Billy for all the suffering he had caused. The loss of each other... our marriage... our family. Hidden behind years of prayers, the hurt was still there, buried deep within. The betrayal of my husband with Floozie, his drinking partner and girlfriend, had threatened to destroy me financially through the divorce. Painful memories. Even though I was sincerely touched by Billy's conversion, I questioned if I could ever truly forgive and forget.

One of God's biggest miracles occurs in our hearts. Where rage and hate once resided, compassion and love now lived. Life doesn't hand out prizes for carrying the weight of a stony heart (Ezek. 11:19). Jesus, Himself, gave us the example to follow as He hung from the cross, praying for those who were crucifying Him. "Forgive them Father, for they know not what they do" (Lk 23:34).

"Dear God, help me to *authentically* be able to forgive and sincerely celebrate this moment of salvation with Billy. Help me to wipe the slate clean. Help Billy and me to both become stronger because of this moment together. Help us to become what *You* always meant us to be. Thank you. Amen."

Lo and behold, an older version of the younger man I once loved suddenly emerged. Billy was quite dapper, even with his gray hair. I began looking forward to our times together. God's gift of forgiveness had entered my heart and now, after the devastating breakup of our twenty-five-year marriage, my ex-husband was back in my life and making my heart go *Pitty-Pat*. I was astounded how well we still fit together. In more ways than one. And, how fast the windows steamed up when we were alone.

His drinking had left. My trust had returned. Without the thorns of an unforgiving heart, my nemesis had become my soul mate. It was magical being able to talk about the good ole days again without thinking of the pain. We laughed. We teased. We hung out together. We enjoyed one another, even in silence. It was fun getting to know each other again. We had won back the loss of each other through the miracle of forgiveness. And, within a few months, our friendship blossomed into more than friends.

Walk as children of light
Ephesians 5:8

The Holidays were quickly approaching. I decided to give Billy a Bible for Christmas, something he didn't have. It was to be the first gift I had given him in years, and I wanted it to be special. Something meaningful, and I knew just how to accomplish it.

During the summer when Billy and I were married, we would take the boys camping. I did the cooking and Billy was in charge of the campfires. His ability to create beautiful and sustaining bonfires drew the admiration of fellow campers, and they began calling him *Chief.* With his chiseled features and swarthy complexion, people began speculating Billy may be of Indian descent, instead of the Black-Irish brood he came from—a family of stubborn Irishmen who had a fancy for the brew. Billy's nickname stuck of "Chief" stuck lasting long after our divorce.

One afternoon, years after those fond camping trips, I became so irate over Billy's stubborn and ignorant behavior, watching him laugh and encourage Derek to have another beer. I began yelling at him in a moment of blind anger. "I'll never call you *Chief! Do you hear me?* You're not worthy of that name. You can't lead *anyone… anywhere.*" The words echoed in my ears as I headed toward the Christian book store on the other side of the island… to pick up Billy's surprise Christmas present… an engraved Bible.

Christmas morning arrived. We were both delighted as we opened the gifts we had purchased for each other. Inside his simply wrapped gift for me were two Elvis Presley cassettes. One had Christmas songs we had always played when we were together as a family. The second was *Love Me Tender,* recorded the year Billy and I were married. Tears sprang to my eyes at the thoughtful, heartfelt gift he had given me. I was shocked and touched, and couldn't find any words to say. I finally looked up and mouthed, "Thank you."

Then it was his turn. He took the gift from me and began opening it. When he peeked inside and saw the Bible, moisture filled his eyes. He stared at it, tracing the gold letters with his fingers, *C-h-i-e-f.* Then, placing it on the table, he walked over to the couch where I was sitting and sat down beside me.

For a moment we sat there, motionless. Neither of us moved. I could hear Mynah birds squawking in the trees outside as they frolicked together. I felt awkward. The urge to jump up and begin Christmas breakfast was squashed, however, when Billy took my hand and pulled me toward him. We sat there again, saying nothing, looking into each other's faces. The only noise that could be heard was the chatter of the birds outside and our own heartbeats pounding inside.

Slowly, Billy turned and put his arm around me, pulling me closer. Then he leaned over and tenderly kissed my cheek. Then he kissed the other. Then my forehead. And eyes. And then, my mouth. His breath was familiar, as were his lips. They found their way down to my neck. He had not forgotten. My body began to pulsate, as did his. One thing led to another, as one hour turned into another. The Christmas ham was forgotten, as well as our plans to attend a church gathering scheduled for later in the day.

We emerged December 26th, with kinks in our necks from both of us sleeping on my twin-sized bed. But we had smiles on our faces. It wasn't long before there was a double-sized mattress to replace the twin, for our new-found entertainment.

Blissful months followed one after another, and soon it was Father's Day. A large baptism was scheduled by Kumulani Chapel. Billy signed up. He felt compelled to outwardly display the inward commitment he had made to Jesus. Everyone saw a miracle that day when Billy stepped into the waters at Fleming Beach, announcing through his actions to the cheering crowd who watched from the shore, that the old man had died and a new one had been reborn (Jn. 3:3).

The real baptism had actually began eight months earlier, on Halloween—the day Billy invited Christ into his heart. After centuries of struggle and strife, and much prayer from Godly women, the Powers men were being given a new family tree. Billy, the earthly father, had surrendered his life to the Heavenly Father. I knew it was only a matter of time before our son would do the same and follow in the footsteps of *his* father.

For decades, behavioral sciences believed newborns came into the world devoid of personality, believing the environment stamped its unique characteristics on boys and girls during their developmental years.[1] Most of the best-known psychologists in the world ascribed to this theory. Thank God, they were wrong.

Their later findings stated that heredity plays a huge role in the development of human temperament, impulses, inclinations. "Though we don't act on every urge, despite our genetic underpinnings, heredity does provide a nudge in a particular direction. One that can be brought under control by rational processes."

You are the God who does wonders
Psalm 77:14

Billy's decision to be publicly baptized was a big deal. *It was huge!* It was done with a deliberate purpose. He and I both knew how imperative it was to stop this cycle of darkness that continued to haunt our family. When Billy stepped into the warm ocean water of Hawaii, the angels in heaven were singing. The joke was on the devil! The Heavenly Father was having the last laugh. The devil hadn't lost just one soul. He had lost an entire family. One old man had broken a family's legacy of bondage.

Billy's family had a history of wild men. They were known for living by the motto, "Let's drink and be merry, for tomorrow we die" (Ecc. 9:7). And, die they did. Died by their own hands. Died at the hands of others. Died inside prison. And outside. Young and old alike. Men who believed only women and children go to church. Men who thought rules didn't apply to them. Handsome rebels who left a string of broken hearts, including their mothers, wives, and children. It appeared that the Powers family tree was destined to wither and die. But all along, the tree had been going through a slow transformation of painful graftings and transplants. Until finally there sprouts blossomed. The power of God's Love can not be denied.

As Billy walked into the ocean for the baptism with Pastor Craig and an assistant, a large wave could be seen in the distance. However, the trio seemed oblivious to it. They stopped and turned their backs on the ocean. With bowed heads, they started to pray. As they began Billy's submersion, the powerful, frothy wave crashed down upon them from behind, tossing all three to and fro. In one of the photos taken, Billy's face could be seen peeking through a wall of sudsy, white foam as he body-surfed to shore.

Safely back on land, people came up to him and teased. "Hey. Congratulations. Not only did you get baptized... you actually survived it!"

"Yeah, thanks," he chuckled, reaching for his towel. "The church nearly drowned me."

A woman nearby chided, "Oh Mr. Powers. I don't think the church tried to drown you," she teased. "You must've just had a lot of sins that needed cleansing" (Isa. 1:18).

Delight yourself in Me He said, and I will
give you the desires of your heart
Psalm 37:4

God promises to give us an inheritance as a reward if we follow Him (Gal. 6:9). He certainly kept His promise to me in ways I could have never imagined. He brought Billy and me back together, in spite of ourselves, forgiving the mistakes we had made in our past and offering us a future filled with comfort and joy. A phoenix had emerged from the ashes of our dead marriage. God had blessed Billy's and my relationship and revealed to us the secret for a successful marriage. Something we had not known. We thought love between a husband and wife was enough. It never was. It always takes three. *The Eternal Triangle.* If Billy and I had placed God at the top of our relationship and focused on the Source of our love instead of upon our ourselves and each other's shortcomings, we would not have gone through such torment here on earth.

Having fixed the blame for the destruction of our marriage upon the other for so long, and then receiving the Healing Balm of God's Forgiveness in our hearts, became Billy's and my miracle. It was an opportunity for a second chance to win back what we had lost. The two of us had always needed Jesus... and not just the blessing at our wedding. Our love was never meant to be enough to sustain a marriage… a marriage birthed by two dysfunctional families, even though we did start out with a hope for a *grand* future. We eventually came to realize in order for us to *ever* have a happy ending, Billy and I would have to have Jesus as the Third Partner in our marriage.

###

Billy's Baptism

PRAYER

Where two or three are gathered together in My name,
I am there in the midst of them
Matthew 18:20

chapter fourteen

THE FEARS

He who walks in darkness does not know where he is going
1 John 2:11

Everything that could have gone wrong began to go wrong. It was a slow decline into the mire that appeared to be nothing more than a string of bad luck. It started when Derek awoke in the middle of the night and saw two dark, ghostly figures standing at the foot of his bed.

When he told me and saw my reaction, he said, "Don't worry, Moms. They were good angels." He wasn't a bit concerned over the strange visitation, but a red flag went up for me. I was very much concerned. I knew darkness comes to us as a tempter, disguising himself as light, the meaning of Lucifer, his given name (2 Cor. 11:14).

My prayers intensified. I felt Derek's vision of the two dark figures had been an ominous premonition. Sadly, I was right. Several weeks later, Derek was hurt on the job and ruptured a disc in his back, forcing him to undergo surgery. It was the same disc I had ruptured years earlier when I was pregnant with him! It seemed to me a sign that the forces of darkness were actively working against him.

As Derek's life grew darker, so did his erratic behavior. He was moody. Explosive. Angry one minute, charming the next. His life seemed to be in harm's way. He was unable to work, and with the loss of income he only became angrier. Even Kaya, his favorite wolf-hybrid dog who supplemented his income with litters she had given him over the years, had tragically died.

Apparently the rope meant to keep Kaya in the yard while Derek was away was too short. She had jumped over the fence in hot pursuit of a neighboring chicken and was unable to touch the ground on the other side. So in addition to everything else, Derek was now grieving the loss of his beloved Kaya, and was in pain both emotionally as well as physically.

Billy and I watched from the perimeter of Derek's life as it began to unravel. He was under attack. Our hearts wept as our son faced one obstacle after another. We prayed for him, yet we continued to see more of the same. Trouble. Misfortune. Lots of *bad attitude,* and the repercussions that go along with it... making it difficult for us to be around him.

A prudent person foresees
the danger ahead and takes precautions;
the simpleton goes blindly on and suffers the consequences
Proverbs 22:3 NLT

Derek always pushed the envelope. Twisting and distorting the truth. Breaking the rules whenever he pleased. Choosing which ones he wanted to follow. House rules were always changed to "his rules."

Like a man struggling in quicksand, Derek's misery was brought on himself, by making choices that sent him deeper into mire (Deut. 30:19). My spiritually blinded son wasn't able to connect the dots. Somehow he couldn't see the correlation between his actions and all the darkness that was coming his way (Ps. 7:14-16). *Was he crazy? Had I dropped him on his head as an infant?* My son's spirit was drowning in the "ocean of life," and I could hear him screaming for help through his volatile behavior. To survive, he would need a strong life-raft of prayers.

Once I attempted talking to him about it. But it was nearly impossible. Before I could get two words out of my mouth, he turned and scowled, "You're so full of it! No wonder I don't like you." *Wow!* His words echoed my mother's—cutting and stinging.

Derek said he knew Jesus, but the way he behaved, it was difficult to see much evidence of it. He attended our beach ministry for awhile, but I wondered if he ever really heard the scriptures that I quoted each week—sitting in the back with the distractions of bikini-clad girls strolling by. When I brought the subject up one day, he responded, "I don't need to sit up front to hear that crap."

"Wow. Where's my squirt gun?"

We sat in silence for a moment. Finally he looked at me. "I don't know what's going on with me, and the things that have been happening. Maybe God's paying me back for something I did in a past life of mine."

"Sorry, Big Guy. You're not being paid back for some transgression you made in a past life. You know better than that," I said, shaking my head. "You only get one life, Derek (Heb. 9:27)."

"Well, you believe your way, and I'll believe mine."

"Okay," I paused, wondering if I should continue. "I just hope you enjoy your time in Hell, because that's where you're headed if you don't change your ways."

"Yeah? Well I don't like ultimatums," he retorted as he stormed off.

I questioned if Derek understood what I was trying to say. He looked at me sometimes like I had two heads—an eccentric old lady who had suddenly "found Jesus." In a way, I suppose that was true. God had been a part of my life numerous times. But it wasn't until I reached my forties that I truly began to walk with Christ. He was the One who had saved me from myself and… my stinkin-thinkin. (Is. 55:8,9).

Whatever a man sows, that he will also reap
Galatians 6:7

When there seemed there couldn't be any more surprises for Billy and me, Derek slammed us again with ugly news. Someone had torched his and his girlfriend's house. Everything they owned had gone up in flames. Derek had been the victim of a jealous neighbor who paid him a visit while he was at work. Though the police were called, there wasn't enough evidence, and no arrests were made.

"Moms, it's gone. The scrapbook you made me. Everything. All my belongings and keepsakes. Even the baby's new crib." Tears streamed down his face. I stood there, in shock. All I heard was *the baby's crib.*

"What *baby's crib?*" I asked.

"Don't get excited, Moms. We were going to tell you. So, now you know. Congratulations, you and Pops are gonna be grandparents... to a baby whose house just went up in smoke." Again sobs broke from him as he turned away.

My head reeled. I didn't know what to say. Should I address the shocking news of a grandchild? Or, the devastating fire?

"What can I do?"

"Nothing. We took care of it."

I didn't like the sound of my son saying, *We took care of it?*

"Oh Derek, please tell me you didn't do anything foolish. Two wrongs don't make a right."

"Yeah? Well the Good-Book says, *An eye for an eye* so don't lecture me." He bent over and pulled off one of his shoes, revealing a bloody foot.

"Dear God, what happened?" I cried.

Ignoring me, he limped off toward the bathroom asking, "Do you have any bandages?"

Vengeance is Mine... saith the Lord
Romans 12:19 KJV

The joy of hearing the news that Billy and I were going to be grandparents didn't offset the fears we had for our son. There was nothing in Derek's behavior that made either of us feel confident that he was handling the obstacles in his life wisely. He was at a fork in the road. He held the steering wheel for his future. He could do his life his way, or God's way.

Derek knew right from wrong, having learned it in Christian schools when he was young. Mamo had encouraged us, "Raise up a child in da way it should go, an when they is grown they won't go wrong" (Prov. 22:6). I hoped she was right.

Derek would make a great catch for the devil. He was easy prey. Vulnerable. Desperate. Reacting emotionally to what life was throwing at him, instead of responding by praying and thinking things through. His body was still mending from his recent back surgery. He had little money except for the disability checks he received. His job prospects were limited. Now, his house was gone. With a baby on the way, and no place to live, his future looked bleak. A blank slate set before him. A *slate* I was frightened he may fill with more bad choices.

The devil plays his ace in the hole when we're at our lowest. He did it when Jesus was in the desert at the end of His forty days of fasting. Jesus had no water or food when Satan came calling, tempting the Son of God when He was at His weakest (Mt. 4:1-3). Just as the devil had tempted Jesus, the devil was also seducing my son—coming to him at his weakest. And his weakness was his *spiritual blindness.* It tore at my heart, adding weight to my already slumping shoulders and more gray hairs to my already silvered hair.

And then it happened... right in front of my condo. I screamed as the police handcuffed Derek and put him in the back of the squad car. My knees buckled. My head spun. I began to fall. Someone from behind caught me and helped me back to my apartment. My son was being arrested for taking revenge against his neighbor for setting his house on fire. He had broken into the evil-doers home and trashed it with an axe. However, in his act of retaliation, he cut his foot, his blood was found at the scene, and Derek was arrested.

After everyone left, I went into the bathroom and took a long shower. The suds felt good as I washed my body. But soap wasn't able to wash away the vision of my son being handcuffed and taken away. My spirit needed more than a bar of Ivory Soap. Nothing I said had made any difference. Derek had followed his own ways, treating many of God's laws *like trash* (Ps. 50:17). Solid judgment had surely left him. And his actions confirmed it. He struggled with arrogance, false pride, and misplaced loyalty. God wanted him to be loyal only to Him, doing what He says. Not what Derek thought he could get away with.

Derek wanted to be a rebel… a rogue… and not a conformist. Yet, by throwing away the rules when it suited him, he not only hurt himself, but those who loved him. His emotions jerked him around, and blindly he walked away from the Light.

Derek had done as he pleased, and what pleased him was to please his girlfriend. So he followed her into revenge and received a felony sentence—all because of his destructive retaliation against his neighbor who had set his house ablaze.

There is no joy for the father of a rebel
Proverbs 17:21 NLT

Derek was sentenced to five years behind bars. My heart was broken, but poor Billy! I had never seen him so devastated. From the time we were kids, Billy was fiercely determined to never follow in his older brothers' footsteps. Most of them had been in prison. Billy joined the Navy at seventeen to get away from the bad influence of his family. Now, four decades later, his own son is caught in the same veil of darkness.

Billy's sorrow was beyond words. He had recently given his life to the Lord. Then he was baptized. Now, he was facing one of his worst nightmares. Thank God Jesus had come into his life when He did, because Billy's grief seemed insurmountable. Even when Mother Powers, his beloved mother, passed away, Billy's sadness paled in comparison. The past flooded his mind. All he ever wanted was to be a better father than his had been. Billy nicknamed Derek, *Buddley*. He wanted Derek to be his buddy, his friend. He had always tried to shelter and protect him. To be his confidant. *And now?*

Our car ride from the courthouse was spent in silence. When we got home, Billy immediately headed for the bedroom, I assumed to take a nap. A few moments later, I heard noises. As I opened the door, there was Billy slumped on the floor, sobbing uncontrollably.

I dropped down beside him. "Oh, Billy, my darling, are you all right?" He looked up with utter despair on his face. Gut-wrenching sobs gushed from deep within. I gently placed my arms around him.

"Oh, Sam," he sobbed, water pouring out from his nose and eyes. His shoulders jerked with each sob. His body rocked back and forth, writhing in pain.

"Sam, our son... he's in prison... just like my brothers." Once again, he leaned forward, placing his head between his knees. I tried to comfort him. But all I could do was weep alongside him.

After awhile, he sat up. Shaking his head and reaching for the box of tissues beside the bed, he whispered, "Honey, how did this happen?" His eyes pleaded for an answer.

"I don't know, my darling," I paused. "All I know is, we have to keep praying. Derek is behind bars, Billy. But so is the Lord. He's aware what's going on. Maybe that's where God wants him right now. I don't understand. But sweetheart," I reached for his hand, "we have to believe God has a plan and knows what He's doing" (Jer. 29:11).

We are to leave the present,
along with the future, in Christ's Hands,
knowing He can bring order out of chaos, good out of evil,
and peace out of turmoil.
We are to trust God and not be afraid
A.J. Russell--God Calling[1]

In the midst of our fears, God delivered our first grandchild, a beautiful bundle of joy. They named her Makena after the beach where she was conceived. We were grateful she hadn't been conceived at Haleakala, Maui's National Park!

I was scheduled to perform a wedding at the Embassy Suites Hotel. It was the first wedding in their newly built Gazebo on the beach-lawn overlooking Kaanapali. It was a gorgeous day! As the bride, groom, and I entered the open-air pavilion, a warm breeze began to swirl around us. Within moments, we were engulfed in a funnel of beauty made up of loose rose petals that had been placed in large vases as decorations. We were surrounded with the petals as they twirled around us. At that moment I knew my grandchild was being born. A child of God. And, a great, great, grandchild for Mamo.

Two days after she was born, Makena was dedicated to the Lord. I was filled with wonder. After sprinkling her little body with the Holy Water I had brought home years earlier from Israel, I captured the moment by taking her photo. The black and white photo became my Christmas Card that year and titled, *A Child Is Born.* God had truly sent us a little angel.

When Derek was convicted, he lost his freedom, his county lifeguard job, and custody of his daughter. Now she would be *required* to live with her mother, Derek's former girlfriend, who was known for her tremendous dislike for me. The day Derek's sentencing hit The Maui News, Makena's mother raced over to the church camp where we were spending the day. As she drove off with the child, she shouted, "You'll never see your granddaughter again!"

"Oh, sweet Jesus, help me! I need You," I cried as I sat on my patio later that day. My head was bowed. My eyes closed. I needed His touch. I could hear the surf. After awhile, the repetition of the waves hitting the shore became rhythmic. *Here I am. Here I am*, it seemed to chant. *How long had I been there?* Then, as if standing inside the living room, I saw my silhouette seated outside at the patio table. My legs were crossed, yoga-style. My head was bowed. My loyal Abyssinian cat, Kitty, lay curled next to me, on the patio table. But, there was someone standing beside me. I couldn't make out who it was. The scene was backlit from the glare bouncing off the ocean. All I could see was the form of someone. But who was it? Their hair was medium length. The person wore a long beach robe.

Suddenly I froze. *It couldn't be.* "Oh, sweet Jesus," I muttered. There, standing on my patio, was Jesus, His hand resting on my shoulder. I felt His peace flowing through me, filling me with the assurance of His presence.

I began to weep. I knew Jesus had come to set the captives free. And, I knew He had come today to set me free from my frightening fears for my family and future.

He is at my right hand
Psalm 16:8

Derek had been born with a huge lump on his forehead. My broken tailbone of *yesterday* had gotten in the way of a having a smooth delivery *today*. With the raised knot on his head, Derek resembled a unicorn. I had thanked God there weren't two horns. Yikes! One was enough. Maybe that's why God choose me to be his mother. He knew I was a ferocious opponent, with tenacity and perseverance (2 Tim. 3:10).

As I entered Maui County Correctional Center, I did so as a mother. Not as a chaplain. I was frightened. I thought of St. Monica of Hippo, a devout Christian woman during the 4th Century. I had often given a sermon on Mother's Day on the strength of this woman. Her love, worry, and long suffering for her son, Augustus, was admirable—an example for all mothers, everywhere.

Year after year, Monica prayed in hopes of saving her son from his wicked ways. In every way, he was a true prodigal. When he was sixteen, he fathered a child. For ten years, he lived with an Ethiopian woman, at a time when integration had not yet been heard of. Augustus was agnostic and greatly influenced by Manichaeism, a dualistic religious system of conflict between light and darkness. For seventeen years, Monica traveled hundreds of miles following her son over treacherous terrain no woman dared to go, praying for his salvation each step of the way. After years of his mother's prayers, Augustus woke up one day, stepped out into his garden and met the living God. Monica's prayers had been answered!

Just as Saul, a trained Pharisee from the Roman days of Israel, met the living God on a road to Damascus (Acts 9:3) shortly after Christ's execution, Augustus met the same Spirit in his own back yard. Saul went from being a persecutor of Christians to a preacher for Jesus. Saul was renamed Paul. His future was completely and radically changed when he encountered the Spirit and Presence of the Lord. His life was never the same. His past was forgiven and used for the future. He went from blindness to vision after coming face to face with Jesus on a road ironically named, Straight.

So it was with Monica's son, who went from a prodigal to a prodigy. Within a week of his conversion, Monica died. But she died a happy woman. She had lived to see her prayers answered. However, she did not get to see her son's many accomplishments. Years after her passing, Augustus was ordained by the Catholic Church and given the name *St. Augustine*. And it all began with one woman determined to save her son from the grips of Satan. Of one mother's undaunted love. The story brought me so much courage.

Likewise, the apostle Paul had been transformed from being a militant Saul, who killed Christians for a living, into to an *Apostle for the Gentiles*, and authoring thirteen of the twenty-seven books of the New Testament. Just as Augustus and Saul had been turned into vessels for the Lord, I prayed that my son would turn from his ways to God's ways.

A foolish son is the grief of his mother
Proverbs 10:1

I was thankful Billy had not come with me to visit Derek. He hadn't been feeling too well. Before I left, we came together in prayer. Before Derek had been convicted, we had prayed God would deliver our son from the wrong path of life, and not in a subtle way. We wanted God to thump Derek on the head. But we hadn't meant for Him to send him to prison. Yet, there he was. Maybe this was God's way of answering our prayers.

My heart broke as I entered MCCC. A guard I knew from our Sunday night ministry patted me down. He was kind. He searched my purse, then led me to the waiting room where visitors were waiting. It was mostly women with children, all attempting to make the most out of an uncomfortable situation. I immediately went over to the corner and turned around. I couldn't control my tears.

We were escorted into a room where, ironically, Pastor Kamai and I had once led our Sunday night worship services. Derek entered, wearing the orange prisoner's jumpsuit and weighing fifteen pounds less than he had ten days earlier. I gasped. He had dark, green circles under his eyes, and his skin was yellow. He was shivering and his hands were blue. His knuckles were red, showing signs of a fight. The purple bruises on his face revealed the inmates weren't taking too kindly to Derek's turbulent behavior. He was spending most of his jail-time in the *hole,* isolated from other prisoners, most of whom he had alienated. He was a haole with an attitude, whose rage was out of control.

I knew his temper. Derek often lashed out at *me* using foul language, and I was his mother! I had wondered how his mouth was doing with the fellow inmates. Now I knew. Obviously not too well considering the amount of time he was locked away in an 8'x12' windowless, dank cement cell—alone, with only a Bible for company. God truly had my prodigal's undivided attention. I suspected the angels in heaven were rejoicing. However, I wasn't. The searing pain in my heart seeing my son under lock and key was so traumatic for both Derek and me, we agreed my first visit would be my last. It would be three years before this broken-hearted mother would see her son again.

###

chapter fifteen

THE HOPE

There is no miracle I cannot perform,
nothing I cannot not do.
No eleventh-hour rescue I cannot accomplish.
A.J. Russell--*God Calling*[1]

Squeaky. Bossy. Cutie. Those were the names Makena called some of the birds when she was allowed to visit... the same birds that also visited me each morning wanting to be fed. Inside the tin container that sat on my patio table was a bag of wild bird seed. The birds were wise enough to know where their food was. If I were tardy in my daily routine, one of the birds (usually Grumpy, the dove) would come up to my patio window and peck at the glass.

Mamo had always loved birds. That's probably where I got my love for them. She raised all kinds of winged critters, from yellow, singing canaries to chattering parakeets. Sergeant, the militant mynah bird, would strut his stuff and greet visitors at the door with, "I can talk. Can you fly?"

To Mamo they were all God's creatures. Charlie, her favorite cockatiel, would waddle across the floral carpet bringing Mamo more yarn for the doily she was crocheting. Her feathered friends were her family.

My phone rang in the middle of the night. My heart sank. Rodney, an eight-year-old Amazon Parrot, was dying. Rodney was my friend, as was his owner, Valerie.

She was hysterical. Rodney was more than a pet to her. Even more than a best friend. He was her business partner. Together they earned a living as Rodney charmed and entertained tourists on Front Street by posing for pictures. Now her cherished partner was deathly ill.

During the night, he had eaten part of a bell that hung in the corner of his cage. The salt air had corroded the toy, and Rodney had eaten much of the metal, severely slicing his insides. He was bleeding from both ends, and things seemed dire.

She telephoned me after finding Rodney on the bottom of his cage. She had immediately called the Vet and learned their office wouldn't be open for several hours.

"He'll be dead by then," she cried.

Over the years, Valerie assisted me with the prayer meetings I held each week. She was a harpist, and would show up with her small harp under one arm and Rodney on the other. He was always polite and well-behaved.

After opening songs and group prayers, the women took turns giving updates on their lives since we last met. They shared areas of their lives where God was moving, and in areas still needing prayer. Sometimes it concerned health. Sometimes finances. But mostly, it was about relationships.

At the close of each meeting, we took a few minutes and wrote a prayer request on the colored tablets we received when we originally signed up. Then, we'd place them into a jar we called our *Prayer Chest*.

The following week, if any prayers had been answered, the request would be retrieved, recognizable by its color, and placed in the half-gallon apothecary jar we named *The Glass Jar of Answered Prayers*!

At first, the few slips of paper in our tall mason-jar appeared as colorful drops in a bucket. But within two years, our jar was filled with folded pieces of multicolored paper, all witnessing to God's faithfulness. Literally, our *cup runneth over* (Ps. 23:5). As our relationship with God grew, so did the contents in our jar. Valerie had seen first-hand what God had done.

Sobbing softly over the telephone, she cried, "He's gonna die, Beverly. He's gonna die."

"Shh, wait a minute, little one. We don't know if he's gonna die or not." I paused for a moment. "We have to practice what we've learned. Jesus loves you, Valerie. And He loves Rodney along with all His other creatures."

After we prayed, I reminded her, "Don't forget, things often get worse before getting better. Don't get discouraged. Hang in there, and hold onto your faith (Rev. 14:12). Don't stop believing."

All things are possible to him who believe
Mark 9:23

The following Tuesday night, we rejoiced when we saw Valerie show up at our prayer meeting with Rodney sitting on her shoulder!

"After Beverly and I hung up the phone that morning," she told the women, "I went over to Rodney's cage and placed a newspaper over him in hopes it would keep him warm. Droplets of blood covered the lining of his cage."

She stopped for a moment and bowed her head. Her long golden hair covering her face. Softly, she said, "I began to recite the Lord's prayer (Mt. 6:9-13) like we do here each week. When suddenly, Rodney started coughing. I could see he was vomiting green bile. I didn't know what to do. I began to pray harder than I've ever prayed before in hopes the Lord would hear me."

As Valerie told the story of his miraculous healing, Rodney swayed back and forth flaunting his magnificent feathers. He had been victorious, and he seemed to know it. Within a week, Rodney returned to work—posing for pictures... happy to be earning his keep once again.

Rodney was healed by God—a healing no one could deny. People can lie or exaggerate about miracles, but not a parrot. Rodney was alive today because God miraculously had healed him, as He had done throughout the ages, and will continue doing throughout the tomorrows (Heb. 13:8). God doesn't play favorites (Gal. 2:6). He loves all His creations. As I looked at Rodney who had been saved by prayer, I thought of my wayward son Derek. I had to believe that my prayers were also being heard... and an answer was on its way.

Nothing Derek did could squash the unconditional love of his Heavenly Father. At some point, we all have been given a second chance. Some of us have had third and fourth chances! Derek was a child of God. No matter where he was, or what he had done, God was rooting for him. Calling him out by name (Jn. 10:3). He was in my son's corner and had a plan for him. A plan of good. And nothing he did could erase that. Postpone it? *Yes.* Erase it? *No!* (Rom 11:29).

I didn't have any idea how this nightmare would end. I knew my prayers would be answered with a *Yes*, a *No*, or a *Not Now*. Those were the only possible answers. I reminded myself *delay* didn't mean *denial*. And that *doubt* wasn't allowed! I had to hold onto my faith—and pray. And, stay out of the way. I had to stay focused and believe in the God who believed in me, knowing if I did my best, He would do the rest. That somehow He would untangle the web that Derek had spun for himself and release him from the clutches of Satan.

The Bible tells us not to worry (Mt. 6:25), that it only brings harm (Ps. 37:8b). My choices were to worry, or trust God. I couldn't do both. I had to choose the thoughts that would empower me. It wasn't easy. Sometimes Satan had his way with me, and I played, "What if I had done *this* instead of *that?*" Or, "Maybe if I had picked my battles more carefully *yesterday*, Derek wouldn't be in jail *today.*" My thoughts seemed to have a mind of their own.

The *Maybes* and *What-If's* could hound me "till the cows come home," as Mamo would say. But they wouldn't help. The past was *pau*—the Hawaiian word for gone. All I could do today was to step into my tomorrow, do the best I could, and let God do the rest. And pray! Hard, like Valerie, trusting it would be sufficient to protect my son locked away in a dungeon. A dungeon of blindness.

Derek was caught in the worldly pit of seduction and "miry clay" (Ps. 40:2) as I once was. He was a grown man, but he still needed the prayers of his mother. But I also needed prayers. My sleep was being affected. My appetite. My concentration. My *long suffering* (Gal.

5:22) was growing short. Scripture promised me fruit *IF* I didn't lose heart, grow weary, or get discouraged (Gal. 6:9).

"Oh, Heavenly Father," I cried. "I've already grown *weary*." *If* was such a tiny word describing such a big umbrella, capable of blocking God's Sun-rays of Hope from shining on us. It demonstrates a chink in our faith. If I really believed all things work together for those who believe, how could I worry about the outcome? (Rom. 8:28)

I had to fight the doubts that entered my head. I knew what Doubt and Fear are capable of. They are two of Satan's best allies. They paralyze people, leaving no room for God's soothing balm of hope to be applied. The spirits of Hope and Encouragement were needed to fight the Goliaths (1 Sam. 17:44) in my life.

Satan's ace in the hole is *Ignorance*. It's the damaging card that blurs our vision. That's what happened with Derek. He couldn't see where he was headed. Darkness had temporarily gained the upper hand.

Our family had lived in a dim light for generations. Our sight had become so accustomed to the dimness we became desensitized. *Jealousy, anger,* and *wrath* became the norm. We were blinded by the shadows. It was the blind leading the blind. I prayed the echoing of darkness would someday cease to exist. It was imperative I hold onto my faith and not be swallowed up by fear.

Mamo once told me of the speech she heard over the radio in 1933 of President Roosevelt's first Inaugural Address. It was about fear. The nation was crippled with fear during this time of the Great Depression. His encouraging words were forceful as he spoke over the air-waves to the impoverished.

"The only thing we have to fear," the President said to a hurting America, "is fear itself." I understood what he meant. Fear is bad. But fear without hope is the worst kind of fear.

Be anxious for nothing
Philippians 4:6

If Satan's purpose is to steal and rob (Jn. 10:10), he was doing a good job. Derek was over there locked up behind bars. While Billy and I were over here praying. But Jesus was our *Ace in the Hole*. How things appeared was not my concern. I believed God would give Derek a second chance. But, I also believed Lucifer was working so that he wouldn't take it. He had always been a tempter in Derek's life, and hoped Derek would continue to be loyal to him by staying desensitized to God's promise, thereby continuing to be easy prey. Satan never sleeps. He prowls the earth like a roaring lion, seeking whom he can devour (1 Pet 5:8).

Well, he wasn't going to devour my son if I had anything to do with it. If the devil wanted Derek, he was going to have to go through the Son of God to get him. Because that was who was interceding on Derek's behalf. God had interceded in my life on numerous occasions over the years, but this time it was different. This time the war was second-generational, and now I prayed God would do the same for Derek. It was the same enemy we fought, the father of lies. It was the same principality, just different personalities (Eph. 6:12). Derek and me.

It was imperative I stay focused on God to rid myself of negativity. I wasn't willing to let Satan have the slightest opening into my mind. I focused on scriptures that promised victory and freedom from fear. I printed them on index cards and taped them throughout my house.

Do your best and I'll do the rest became my daily reminder tool. *The Lord is my helper I will not fear* (Heb. 13:6), I taped on my refrigerator. On my bathroom mirror I placed, *God will never leave me or forsake me* (Heb. 13:5). Under my pillow, I kept, *He who keeps you will not slumber* (Ps. 121:3). And on my closet, I was reminded, *God is standing beside me* (Deut. 31:6). And finally, on the inside cover of my Bible, I placed, *Do not be afraid. Only believe* (Mk. 5:36b). However, sometimes negative thoughts got so loud, I would scream, *GET BEHIND ME SATAN!* (Mt 16:23).

Before going to sleep each night, I closed my eyes and mentally covered Derek with a blanket of prayers, asking God to protect him and to keep him safe. To deliver him from the forces that were attempting to destroy him. I would envision a hedge of protection surrounding him. I would cling to God's promises. I believed somehow the Lord would set my son free. I prayed night and day, and waited for answers.

One morning as I prayed, I envisioned myself back in time entering St. Elisabeth's parish, the oasis for me during my teen years. I am alone. As I enter, I see the rows of wooden pews lining the long center aisle. The sanctuary is walled by massive stained glass windows depicting various Saints. Shafts of morning light shoot through the silence. I can hear the echo of my footsteps as I walk toward the podium. Candles are lit under the statue of Mary. Behind the lectern, on the front wall, Jesus shines down holding in His arms the *Book of Life*. His countenance lures me toward the altar. He beckons me to come and rest. *All is well. Trust in Me. I have a plan. A plan of good* (Jer. 29:11).

Nearly half-a-century has passed, yet through the gift of memory, my mind travels back in time to the place that offered me peace. As my eyes open, once again I see reality. The ocean and majestic palm trees are swaying gently in front of me. Familiar and comforting, like the place I just visited.

I think of Mordacai from the Old Testament, who had been a great source of comfort for his young cousin Esther. She was an Israelite, a Hebrew who became Queen of Persia; who by disguising herself as a gentile, saved her people from tyranny! It was a treacherous time. God used Mordacai and his faith to comfort and encourage this vulnerable child of God. (Est. 2:7).

St. Elisabeth's Church had been my Mordacai! It had encouraged me—grooming me for the future. The safe-haven that comforted me as a child was still comforting me today. I wept as I recognized God's thread of tapestry. He *always* had a plan for me. He knew what

He was doing. He knew everything about me. He was the One who made me. He knew *making a difference* would be the only purpose that would be capable of filling the hole within me.

Focus on the Lord, and He shall give
you the desires of your heart
Psalm 37:4

The Sheraton Maui Hotel had closed for renovations. After preaching for five years under Black Rock, a local church asked if I'd be interested in co-pastoring their small church in Honokowai. Without hesitation I said yes.

The Lahuiokalani Congregational Church was built in 1850 and mainly catered to vacationing snowbirds, hiding out in Hawaii while winter's snow covered their homes. The old chapel reminded me of the one Mamo and I attended when I was a child, living in the predominantly black neighborhood. Except for the Pastor and his family, Mamo and I were nearly the only white people in the congregation.

I could hear Mamo chuckling. "Sittin' in there with all those black folk, weez looked like an Oreo cookie."

My first Sunday, as I stood in front of the congregation made up of Hawaiians and visitors, Mamo's words rushed back to me. I could see the surprise on the parishioners' faces, that I was the new Pastor. And, I wasn't Hawaiian, or a man with black hair. I was a white-skinned, blue-eyed woman with silver hair. *Unheard of!* As I stepped up to the altar, I uttered a silent prayer. A five-foot illuminated Cross hung on the wall behind me.

Stepping up to the microphone, I heard myself say, "I bet you're surprised to see a white-haired haole standing up here behind the podium, huh?" No one moved. They just sat there.

After a moment, I leaned forward, smiled and asked, "Would you believe I'm really an *albino* Hawaiian?" With that, everyone laughed.

Feeling the warmth from the people brought back memories from the good ole days, standing on stage with Red Skelton. It felt like a big hug. Everyone loved Red Skelton. And, I reminded myself, the people sitting in front of me loved God. They loved Him so much they couldn't go on vacation without visiting His house. The gift of laughter given me years before was still opening hearts today. But things were different. Today my *Hollywood Scripts* had been exchanged for *Holy Scriptures*!

The quaint church is steeped in tradition, from the ringing of the steeple bell to the standing when the Pastor enters. Hawaiian Hymns from long ago are still sung. The first time Makena and my niece attended the church, the usher sat them in the front row directly in front of the lectern. My heart gasped when I saw where they had been seated. My energetic four-year-old grandchild was right up front!

As I waited to enter, from the back of the room, I could see her tiny head bobbing up and down. Inquisitive. Looking around. When the elder asked from the back of the room, "Will everyone rise?" Makena stood up and peeked down the aisle to see who was coming. When she saw me, she squealed. "Oh, it's only my Grandmama!" Everyone spontaneously laughed. The *genes* of creating laughter had been passed on.

A merry heart does good, like medicine
Proverbs 17:22

Walking across the street to get my car one Sunday after church, some guys I recognized from MCCC were sitting at the picnic tables near the park's entrance. "Yo, Rev Bev," they hollered, waving me over. I knew a few of them from the Prison Ministry. A few even knew Billy from the old days and had been his drinking buddies.

"Come. Sit. Have a cerveza with us," they invited me.

Pointing to the Clergy Robe I was wearing, I smiled. "I'm sorry, you guys. But I don't think I'm dressed for beer today."

Everyone laughed. "That's cool."

I waited a moment. Then nodding to the church across the street, I said flirtatiously, "Why don't you guys go over there on Sundays and visit me?"

There was some stammering. Finally, "Yo...uh... we're not dressed for that either," one of them teased. Again, we all laughed.

Gazing across the street where I had just preached, I looked up at the steeple. For the first time, I realized there was no Cross. Just a four-by-four, two-foot tall piece of painted wood perched on top of the bell tower, symbolizing a needle pointing to God.

"Where's the Cross?" I asked. The guys didn't know what I was talking about. But, I did. The men in the park deserved to see a Cross perched on top of a church's belfry.

Years earlier I had been touched by a Cross. I was returning home after seeing a divorce lawyer, and was extremely despondent... wishing I were dead. I sobbed as I sat on the 101 Freeway stuck in a traffic jam. *Please, Heavenly Father, please, take me Home.* Mamo was gone. As was my marriage of twenty-five years. Both boys had left home. And, now, *I just wanted to die!* Glancing up toward the heavens as I cried, I saw hovering above me... perched on a rooftop adjacent to the freeway—a fifteen-foot illuminated Cross! That's when I heard a voice say, "My child... *you* want to die. But... *I* want you to live."

My life was never the same after that. These men in the park deserved to have a Cross sitting on a steeple and speaking to them. A Cross offering hope. I wanted everyone to know how much Jesus cares.

The following Sunday, I led the congregation in prayer asking for a Cross to be placed on top of the little church. There were only a few protests from the regular attendees who claimed, *tradition must always dictate.* After much prayer, the one-hundred-and-fifty-year old "Needle" that *pointed* to God was replaced with a "Cross" that *showed* people *the way* to God.

Hope that is seen is not hope
Romans 8:24

One day while puttering around the house, I noticed how thin Billy had become. With most of my attention mainly on Derek, I hadn't noticed how frail he was. My Billy was sick. After decades of smoking, Billy was diagnosed with severe emphysema and placed on oxygen. He hated the restrictions and loss of independence that the oxygen-tank placed on him.

"I hate using this stupid thing," he said pointing to his new oxygen tank. When he finally stopped grumbling he smiled and said, "Especially when I can't chase you around the bedroom at night." We both giggled. He still could make me laugh. Even as a teenager, in a world of sadness, Billy was able to make me laugh.

Pride was stopping him from going out for his daily moped rides. He stopped attending church. Yet, as weak as he was, he remained my strongest prayer partner. We both believed if the two of us would come together in Christ's name, as the Bible told us to do, anything we asked would be given to us (Mt. 18:19).

So, every morning Billy and I prayed together, believing our combined prayers would make a difference. Life had taught us that hope is often called blind faith because it hopes, against all hope, that everything will turn out all right—despite evidence to the contrary. It is filled with high expectations. It isn't a wishbone, a coin tossed in a fountain, or a wish made upon a star. Hope believes in the unseen. And, Billy and I both believed Derek would come home to us somehow—some way—safe and sound.

However, the thought that I might lose Billy to sickness shook me to the core. When we were separated decades earlier, there were numerous times I wished he were dead. Now, I was desperately afraid that may happen and I'd be left alone without him. God had brought us full-circle back into each other's arms. We were designed to be a blessing for each other.

[God] comforts us in all our tribulations that
we may be able to comfort those who are in trouble
2 Corinthians 1:4

###

Makena with Beverly, Christmas Eve Church Service
@ Lahuiokalani Congregational Church
Honokowai, Maui, HI

chapter sixteen

THE LOVE

God is Love
1 John 4:8

The long-anticipated blooming of the large *Century Plant* was unfolding right in front of my unit. I felt blessed witnessing the miracle of the blossoming flower, and at having Makena spend the night with me. That evening as I sat on the patio, with her in my arms, I watched the sun set on the horizon for the last time of the 20th century. A new century was beginning.

I wondered if Mamo, who was three at the turn of the last century, was held in the arms of her grandmother as the sun went down. Being a Godly woman, I suspect she probably prayed as she held Mamo as a child in her arms, watching the sun disappear, "Dear Lord, bless this child I hold in my arms, and all the generations that will follow after her. Thank you, Jesus. Amen."

Her prayer had been answered. Mamo was not only a blessing to *her* grandmother. She was also a blessing to many others, and especially to me, her granddaughter. Mamo passed the baton of light through her example of Godly love. I prayed I'd do the same.

The year 2000 began with an abundance of joy. Derek was being released! Our prodigal son was coming home. Years of prayers had been answered! The prisoner was finally being set free, and in more ways than one. Physically, as well as spiritually.

Before Derek went to jail, he was in the dark, dead to his sins and trespasses (Eph. 2:5). He had trespassed right off God's path. He had gone his own way and become lost. All that was left was a shell of a human who resembled my son. He had been filled with darkness when he entered MCCC, rebellious and arrogant. No one could force him into salvation. He was way too big to spank!

Then one day I looked up from my patio table, and there he was, my Derek, walking towards me, smiling and radiant. My son had been set free. Free from the shackles of anger, sorrow, dread, and guilt. The darkness within him had vanished. God had turned on the lights. What was once lost had been found. Derek radiated God's love and forgiveness. As he stood before me with his arms outstretched, we both cried as we embraced in a long overdue hug.

When things appeared hopeless, God had given him a new lease on life. His sentence was reduced. And my son was home. I wept for joy. God had turned the ugly into beautiful. The dark into light. Death into life. The caterpillar had been transformed into a beautiful monarch butterfly. And, through his redemption, I, too, felt I had been redeemed.

Your son lives!
John 4:51

In the twilight hours after his early release, our friend Pastor Craig picked Derek up from MCCC and drove him to Airport Beach, where Derek was baptized. It was Derek's 40th birthday. Ironically, the Israelites from the Old Testament had also wandered for forty years before reaching their Promised Land (Ex. 12:25). They, too, kept repeating the same behavior and expecting a different outcome. What should have taken less than a month to achieve took them forty years. It was the same for my son... it was now the time for Derek's cycle of blindness to be broken. Derek suffered from the same seed of myopia as the Israelites. But the morning he stepped into the ocean and was baptized, acknowledging what God had done, he was saved. God had saved *the son of His maidservant* (Ps. 86:16), and my heart wept for joy.

After being released and regaining custody of Makena, Derek and my beloved granddaughter moved to Honokohau. Their new home can only be described as heaven on earth. Tall eucalyptus and coconut trees dotting the landscape sway in the breeze. A stream rambles through the property and flows into the ocean, only twenty-five feet away. Each day before breakfast, they would go surfing; and before dinner, they would surf again, as they watched the sun set before them. Derek and Makena were living in paradise.

"Why doesn't evwy-one go surfin' before school?" Makena asked me one day. Even at such a young age, she reminded me of Derek in many ways. She loved the water and took to it like her father. Her hair was super curly like Derek's. She was tall and slender for her age, and fearless. Together they enrolled in Taekwondo, and within a year had received several colored belts, showing the level of their accomplishments.

As a child, Derek had placed fifth in the Junior Olympics. His nickname had been *Sharkey*. Now with his renewed freedom, he returned to his love of swimming and entered the Masters swimming tournament, taking Gold in his class. I thought Billy would bust his buttons.

Derek had become the son we had prayed for. Free. Happy. Derek had also become the epitome of the father Billy, nor I, never had. Caring. Devoted. Giving Makena memories of love instead of bad ones like our fathers. Derek would do anything for her. He wasn't embarrassed to act silly and be seen in public with pony tails all over his head that Makena had coifed for him. He also brought smiles and joy to the nursery school children the year he put on a beard and played Santa Claus.

During Thanksgiving, Derek became known as the *Gravy Man* at church, making gallons of brown gravy for the four-hundred or so guests who attended Kumulani's annual Holiday feast. The first year we volunteered, Derek was given the job as gravy-maker and handed a ladle and pot; I was assigned to the *Bun and Butter* detail and given prongs to serve the food in front of me; while Makena, my four-year-old granddaughter, stood beside me, placed on the *Black Olive Brigade*.

"Happy Tanksgivin," I heard her say as the patrons moved up in line. "Would you wike an *owive?*" Her little voice sounded so cute. I turned to smile at her but was shocked. There she stood, reaching out to the person in front of her with a black olive stuck on each finger! The people chuckled and smiled… but also declined.

Derek was given permission to deliver frozen turkeys to MCCC for the inmates' Thanksgiving dinner—to the very prison that had held him captive! Derek revealed no fear when he returned to where he had been an inmate. Eventually he became part of the prison's ministry, going back inside the prison walls every Sunday to deliver God's word—then being allowed to leave! It had to be God's sense of humor. The Lord was using Derek. He could talk to the homeless, the wayward, and other prisoners, for he himself had been one, as had the Apostle Paul (Acts 16:36).

After church the following Sunday, a young couple asked if I would be willing to do a baptism for them. They were on their honeymoon, along with their cousin and wife. They wanted to be baptized in the waters of Hawaii.

"Could you do it today?" the woman asked. "We're leaving tomorrow to go back home." An ocean submersion is difficult no matter how small the waves are, especially if you're doing it by yourself and have a weak back.

I began to stammer, when Derek walked up. "I'll help you Moms," he said.

Wow! I thought to myself. I looked at my son and then the honeymooners and smiled, "I guess today will be no problem." The six of us met later that day at Baby Beach. It was thrilling. Derek's newfound faith glowed. His muscular body effortlessly assisted me with the water submersion and kept us safe from the current of the ocean. The faith displayed by the six of us that day was palpable. Electric. The Holy Spirit was evident.

That night as I lay in bed, I tried to express my gratitude for the exquisite day God had given me. "Thank you," seemed shallow for something so momentous. This was God's handiwork. It hadn't happened overnight. It started long ago. Purchased with much suffering and sorrow, and prayer. God had truly answered a mother's fervent prayer.

Speak to the children
Exodus 25:2

"Throw a Jesus Party," the small voice within me whispered. A spiral notebook always sat beside me during prayer-time, in case I needed to jot something down. *Throw a party?* I must have misunderstood. God knew I didn't have the money for that right now. I barely had two nickels to rub together. The ministry was called a *nonprofit* for good reason. How could I do what I think God just asked me to do? But, the directive was strong. "Throw a celebration to honor your granddaughter and her graduating class." They were leaving pre-school and entering Kindergarten.

"Have hot dogs, sodas and cake," the Voice instructed. "The children are to bring swimsuits to wear in the pool. Derek will be your lifeguard, and Billy, the cook."

I received the names of the children to be invited from the school. Twelve in all. Each child was to receive a personalized gift. Pictorial Bibles. Small crosses. Coloring books. Crayons. I made up awards for the most patient, most kind, most joyful—all gifts from the spirit (1 Cor. 12:4). I looked at my notepad and shook my head. How was I going to afford this? "Maybe if I invited a few of these kids, and ignore the idea of giving out presents..." Finally I had to admit, if God wanted me to have this party He would need to show me the way.

I was still in thought when a knock came from the front door. It was Karin, the young German neighbor who lived in the building. She was crying. I could see a taxi in the driveway. I invited her in. Her aging mother, who lived in Frankfurt, had fallen ill and was not expected to live. Karin was on her way to the airport and stopped by my condo in hopes of having a prayer. After I offered a prayer for her and her mother, I gave her my daily devotional for the trip. She hugged me, then left.

Moments later, she returned with an envelope in her hand. In broken English, she explained she had picked up her mail before receiving the dreadful phone call. "Von of the letters vas from my Mother. It vas posted a veek ago. I think this is for you," she smiled handing me the envelope. Then she rushed back to the waiting taxi. Inside the envelope was £250 with a note from her mother that read, "Dear Karin, use this as you see fit. Love, Mums."

I began to cry. I didn't know how much £250 was. But I knew it would be enough to cover the expenses for the *Jesus Party.* And I was right—with $12 left over!

Why had I questioned God? He is always the *Ways and Means Committee.* Right in front of my eyes, I witnessed again His Omniscient Power, and Unconditional Love, as He prepared a banqueting table here on earth, fit for His beloved children.

[We] are but flesh, a breath that passes away
Psalm 78:39

Billy was still handsome, even with his frail body. The tattooed heart on his arm that read "Bill & Bev Forever" was fading but the love in his heart was not. Years of smoking had destroyed his body. His lungs could no longer function on their own. But, his spirit had never been stronger.

My Billy was dying.

The day he was rushed to the emergency room, he moaned, "Sam, if only I'd known better, I'd have done better."

"No, you wouldn't," I softly chided. "Who do you think you're kidding? You were the *cool* sailor, with a pack of Lucky Strike cigarettes rolled up in the sleeve of your T-shirt, and your hair slicked back with pomade." I could see his eyes grinning behind the oxygen mask.

"Sam, lay down beside me." He patted the bed beside him.

"Okay," I said putting down my purse and lowering the bed rail. "But only if you promise not to get frisky with me." His eyes twinkled. I always loved the way he looked at me. As we lay there together, my head resting on his chest, his arm wrapped around my shoulder, I could hear his heart beating. I could feel his breath.

"Sam," he said softly, "I don't want to leave you."

"I know my darling," I choked, "and I don't want you to leave me." Lifting my face toward his, I added, "But Billy, don't forget, we'll be together again. I promise."

The next morning, Billy was in and out of consciousness. Derek, Darin, and I stood beside his bed, attempting to comfort him, and each other. Slowly, Billy opened his eyes and looked up at the boys.

"Buddley," he whispered, a nickname he used for both the boys. "Don't be so sad. We're gonna see each other again, remember?" He reached out and touched my hand. Whispering to the boys, he said, "Take care of your mother for me, okay? The greatest thing that ever happened to me was your mother falling in love with me, *and* introducing me to Jesus." He tried to smile, then closed his eyes. That night he slipped into a coma.

The following day, we gathered around his bed again. Holding hands. Taking turns to be near him. Suddenly Billy's eyes popped open. Excitement filled his face.

"Oh-h-h-h, it's so beautiful," he exclaimed softly. His eyes twinkled as they darted across the hospital ceiling. "Oh-h-h-h," he repeated. "It's so beau-ti-ful." After a few moments, he closed his eyes. *He was gone. My Billy was gone.* Had he seen angels before he left, that had been sent to take him home?

As the coroner pushed the green corduroy body-bag onto the gurney, my knees buckled. I began to vomit. I knew Billy would eventually die. One of us had to be the first to go. *Until Death Do Us Part,* I knew that was the vow we had made to each other. But

I wasn't ready. It seemed we had been together forever! There had always been a Billy.

We had loved. We had fought. We had made up. God had healed us. We had renewed our wedding vows! Our love for each other had never died. Even during those horrendous years of havoc when we were separated, I knew I could always find Billy if I needed him. But now? No matter how hard I searched, he was nowhere to be found. God's messengers had taken him home and my heart along with him.

Tears streamed down my face at his memorial on the shores of Fleming Beach, where his baptism had also been. I knew on the *shores* of Eternity, heavenly angels were singing and cheering as Billy arrived home. He was now with Jesus, his mother, and my Mamo. My comfort came from knowing I'd someday see him again.

###

BEHOLD

If anyone is in Christ, he is a new creation;
old things have passed away;
behold, all things have become new.
2 Corinthians 5:17

chapter seventeen

THE CHILDREN

Here am I and the children whom the Lord has given me
Isaiah 8:18

Makena was excited to start camp. So was I. Team leaders were encouraged to dress silly for the first day. In addition to wearing our team T-shirt, we could blacken out a tooth, paint freckles on our nose, wear a wig. "Just have fun," the volunteers were told. I decided to wear my hair in two long pony tails like Pippi Longstocking.

The moment I entered the recreation room, I felt the excitement. It was electrifying. Approximately a hundred children, Kindergarten through fourth grade, gathered to begin the annual five-day church camp offered by the Kumulani Chapel. It was free of charge and filled with fun and food for both the body and spirit. Makena was now old enough to attend, so we signed up together. She as a new camper, and me as a volunteer.

The *keikis*, Hawaiian for children, were divided into three teams divided by the grades they would be entering when they returned to school. Each received a camp shirt identifying their team. Makena and I were on the "Red Team."

Each morning the teams gathered together for opening prayers and lots of singing. The joyful noise was deafening. And infectious. The teams would then break out into their individual groups and head off to start that day's activity. There was story-time, play-time, and eating-time. Snack-time was the kids' favorite part of the morning.

Twenty-one kindergarten and first-graders comprised our team. The first morning everyone danced! Twirling, clapping, and do–si–doing, someone grabbed one of my ponytails as I spun around, nearly yanking me off my feet.

"OW," I hollered, grabbing my neck. "That hurt!" I wasn't kidding.

"Who did that?" I whined. Some of the kids glanced toward Brighton, a kid large for his age and oldest of the group. "Did you do that?" I asked.

He looked about. There wasn't anywhere to hide. He nodded.

"Oh dear," I said. I could feel the childrens' eyes upon me. Everyone was waiting to see what I was going to do. Including me. I had no idea. This wasn't covered in the camp's Manual.

There was a time when I would have exploded in rage had someone done what Brighton had just done. However, God had tempered my temper, and now instead of acting out my anger, I tried to act out His plan. I motioned for the boy to come forward and heard myself say, "Let me look inside your T-shirt."

With an attitude, the seven-year-old stepped up and pulled open the neck of his red shirt. I peeked inside and jumped back. "Just as I thought." I pretended to cry. "You have the devil in your heart!"

After a moment I composed myself, and the children and I continued on with our square-dance. However, when I got home, I spent the rest of the day on the couch with a bag of frozen peas wrapped around my neck, praying my sore muscles would feel better by morning.

The following day, I wore my hair in an *Up-Do* and gave thanks that my body didn't ache. For *Game Time*, the team was split into halves. As fate would have it, Brighton's name was drawn to be with me.

He protested when his name was called. "I don't want to be on that ugly old lady's team." I was shocked. I had never been called *old* or *ugly*. At least, not to my face. And by someone of such small stature! The actress within me broke out in tears as I had the day before.

"You hurt my feelings," I wept. Again, I could feel the childrens' eyes upon me. Without skipping a beat, I again said to Brighton, "Come here. I want to see what's inside your T-shirt." Slowly he stepped forward and stretched out the crew-neck of his shirt as he had the day before. Again, I jumped back. "Just as I thought," I gasped. "The devil's inside your heart again. Yikes." I turned away, frightened.

When I arrived at camp the following morning, however, I discovered Brighton standing in the parking lot waiting for me. He was excited for me to open my car door. "Look inside," he grinned, pulling out the neck of his soiled T-shirt. I took a peek and jumped back.

"Is that Jesus I see?"

"Yup," he answered proudly. "I asked Him to come into my heart last night." I placed my arm around Brighton's shoulder and gave him a huge hug. We turned and walked into the rec room together with Makena beside me.

The following day, as I was carrying the activity toys up the stairs to the playing field, Brighton ran up and took some of my cumbersome load from me.

"So how are you, Brighton?" I asked as we continued up the stairs.

"Okay, I guess."

He seemed sullen. "What's the matter? Is everything all right?"

"Yea, I guess."

"What's wrong, honey?"

"Oh nothin.' He paused. "It's jus' that I noticed it's real hard for me to keep Jesus inside my heart."

I smiled. Chills ran through my veins. "Yeah, I know what you mean. It's hard for me, too." We looked at each other, then continued up the stairs to play ball.

Friday morning, Brighton was at the rec room early. He had a friend with him. "This is Jimmy," he said. "He lives next door to me." I saw a Downs Syndrome child about Brighton's age. "I want you to introduce him to Jesus."

Fighting back tears, I leaned forward and shook the small child's hand. "Jimmy? Why that's my brother's name." The boy smiled. So did my heart. God had given me the privilege of being a *Barnabas,* an encourager (Acts 4:36), to one of His children. Brighton was now encouraging another by passing the baton of God's light.

I remember how Mamo had fought my mother sixty years earlier to permit me to attend a week-long church camp. Mamo had been my *Barnabas*. She even paid the tuition from the money she earned as a maid. Now, decades later, I was given the honor to be a *Barnabas* and touch these children for Jesus. Little did I know that someday God would use those scars made in my heart to comfort and help other children today. He didn't cause the pain, but He certainly used it.

The children reminded me of newborn hatchlings, their mouths opened in faith, trusting they would be fed and gobbling up the nourishment. Christ's words, and the examples Brighton witnessed at camp, had touched him. He then turned and did the same with his young neighbor, revealing another side of himself that had been buried away. The little boy wanted what Brighton had found, and Brighton wanted to share it. And, he did! He had been a *Barnabas* to Jimmy.

Nobel Peace Prize winner Dr. Albert Schweitzer wrote, "I don't know what your destiny will be. But one thing I know: The only ones among you who will be truly happy are those who have sought and found how to serve."

Everyone wants to make a difference. But rarely do we have an opportunity to see it in the actions of a seven-year-old. I had witnessed it at its best! Brighton *sharing*. Brighton *caring*.

A child shall lead them
Isaiah 11:6

That Halloween, Makena and I were in the Lahaina Keiki Parade. In honor of the holiday, Front Street is blocked off for seven blocks. The day is referred to as *The Mini Mardi Gras of the Pacific*. Approximately 20,000 visitors come to Maui each year to celebrate.

My little white convertible with its *GOD BLS* license plates was one of the "floats" in the parade. Mayor Linda Lingle waved as she sat on top of the back seat. Costumed children sat around her, tossing candy Kisses and Almond Joys to the onlookers.

The crowd waved and cheered. Memories flooded my mind of other parades I had participated in. One with Elvis Presley caravanning down the mountainside of Big Bear as we filmed *Kissin' Cousins*. Another when I worked with him playing *Miss Speedway*, in the movie of the same name, and circled the racetrack waving to the crowd. And, the wonderful memory of walking down the Red Carpet with famous celebrities on *The Lucy Show* amongst a flurry of screaming fans and photographers. Many processions, with many famous people. But, none thrilled me as the memory of the parade I did with the little children of Lahaina.

Teach us to pray
Luke 11:1

When Kumulani Chapel asked if I would participate in their newly formed children's choir, I was ecstatic. My title would be the "Praying Partner" for the *Keiki Korner*, ages 4-7. There was nothing I'd rather do than have an opportunity to teach God's little children how to pray. Ironically, I recently had received a present from a friend: an eighteen-inch talking Doll with Golden hair. When her hands were placed together, she recited the Lord's Prayer. I named her *Angel*. Each week at the close of choir practice, the children and I would hold hands and make a circle of prayer. I always asked if anyone had anything they would like us to pray for.

The first week there was no response. Just blank stares. But the second week, a little girl in pig-tails shyly said, "Would you ask Jesus to make my big brother stop being so mean to me?"

"Yeah," a little boy agreed.

"And ask Him to make me brave tomorrow when I get a shot." There was silence for a moment. Everyone's head was bowed.

Then a soft voice whispered, "Pray for my Grandma. She's sick," the child sobbed. Another spoke up. "Pray for my mommie." Pause. "My Daddy jus' put her in da' hospital."

It didn't take long to figure out that the little ones needed the Lord just as much as the big ones do. Children can have big concerns in their short lives, and also need to know the power and comfort of prayer. So, Angel and I taught the children Christ's model prayer, closing with a personal request for the children.

"Jesus, You've showed us how much you love us. You've showed us how to pray. You taught us that if two of us would pray together in Your name, if it be for the highest good, it will be given to us." Prayerfully they understood what I was saying. "So, Heavenly Father, be with these children and their families. Protect them. Let them know You are standing right there beside them—that they're not alone. Thank You, sweet Jesus. And, so it is. Amen."

The children would then disburse and return to the world from whence they came, prayerfully better off than when they arrived. It was during this period of time while in a circle, holding hands with the children, that I saw one of God's important plans for my life. To bring the little children to Him.

For this purpose I came
John 12:27

I felt the Lord leading me to attend *The Call,* a Christian youth rally, in Pasadena, California, at the Rose Bowl. Ten-thousand enthusiastic teenagers and pre-teens were expected to attend. I brought my granddaughter and grand niece with me and together we sang, prayed, and committed ourselves to God's leading. The one-day event was only twelve hours. Prayerfully, for the children, it would last a lifetime. As for me, and my achy body, it took several weeks before I felt like my ole self again.

God continued to expanded my territory (1Chr. 4:9,10). A new ministry was born. *Women Helping Women* was opening a new center in West Maui, and they asked if I would like to assist on Thursday nights with women in need of counseling. Most were court-ordered sessions, and nearly all had children that tagged along. The invitation to be the new counselor was flattering, and like in Titus 2:3-5, I would be a senior woman counseling the younger ones. But, I declined. Instead, I was being led to a different purpose. I offered my services as the caretaker for the children while their mothers were having their counseling sessions.

The next Thursday, I'm sure the heavenly angels were singing as the keikis and I skipped down Front Street as we played Follow-The-Leader, heading to Lahaina's famous banyan tree. I allowed the older children to try balancing on the lower branches of the massive tree as I walked beside them. Each week we ended our time together by skipping single file to Baskin Robbins for ice cream singing *Jesus Loves Me*. Onlookers smiled and sang along with us as we passed. I had as much fun as the children, although I was far more exhausted when we returned to the women's center where their mothers were. I became known as the *Nice Lady with the White Hair*... making me wonder if there was a *Mean Lady* with the same color hair!

"The children think you're one of them," a mother said one evening as we returned from our outing.

"I am," I smiled. "The only difference is that my skin hangs."

After obtaining permission from the parents, I spent birthdays with each child individually, taking them to Maui Ocean Center. After spending hours at the aquarium visiting the stingrays, jellyfish, sharks, seals and turtles, we would dine together in the Harbor Restaurant. I always requested a cake with candles, and after dinner would present them with a special birthday gift. Then, together we would head home with the car's top down, and the wind blowing through our hair. Glancing at the child sitting beside me, I often thought of Philip, the deaf mute I cared for many years before when I was a child. The same feeling of love that radiated through me back then would surface. Again I saw the thread of God's tapestry.

You guard all that is mine
Psalm 16:5 NLT

Just like her father, Makena adored animals and had a special bond with them. In the Valley where they lived, they were allowed to have pets. They had Duchess, the rabbit. Penelope, the pig. Kala, the horse. And Nanuk, Sequoia, and Dakota, the wolves that Derek adored. I shouldn't have been shocked when the phone rang, informing me Makena had been attacked by something she loved... an animal.

"Mrs. Powers?" the caller asked. "I'm calling to inform you your granddaughter is in the hospital. She's gonna be okay but she's pretty shaken up."

While Makena was visiting her mother Upcountry, she crawled under a fence behind the house and wandered off into a pasture where she befriended a baby calf. Her unbridled love for animals drew her near. She began petting the precious animal, when she heard the snorting and pounding of hooves coming from behind. She turned and saw an angry Mama cow coming over the knoll, headed straight towards her with horns ablaze. The thousand–pound animal charged the fifty-pound child, who was quickly overtaken.

Knocking her to the ground, the massive cow began mauling Makena with her hooves. With one of her large horns, she hooked Makena's outfit and began tossing the terrified child to and fro. Then, out of nowhere, three barking dogs mysteriously appeared and chased the angry Mama cow and her baby back over the hill.

Makena was badly bruised, but thank God she would be all right. A large hoof had sliced her tiny leg. Open cuts, gouges, and abrasions ran up and down the left side of her small frame. One knee was badly sprained. She could barely walk. My grandbaby was hurt, but she was alive! God had miraculously saved Makena as He had for me numerous times over the years.

"It's amazing," the doctor said. "She has no broken bones. No internal injuries from what we can tell. Nothing crushed." The doctor shook his head in disbelief as he completed the exam. "She's lucky to be alive," he said. I smiled to myself. Deja vu. Luck had nothing to do with it. The thought of what could have been, but didn't, filled me with profound gratitude.

The following morning, as we sat on my lanai feeding the birds, I nonchalantly said, "I wonder where those dogs came from that chased away that angry Mama cow." She didn't know. Derek confirmed nobody in the neighborhood knew of any such dogs. No one had seen or heard the barking that morning that had herded the bovine and her calf away from Makena.

"So, I wonder who sent those dogs to protect you from that angry cow," I asked. I could see the wheels in her head spinning. Finally she turned and looked up at me with wonder in her eyes and said, "It was Jesus, huh?"

"Yes, my darling," I smiled. "It was Jesus who sent you His protective *Spirit Dogs*."

Kamp Kumulani

Keiki's Halloween Parade

Keiki's Birthday "Alone-Time" with Beverly

THE CHILDREN

Darin with sons, Jacob & Evan; Derek with daughter, Makena

chapter eighteen

THE BLESSINGS

I will bless you so you can be a blessing to others
Genesis 12:2

Right in front of my eyes, I had grown old and hadn't even seen it. One day I was young—the next I wasn't. However, recently I had noticed the reflection in the bathroom mirror was beginning to resemble my mother. I tried ignoring it. I lowered the light wattage. I took down some of the mirrors in my home. But when an AARP membership card arrived in the mail with my name on it, I couldn't ignore it any longer. I was getting older. In my mind I was still young. Maybe I had a few extra aches and pains here and there, but I still felt there were things God wanted me to do before taking me home.

In the book *The Prayer of Jabez* by Bruce Wilkinson, Mr. Jones goes home to heaven and discovers a box with his name on it. Inside he finds unopened presents with their bows still intact. Undelivered gifts addressed to him. Blessings his Father wanted to give him while he was on earth... that Mr. Jones had blindly rejected.

At birth, Mr. Jones had received an irrevocable gift called *free will* (Deut. 30:19) from our Heavenly Father. But, for over the majority of his life, Mr. Jones mishandled the legacy... choosing to do things his way and not God's, depriving himself of the blessings his Father had intended for him. *What a travesty!*

I didn't want to be like Mr. Jones, and get home and hear God say, "Let's look at your life, Beverly Jean. Let me show you what I wanted for you, and tried repeatedly to give you, to accomplish through you... but you wouldn't let me."

THE BLESSINGS

When I get home, I want St. Peter to show me an empty box... a box with my name on it, but empty. Not because I'm smarter or better than Mr. Jones, but because I had a praying Grandmother who covered me each night with a blanket of prayers, asking for God's light to shine down upon me wherever life took me.

And for sure, life took me many places. Some places I'm ashamed of. Places filled with obstacles, distractions, and confusion. But always, God was there beside me. From my youth He surrounded me. No matter how far I strayed, He drew me back to Him. My life was like a stretched out rubber-band. But, once I authorized God to use me as He pleased, my life boomeranged back to its intended path that God had originally planned for me... long before I was even born (Ps. 139:13-16). And, my life was never the same.

When I was young, I searched for answers in many wrong places. But even when I was on that crooked path, my walk was not in vain. God used it all. The good, the bad, the ugly, reflecting His light out through my darkened past. I never could have contemplated the heights God would raise me to from the depths I had come from. Nothing from my past was wasted. My sins; my search for purpose and meaning; the Hollywood movies; self-realization courses; Eastern philosophies. God had used them all.

My life began as an accident. But as Mamo always said, "God don't make no mistakes." And over the span of seven decades, my life proved her right. I went from being an unwanted child to being a woman that God wanted, and used in ways I could never have imagined. God used my past to speak to my future.

When I look at the tapestry of my life, I see God was always there walking beside me into places I should never have taken Him. Yet, He turned my lemons into lemonade, and orchestrated a new life for me, despite the obstacles I had placed in His way. The day I surrendered my life to Christ, out of sheer desperation, my life became a learning curve that never leveled out—that kept curling further and further upward toward Him.

I once wondered what my future would have held if I had given my life to the Lord any earlier. Today, however, I realize the search for my purpose was actually a treasure hunt, retrieving information as I went along life's bumpy road. And, I wasn't disappointed at my discovery.

I identified with Rahab, a woman with a questionable past from the Old Testament (Josh. 2:1-21). She believed in the living God, and helped save His people when the walls of Jericho came tumbling down (Josh. 6:20). She had made many bad choices, yet she became the mother of Boaz (Mt. 1:5), mother-in-law of Ruth, the great-great grandmother of King David (Mt. 1:6), and part of the lineage of Christ Himself! Rahab went from harlot to a woman of faith (Heb. 11:31), saving herself and family. God had given her a new beginning, as He had me. From stripper to minister. I had done nothing to warrant His favor. All I did was surrender my life to Him, and He did the rest. I wonder if, like me, Rahab also had a praying grandmother.

Heaven's door opened up the day I gave the reins of my life to the Lord and was given the gift of the Holy Spirit. I was able to do what I had always desired (Ps. 37:4), to make a difference in people's lives. I did it with the help of the many angels God sent along the way—Earth angels who fought for me even when I hadn't asked, guiding me, saying, "Right this way to your promised land."

The Lord has made everything for His own purposes
Proverbs 16:4 NLT

God promises new beginnings for all who believe in Him. That was certainly true for me. He gave me favor that wasn't dependent on my name being in lights, owning expensive jewelry, furs, and apartment buildings. God didn't want me starstruck with earthly possessions. But He also didn't want me filled with sorrow, grief, and fear. His intention for me, as for everyone, was to have heaven on earth (Mt. 6:9). He promised He would never leave me (Heb. 13:5) and He never did.

Throughout my life, God sent me angels that resembled ordinary people. But, they were far from it. They would show up unexpectedly, at the right time, and at the right place. They were part of God's global team, His torchbearers, leading His children homeward. Angels disguised as regular people... like Billy, my soul mate. Even though I didn't always recognize him as such, Billy was always there through thick and thin. Then one day he wasn't... and I thought I was alone.

The day I flew home after attending a memorial service for Billy on the Mainland, my heart ached. I stared out the plane's window at the clouds, at the heavens. I wanted to die.

"Oh please, sweet Jesus," I silently wept. "I can't go on without him... I'm gonna be seventy. Please take me home," I pleaded. "Please let me be with my Billy." At the moment I was flying home wishing I were dead, I suspect Billy was in heaven pleading the opposite.

"Heavenly Father... Sam needs Your help... she's gonna need something to do for the rest of her life. Please help her."

And, help me He did! Obviously Billy's prayer was louder than mine.

Some have entertained angels unawares
Hebrews 13:2 ASV

In the midst of my sorrow, when I arrived home there were three phone messages on my machine. Three earth angels, each bearing gifts in ways I could have never dreamed. I hadn't preached since Billy became ill. So when I heard the messages, I was very surprised.

The first message was from Marlene, a woman who always wore flowers in her hair when she visited, and loved God as much as I do. We had met years earlier when I was preaching at the Sheraton Maui Resort. We clicked instantly. From then on, whenever she and her husband visited Maui she followed me wherever I preached. She was calling to tell me she and her husband were in town and inviting me for lunch while they were here.

"We're staying at the Kaanapali Beach Hotel," she said. "Rev Bev, the hotel here doesn't have a church service, so Carl and I have suggested they start one. Maybe you should give them a call. Anyway, we're here. Hoping to see you before we leave."

The next message was from the hotel itself. Lori Sablas, the Director of Po'okela, was calling to tell me they were building a Hale, a thatched-roof pavilion, on their ocean grounds and wanted to ask if I would be interested in having church services there, in their garden, on Sunday mornings for the visitors of Kaanapali.

The last phone message was from a man I met while preaching at the Lahuiokalani Congregational Church. When he and his wife, Joan, vacationed here, they always visited the historic church. "Beverly, this is Bill Brown," he began. "I have retired and recently moved to Maui and was wondering if you could use some help with your ministry."

Was he kidding? Mr. Brown had assisted Billy Graham for forty-seven years, working as his Crusade Director and President of Graham's film ministry, World Wide Pictures. He had produced successful films such as the award winning film *The Hiding Place*, the true story of Corrie ten Boom in Holland, during World War II, featuring Julie Harris. Mr. Brown's offer to assist me was like receiving a kiss on the cheek from God Himself.

"Just let me know if there is anything I can do." I couldn't believe it. As it turned out, he assisted me for over three years at the beach ministry. He truly was a Godsend.

> *The Lord... is right beside me*
> Psalm 16:8 NLT

My heart races in the predawn hours, as I approach the darkened beach to place my homemade signs in front of the hotel, inviting the tourists to our service. "Song. Worship. Hula. All Are Welcome." *Were signs allowed?* No one ever said.

I can feel my heart pounding in my chest. I want to have the signs in place before the sun comes up and the weekend joggers come out. Over my shoulder I carry a canvas nap-sack with six 7"x8", two-sided, laminated posters. They are stapled to stir-sticks I purchased at the local paint store. I also have inside my bag a tack-hammer for pounding the sharpened stakes into the packed ground.

I can hear my sandals hitting the sidewalk as I walk. I am aware that I'm alone. There's not another human to be seen. The only vehicles in the parking lot belong to the early morning kitchen cooks and the night desk clerks, who snooze inside waiting for their shifts to end. A harvest moon hangs low on the horizon, creating a wide golden path of shimmering light across the calm ocean surface... appearing as a path leading to heaven. A shiver runs through me. Suddenly I know I'm *not* alone. The Lord was with me.

Tears well up in my eyes. I think of Mary Magdalene. How had she felt in the wee hours of the morning as she hurried along to do God's bidding, heading toward the tomb where Jesus lay? I wondered if she felt as I did. Was she exhilarated? Did she feel vulnerable? Driven? I knew my purpose was the same as hers... to serve the Lord.

The age of a woman doesn't mean a thing.
The best tunes are played on the oldest fiddles
Ralph Waldo Emerson

God gave me a project after losing Billy that kept me busy morning, noon, and night. He knows me. He made me. And, He knows I love to talk... especially about Him. So, each week, God had me open church by singing the traditional favorite, *Savior, Like A Shepherd Lead Us*, except He had us sing it in Hawaiian. The tourists loved it. They also loved the blessing offered at the end of the hour from Numbers 6:24-26. In-between, I wove God's words of encouragement and inspiration, filled with illustrations of men and women from over the ages who had made a difference.

Many couples who attended our Sunday services were on a romantic holiday. I suspect some of the men had been coerced by their spouses to accompany them to our unique outdoor chapel. Many hadn't been to church in years. A wedding, baptism, funeral--that was it. The Lord had given me an awesome gift in my winter years... a new ministry.

Because of Marlene and Carl and their willingness to do God's urging by suggesting a church service be held at the hotel, I was able to lead Sunday services to more than seventy-five thousand people over the next seven years, sharing my love for Christ to vacationers from around the world. It was a ministry without walls... and an opportunity for me to read God's love letters to those who joined us each week. God had given me a new blessing in my old age.

Shortly after arriving on Maui, I met a man who owned a produce stand in the middle of our island. He was one of the earth angels God sent me after I moved here. Terry was always in my corner. When I had needed a dependable car at a good price, he found me one. When I had needed a camera to borrow for the *Photo Ministry,* he offered his. So, I shouldn't have been surprised to see him when I began preaching at KBH. Terry's health was failing, yet each Sunday, he would drive the one-hundred-and-forty-mile round trip from Upcountry to our beachside ministry out of his love for me, and more importantly, Jesus.

Terry was a heart transplant recipient. One Sunday morning, he brought a couple to church with him. During the "greeting" portion of the service, Terry stood up and shocked everyone.

"These are my special friends visiting from the Mainland." He glanced down at the couple and smiled. "A few years ago, they were planning a family holiday to Maui. At the last minute, their grown son was unable to go because of work, but promised he'd be with them the next time they went.

"While they were here on vacation, their son was killed in a car crash." Leaning on his cane for support, Terry reached for the woman's hand. "I was next in line on the National Heart Recipient's list. Of course, we didn't know each other at that time. I was immediately flown to Tennessee where the heart was, and I received the transplant... the heart of a twenty-two-year-old male." Tears filled his eyes. "The heart of this couple's son... now lives inside of me." He paused. "Their son *is* here on Maui as he promised." He bent down and whispered, "Bless you."

They shall still bear fruit in old age
Psalm 92:14

Though I rarely recognized it, God was always with me... through close encounters, physical dangers, spiritual and emotional blindness. Looking back, I can see a thread of God's tapestry in every chapter of my life. As I grow older, my blessings become more apparent. I see the reason *behind* my blessings... to be a blessing to others (Gen. 12:2), and to receive God's light vertically, then reflect it back out horizontally, creating what the Hawaiians call a *'oloke'a,* a cross for the King.

I prayed that I would bear good fruit for the Lord in my old age. Not the sweet fruit of youth. But the delicious fruit of wisdom found in an old olive tree. Often in my golden years, I have felt like these were my *rusty* years. My bones creak and I look forward to seeing Billy again. I miss him terribly. I'm also excited to see Mamo. Together we will all sit at the banqueting table alongside Jesus, as Mamo's famous chicken and dumplings are served on a platter of love.

From generation to generation, the women in our family had attempted to pass the baton of light to the next. There was Mamo, her grandmother, and God knows how many others before them. Women born to pass God's light to others, to be a reflection of Him. The Bible states we are to, "Display our radiant glory" (Ps. 80:1b). No matter where we are planted, God has a purpose for us. We are to take our job seriously, which I didn't always do. I wasn't always a good example, but God's faithful angels kept prodding me forward...

and upward! God had a plan, yet it took me nearly a lifetime to figure out what that was. But when I discovered my purpose... *to be a blessing to others*, I found heaven on earth. Mamo was right. God did have a plan for me... to pass His light on to the next generation, and let them know His plan for us is far better than we could ever imagine.

Because of one woman many believed
John 4:39

One woman with a third grade education made a difference for the Lord, touching thousands of lives because of her prayers. She touched hundreds of people through me alone. Her prayers put into action God's plans for me and my future, to have heaven on earth, and not hell.

Mamo was perceived as a woman in white... with wings, a halo, and a grocery bag containing maid's clothing, who loved the Lord. Her life demonstrates the power, and importance, of one woman. She loved me and even prayed for me when I was still in Mother's womb.

The importance of one praying person, such as Mamo, placing their hands together cannot be measured. Mamo made a phenomenal difference in many lives, especially in mine. In fact, her last present to me came as a total surprise. Thirty-two years after her death, Mamo had one more blessing up her sleeve. And, I almost didn't receive it.

After a serious bout with neurological shingles, a lengthy stay in the hospital, and the subsequent recovery, I thought I might want to take a look at some of my legal papers. I was surprised when I learned that Billy was still the beneficiary in my will, though his ashes were sitting on my living room shelf in an urn! I had always meant to find a resting place for Billy and me, but had never got around to it.

While sorting through my papers, I discovered an unopened manila envelope postmarked years earlier from Mamo's grand niece, my third cousin. I had stored it away unintentionally without ever opening it. Inside the folder, I found faded photographs taken in the early 1900s' of Mamo when she was young, and other people I didn't recognize. I also found a legal document, signed and dated August 7, and a flyer for the mortuary where Mamo was buried. There was also a diagram of the family plot where Mamo and her sister lay side-by-side. The graves around them were filled except for the one next to Mamo. It lay empty... yet unclaimed. *That one had been meant for me!* Mamo had secured a final resting place for me on my seventh birthday! A place beside her for all time.

After learning the news, I walked around for days as if my head was in the clouds. I was overwhelmed. Mamo had given me a precious gift, guaranteeing me a place near her. And to make things even lovelier, I learned I could bring Billy's ashes along with me upon my arrival! *It was a perfect.* Mamo, Billy and me, all resting in peace together... in one place.

A silver thread had always connected Mamo to me. It began with Mamo's grandmother who, at the turn of the 20th century, 1899, on New Year's Eve, lifted Mamo up to the heavens, and asked for a blessing to be placed upon her, and all future generations. Her blessing wove itself through the decades. Her prayers lit a candle for generations to come. One backwoods woman, who picked cotton and raised chickens to eke out a living, made a profound difference right where she was planted. She had passed the baton of God's light to her family members... yet to be born.

> *My life is an example to many*
> *because You have been my strength and protection*
> Psalm 71:7

As I close my eyes, I see myself entering St. Elisabeth's, the sanctuary that provided me comfort as a child. I can feel the Lord's presence as I did back then. I see the glorious image of the Good Shepherd at the end of the aisle. Familiar colored sun-rays stream across the cathedral through the tall stained glass windows.

The church is empty, but I'm not alone. God's angels have come to greet me, and to escort me to the top of the stairs. Slowly I walk toward the front of the room. As I pass wooden pews, I see people kneeling... faces I recognize from my past. There were numerous brides and grooms from the twenty-five hundred weddings God sent me over the years, all decorated with leis of flowers.

To my left, I see a row filled with children from church camp singing *Jesus Loves Me*. In another row, I see blessed faces young and old, patients I prayed with when I was a chaplain at Maui's hospital. All hurting... all in need of prayer. Across from them, I recognize a few of the young faces from *Make A Wish Foundation*, especially the young girl with the pink Cinderella kerchief wrapped around her head.

Continuing up the aisle, I see my two beloved sons and their families, kneeling and worshipping together. My heart skips a beat. I am filled with joy. Darin, his wife, and precious children are there. Derek and his beautiful wife are also there bowed in prayer. And, seated behind them are numerous people Derek had touched with his new life God gave him after his freedom from prison. Even mother is there kneeling in prayer. And *there* on the aisle sits my beloved Makena, Mamo's great, great, granddaughter, radiating and glowing for all to see her love for Jesus.

Again I turn toward the altar. I can see my future. A glorious, timeless future. One without end. One with both Mamo and Billy. They are standing together beside Jesus. I begin to weep.

"Oh, my Savior... my Love!"

I glance back over my shoulder, one last time, and see future generations coming up behind me, and my heart rejoices. The baton of light Mamo passed on *to me* is now being passed on *by me* to the next generation. The thrill of completion fills my being.

"It is finished," I whisper to myself. I am ready to meet my Maker.

I turn toward the Light. Approaching the stairs, I flash a triumphant smile and sing out, "Hallelujah. I am home!"

###

These days [shall] be remembered and kept
from generation to generation
and celebrated by every family [member]
Esther 9:28

<u>PRAYERS</u>
Beverly Powers, Mr. Bill Brown, Pastor Laki Kaahumunu
Kaanapali Beach Hotel, Maui, Hawaii

ACKNOWLEDGMENTS

★ My sincere thanks and gratitude to my friend and mentor Bill Brown, and his beloved wife Joan, who have always been in my corner, encouraging me with their expertise, words, and prayers. They were truly instrumental in getting this book ready for print. As was Randy Elliott of Guideposts—faithful and wise, playing a large part in pointing this book toward publication.

★ I also want to thank Kelly Stanley, my *Grammar Policewoman*, for always being willing to help. With her bright red pen, poised in hand, she gave of her time, knowledge, and support every page of the way.

★ Mary Lynne Boland, another earth angel, deserves kudos for her abundance of knowledge and willingness, day or night, to answer any questions I had, without judgement, no matter how small, or subject-matter.

★ My deep appreciation goes out to Mark Vieth, Editor of Lahaina News, and his trained eagle-eye, for proofreading and assisting me in the preparation of this book.

★ I thank God for Rick Ortiz, known as *The Mac Pro*, for his faithful and loyal support, unwavering patience, and vast knowledge of computers, that kept me going when my frustrations wanted to take over.

★ Finally, to all those who prayed for me, making *Passing the Baton of Light* a reality. Bless you! You know who you are... and so does God. You have truly made a difference. *Thank you!*

NOTES

Chapter 1

1   *Senator Joseph McCarthy, Chairman of the Government Committee on Operations of the Senate*

Chapter 4

1   SAG; AGVA; AFTRA; EQUITY

2   L.A. Examiner Mike Jackson, *Meeting Beverly Hills is a Fascinating Treat*, June 14, 1963

3   The Lucy Show, *Lucy Goes to a Hollywood Premier*, Desilu Studios, 4th Season, Episode 104

4   Sacramento Union, Charles A. Welch, *Drama Critic*

Chapter 8

1   Krishnamurti, *Video* 1972

Chapter 9

1   SIPC; NASD Series 6 & 63; Life & Disability Insurance; Mortgage Insurance

Chapter 10

1   Minister of *Marble Collegiate Church, NY* @52 years; Author *The Power of Positive Thinking*

Chapter 13

1   Nature or Nurture, *Focus on the Family,* James Dobson

Chapter 14

1   God Calling, *Taste and Trust,* September 20, Barbour Publishing

Chapter 15

1   God Calling, *A Child's Hand,* October 6, Barbour Publishing

Printed in the United States
By Bookmasters